Lecture Notes in Computer Science 12515

More information about this subseries at http://www.springer.com/series/7410

Andrea Saracino · Paolo Mori (Eds.)

Emerging Technologies for Authorization and Authentication

Third International Workshop, ETAA 2020
Guildford, UK, September 18, 2020
Proceedings

Springer

Editors
Andrea Saracino ⓘ
Istituto di Informatica e Telematica
Consiglio Nazionale delle Ricerche
Pisa, Italy

Paolo Mori ⓘ
Institute of Informatics and Telematics
Pisa, Italy

ISSN 0302-9743   ISSN 1611-3349   (electronic)
Lecture Notes in Computer Science
ISBN 978-3-030-64454-3   ISBN 978-3-030-64455-0   (eBook)
https://doi.org/10.1007/978-3-030-64455-0

LNCS Sublibrary: SL4 – Security and Cryptology

This Springer imprint is published by the registered company Springer Nature Switzerland AG
The registered company address is: Gewerbestrasse 11, 6330 Cham, Switzerland

Preface

This book contains the papers which were selected for presentation at the Third International Workshop on Emerging Technologies for Authorization and Authentication (ETAA 2020), that was held in Guildford, UK, on September 18, 2020, co-located with the 24th European Symposium on Research in Computer Security (ESORICS 2020).

The workshop program included 10 full papers concerning the workshop topics, in particular: new techniques for biometric and behavioral based authentication, authentication and authorization in the IoT and in distributed systems in general, techniques for strengthening password based authentication and for dissuading malicious users from stolen password reuse, an approach for discovering authentication vulnerabilities in interconnected accounts, and strategies to optimize the access control decision process in the big data scenario.

We would like to express our thanks to the authors who submitted their papers to the third edition of this workshop, thus contributing to making it once again a successful event, even through the difficulties brought by a fully virtual event.

Last but not least, we would like to express our gratitude to the members of the Technical Program Committee for their valuable work in evaluating the submitted papers.

September 2020

Andrea Saracino
Paolo Mori

Organization

Workshop Chairs

Paolo Mori   Consiglio Nazionale delle Ricerche, Italy
Andrea Saracino   Consiglio Nazionale delle Ricerche, Italy

Technical Program Committee

Benjamin Aziz	University of Portsmouth, UK
Alessandro Aldini	Università degli Studi di Urbino Carlo Bo, Italy
Francesco Buccafurri	Università degli Studi Mediterranea di Reggio Calabria, Italy
Gabriele Costa	IMT Lucca, Italy
Francesco Di Cerbo	SAP Lab, France
Carmen Fernandez Gago	University of Malaga, Spain
Vasileios Gkioulos	Norwegian University of Science and Technology, Norway
Jatinder Singh,	University of Cambridge, UK
Jens Jensen	Science and Technology Facilities Council, UK
Erisa Karafili	Imperial College London, UK
Georgos Karopulos	JRC, Italy
Hristo Koshutanski	ATOS, Spain
Gabriele Lenzini	University of Luxembourg, Luxembourg
Mirko Manea	HPE Italia, Italy
Charles Morisset	Newcastle University, UK
Silvio Ranise	Fondazione Bruno Kessler, Italy
Marco Tiloca	RISE, Sweden
Francesco Santini	Università degli Studi di Perugia, Italy
Daniele Sgandurra	Royal Holloway, University of London, UK
Nicola Zannone	Eindhoven University of Technology, The Netherlands

Contents

Deep Learning Based Sequential Mining for User Authentication in Web Applications

Matan Levi(✉) 🆔 and Itay Hazan 🆔

IBM Cybersecurity Center of Excellence, Beer Sheva, Israel
{matanle,itayha}@il.ibm.com

Abstract. Behavioral biometrics is a seamless and transparent way to authenticate or identify users through their interaction with electronic systems. It can serve as an additional security mechanism to existing security methods by continuously authenticating the users, for example when using pointing devices (e.g., mouse, touchscreen). These methods usually aim at extracting meaningful features such as curvature and acceleration using the raw mouse coordinates and ignore the specific elements the user interacts with during the movement. A possible improvement is to combine these methods with approaches that analyze the user path of elements throughout the session. One such previously suggested process proposes using a model-per-user approach, built using the traditional sequence mining algorithm Hidden Markov Model (HMM). In this paper we examine the use of deep learning sequential mining mechanisms for authentication, using mechanisms such as Long Short-Term Memory (LSTM), LSTM with Attention, and a Convolutional Neural Network (CNN). This method has the major advantage of one global model per web application, which drastically reduces the system's required memory and storage resources. We demonstrate the competitive advantage by encouraging results in low false positive rates (FPR) ranges on an anonymized dataset collected by IBM from accounts of more than 2000 web application users.

Keywords: User verification · Continuous authentication · Behavioral biometrics · Deep learning

1 Introduction

User authentication in online systems is fertile ground for many new solutions. Each system has its pros and cons, but most solutions are focused on the login phase, during which users must enter a password, a token (e.g., a one-time password), or even a biometric attribute such as their fingerprint or facial image. Although solutions that focus only on the login phase are effective, they don't protect users against session hijacking after the login phase or if their credentials have been leaked. One emerging type of approach that isn't focused on the login phase uses continuous authentication to complement existing login solutions. The idea behind this approach is that continuous authentication constantly verifies the user's identity throughout an active session.

One of the ways to implement continuous authentication is behavioral biometrics, which verifies the identity of a user based on his or her particular behavioral traits while

© Springer Nature Switzerland AG 2020
A. Saracino and P. Mori (Eds.): ETAA 2020, LNCS 12515, pp. 1–15, 2020.
https://doi.org/10.1007/978-3-030-64455-0_1

using a certain electronic system. In connection with computer desktop applications, behavioral biometrics are usually based on mouse dynamics [1–3], which refer to the particular ways a user moves the mouse. In connection with mobile applications, behavioral biometrics are usually based on touch dynamics [17, 21, 22], the way unique way the user interacts with the mobile touchscreen (e.g., swiping, tap-ping, etc.). The main focus of mouse and touch dynamics is on the X, Y coordinates of the movement, in addition to supplemental information such as mouse clicks and scrolls, touch pressure, and finger size. In short, we refer to both mouse and touch dynamics as pointing device-based solutions. These solutions are usually composed of data collected from an interaction session that extracts features related to movement characteristics such as velocity, distance, curvature, time, etc. The extracted features are input into one of several existing machine or deep learning algorithms or distance metrics that model the user's behavior.

In most cases, these solutions examine how the interaction is done instead of evaluating what the user is doing during the interaction with the system. Websites and mobile applications are usually assembled from layers of elements such as buttons, text fields, images, and so forth. When tracking the X, Y coordinates and combining them with the location of various on-screen elements, one can easily infer the user paths during the session. In addition to elements the user clicked or pressed, each path also includes elements the user just hovered over or swiped through. We suggest that it is possible to profile users based on their paths. This solution can add a complementary aspect to existing continuous authentication mechanisms that examine movement features such as velocity, distance, curvature, time, etc.

The idea of using elements paths to profile user in web applications was first suggested by us in [23]. However, that paper only examined the use of basic sequence-based algorithms. The evaluated algorithms were Hidden Markov Model (HMM) with Linear Regression who show promising results both in desktop and mobile environments. The approach of using HMM with Linear Regression was inspired by a meth-od for detecting cyber-attacks on connected vehicles [4].

In this paper, we extend the approach we previously suggested [23] for pointing device-based solutions in web applications, by exploring more sophisticated, sequence-based algorithms based on neural networks. We specifically examine Long Short-Term Memory (LSTM), LSTM with Attention and a 1D Convolutional Neural Network (CNN) that showed value in sequence-related problems. A major advantage of this work is the use of one global model for all users, instead of separate models for each user. Model per user approach requires the solution to train, save, and load flows for every user accessing the system or website. This results in high memory and storage requirements. A global model allows us to support many users without increasing the load on system resources, such as memory and storage.

Using the abovementioned methods, we profile the user's normal behavior; deviations from that normal behavior can indicate a possible attack on the user's account. The deviations on the neural network algorithms were detected using a static thresh-old on the output of a linear layer that was integrated at the end of each network.

We evaluated the neural network algorithms on an anonymized real-world dataset that was collected from an uncontrolled environment of over 2000 users. Our results showed that this approach exhibited an advantage when low false positive rate (FPR) is required.

2 Related Work

Behavioral biometrics as a continuous authentication mechanism has been researched for several decades and includes several different approaches. One of the most com-mon techniques is keystroke dynamics, which focuses on verification based on the particular way each user types on the keyboard [5–9]. There are generally two types of keystroke dynamics, based on the characteristics of the text to which they are applied: fixed-text keystroke dynamics, which require users to enter a repeat-able text that can be very short (such as a password); and free-text keystroke dynamics, which requires users to enter more text, but text that can be spontaneous (e.g., email) and changed. Fixed-text keystroke dynamics are usually applied in the login page, and in general cannot serve as a continuous authentication mechanism. Free-text keystroke dynamics can be used for this, but only in systems that require the user to continuously type long text, which is not too common in regular internet use (e.g., browsing news, video streaming, and social media). In these types of applications however, most interactions are done through mouse dynamics (on desktops) or touch dynamics (on mobile devices). Therefore, we focus on solutions from the pointing device domain.

For example, Ahmed et al. [10, 11] used mouse movement for user verification. After collecting the movement coordinates and events, they categorized each movement according to four types: mouse-move, point-and-click, drag-and-drop, and silence. Next, they extracted descriptive features such as travel distance, elapsed time, average speed, and more. The feature vectors were aggregated into histograms and used for training and testing neural networks. Pusara et al. [13] worked on the same task, collecting mouse coordinates and click events. They segmented the data by the number of defined movement points and extracted features such as distance, speed, angle, etc., using a C5.0 decision tree to classify the segmented data and produce a score. Feher et al. [12] also used mouse movement for user verification but with additional descriptive features such as curvature, moment, etc. They segmented the movements into actions and proposed a verification method that is applied on each individual segment, using a Random Forest classifier applied on the segments to produce a score for the user identity. Zheng et al. [15] also presented a verification scheme based on the user's mouse movement coordinates and time. They extracted angle-based features and applied the widely used Support Vector Machine (SVM) algorithm.

Shen et al. [14] designed an efficient user verification method using one-class clas-sification and dimensionality reduction. They divided their features into two types: pro-cedural (e.g., speed curve against time, acceleration curve against time) and holistic (e.g., double click statistics, movement elapsed time). They applied several different one-class classification algorithms with Principal Components Analysis (PCA) dimen-sionality reduction, where the best among them was one-class SVM. In another paper, Shen et al. [16] divided the data into what they referred to as frequent behavior segments. These segments are stacked into a sequence of an ordered set of operations, and then integrated into mouse pattern sequence generation, matching methods, and finally into the selected one-class classification algorithm.

Antal et al. [27] used mouse movement to detect intrusion in systems. The mouse movements were tracked and segmented according to three possible user actions: mouse-move, point-and-click, and drag-and-drop. Features taken from various papers were then extracted, such as distance, acceleration, jerk, straightness, critical points, and more. Finally, they applied several supervised classification algorithms, among them Random Forest, which performed best. The authors showed that detection improved as the number of actions grew, and that the clearest action for detecting impostors is drag-and-drop.

Hinbarji et al. [28] used mouse movement to verify user identity, but unlike other methods, they focused on the properties of the generated curves and their discriminative information. The curves are created from consecutive coordinates, and several curves are grouped into a session. For each curve, they extracted features such as efficiency, self-intersection, regularity, and more. The probability distribution of the features was inserted into a neural network built independently for each user. Tan et al. [29] used time-series forecasting for user verification in mouse movement, applying curve-fitting strategies to the data. Here again the authors took the coordinates of the movement and applied a curve-fitting method to the raw data, such as cubic splines, AR, and ARMA. They then extracted features and integrated them with the linear SVM algorithm, showing results comparative to the traditional methods.

Another researched area of continuous authentication using behavioral biometrics is through mobile devices. Patel et al. [21] produced a thorough overview of existing methods and suggested paths for further research in the field. The reviewed works [18–20] that focused on touch dynamics for continuous mobile authentication were also based on the user touch coordinates X, Y and additional metrics extracted from the touchscreen. The authors developed methods that included innovative feature engineering and machine learning algorithms.

Other researchers sought to add additional information to touch dynamics. Feng et al. [22] used touch dynamics to verify user identity, adding the context of the running application. Ben Kimon et al. [17] addressed the same task by monitoring touch gesture sequences and the context of both the user (e.g., driving, walking) and the device (e.g., power consumption, running app). Each user model was trained on gesture trac-es within a predefined time interval using the gradient boosting learning algorithm. Jain et al. [31] combined touch dynamics with motion and orientation sensors to improve verification. The authors used the X, Y coordinates and finger area, in addition to the accelerometer and orientation. They extracted descriptive features and used min-max normalization, and eventually used the modified Hausdorff distance to pro-duce a score.

Other researchers tried to limit the level of information or work in different setups. Yang et al. [30] proposed a continuous authentication method in mobile based on one-class classification algorithms, evaluating one-class SVM and Isolation Forest. They extracted movement-based features, such as velocity and slope, and pressure-based features, such as pressure at start and pressure at end; the process involved removing outliers before the feature extraction and running a min-max normalization after-ward. Ngyuen et al. [32] used touchscreen dynamics to detect user identity across multiple devices. They evaluated verification abilities through three different tasks: reading, writing, and playing a game. They extracted features that relate to the coordinates, time, and finger size, and used multi-class SVM to classify the users. They found that the best task for detection across devices is reading, followed by playing, and lastly writing.

As opposed to many previous works, we don't use the feature engineering scheme to profile users based on their movement coordinates. We use sequence-mining techniques to learn users' element paths through websites. Our method can be used in parallel to existing methods to complement them. To the best of our knowledge, the only work that seeks to verify a user's identity based on their elemental paths within the context of a website is our previous work [23]. In that work, we demonstrated the encouraging results received when using sequence mining over web elements with HMM and Linear Regression. In this work, we present extensive research and further experiments using different deep learning mechanisms (LSTM, LSTM with Attention and 1D CNN) to build a global model (per web application) that can distinguish be-tween benign users and impostors.

3 Suggested Method

In our previous work [23], we introduced a new technique to profile users and identify imposters in web applications. This technique analyzes the user's behavior based on sequences constructed from elements they interacted with during their session on the website. Each element is defined by element name, element type, ancestor element, and interaction type.

The user's pointing device movements during a session form a path that consists of the specific website's elements with which the user interacts. This path indicates the order in which elements were traversed by the user and the action that was taken on each element. The basic assumption we rely on is that people tend to develop habits for routine tasks. Therefore, we assume that each user develops "preferred" paths during his or her sessions on the website. Sharp deviations from those paths could indicate a possible attack.

A path consists of the elements the pointing device traversed during the session. Hence, each session on the website constructs a single sequence or path.

In the following section we introduce a cost-efficient and fast global model approach that uses sequences from different users and previously seen impostors, with the goal of distinguishing between the two.

3.1 Data Collector

We collect pointing device data using a Java Script snippet integrated into the different pages of the website. Each pointing device event (press, move, scroll, swipe, etc.) the user performs is collected and sent to the servers. For each event, we extract the following information:

(Element name, Element type, Interaction type, Ancestor)

Such that:

- **Element name:** Name (ID) of the element
- **Element type:** HTML type, 'FORM', 'BUTTON', 'DIV', 'INPUT', 'LABEL', etc.
- **Interaction type:** Whether the element was hovered over, pressed, or swiped

- **Ancestor:** In a case where the element does not contain a name, our collectors traverse the HTML Document Object Model (DOM) and attach the element name to its ancestor's name

Each such quartet is treated as an event in the time series of events that represent the user's movements over the website's elements. The learning and predictions are performed using different neural networks models: one-dimensional CNN, LSTM, and LSTM with Attention model.

3.2 Sequence Construction

There are various ways in which we can construct sequences, as shown in Fig. 1. We tested the following construction options:

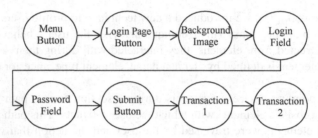

Fig. 1. Example of a sequence of elements a user hovered, pressed or swiped.

- Construct sequences based on all elements the user interacted with (swiped/
- clicked/hovered) during the session
- Construct sequences based on elements that were pressed/clicked
- Construct sequences based on elements that were stopped on (stopping is defined using a predefined period of time in which the user did not move the device)

Each type of sequence construction has its own advantages and disadvantages. The full sequence construction type contains more information and gives us a more precise point of view on the path the user took. However, since the sequence has more data, it also contains more noise, and therefore requires more data for training. On the other hand, the other two types of sequence construction contain less data about the path but are easier to generalize and model. At the end of the process, we built movement sequences based on the website structure for all of the user's historical sessions.

3.3 Training Phase

Pointing device movements can be viewed as a sequence of events, where each event consists of the HTML element in which the pointing device was at time t. Since our data has sequential characteristics; we need a learning algorithm that can use these characteristics. Therefore, we chose to apply our method on several algorithms such as the Long Shot-Term Memory neural network (LSTM), LSTM with Attention model, and the 1D Convolutional Neural Network (CNN).

LSTM is a popular tool for processing time-series data and has been widely used for tasks such as speech recognition [24, 25]. LSTM was developed to encounter the vanishing gradient problem in a vanilla Recurrent Neural Network (RNN). LSTM could be also combined with an Attention mechanism. The Attention mechanism can give the model the ability to focus on certain parts of the input sequence when predicting part of the output. Another approach involves using 1D CNN [26], which can be applied to one-dimensional sequences of data for time-series analysis.

All of the abovementioned models were trained using the output sequences, which are the sequences of elements traversed using the pointing device. Since the deep learning mechanisms require large amounts of data, we learned a global model for each web application (instead of a separate model for each user); the model is designed to distinguish between benign users and impostors.

To train the neural networks, we split the data into train (60%), validation (20%), and test (20%) sets. Each set consisted of different users with different sessions. Training was done using the Adam [34] optimizer with $\beta_1 = 0.9$, $\beta_2 = 0.99$ and $\epsilon = 1e^{-9}$. We tested various epoch values, with a warm-up policy and an early stopping mechanism that was used to avoid over-fitting. To overcome the imbalance in the data, we create new fraudulent sessions by splitting the fraudulent sessions in different locations (without affecting the fraudulent activity) and add class weights to the loss function.

3.4 Test Phase

As a new test session arrives, we extract the session's element-based sequences using the sequence construction technique we chose and test it against the model we trained.

We integrated a linear layer followed by softmax as our network output. The final network score is actually the benign/impostor score. We can easily define a threshold on the score or alternatively choose the label based on the higher score.

4 Experiments

In our experiments we trained LSTM, LSTM with Attention and 1D CNN. All algorithms attempt to detect impostors' activity using the sequential data.

4.1 Dataset

We received mouse data from IBM that consists of data from more than 2000 real anonymous users. The data contained benign data and impostor data. The original dataset we presented in our previous work [23] also contained touch device data; however, due to an insufficient amount of touch device data for a global model, we tested our method only on the mouse data. Nevertheless, the method is suitable for both and we leave the application of touch for future work. The dataset contains both benign and impostor data.

Benign data – the dataset contained sessions from users' web accounts during their daily account actions on the website. The users were monitored over a period of several months in an uncontrolled environment and for each of the 2000 real anonymous users we collected up to 40 sessions.

Impostor data – the dataset contained 75 real impostor sessions that gained control over innocent user accounts.

All sessions were monitored in an uncontrolled environment while users performed their daily account actions. The data was collected using a JavaScript code integrated into the different pages of the website and each session contained the elements related data (element type, element name, interaction type and ancestor) with respect to the user's pointing device movements during the session.

4.2 Model Generation

To generate a global model for a web application that can distinguish between impostor and benign data, we need enough data from both benign users and impostors. After receiving a sufficient number of sessions, for each such session, we extracted a sequence based on the elements (and their attributes) that were traversed during the session. After constructing a set of sequences for benign users and impostors, we trained a global model based on LSTM, LSTM with Attention, and 1D CNN. The models were built in Python using the PyTorch deep learning package [33].

LSTM Architecture. Our LSTM architecture consists of a word embedding layer, where each word is a state in the sequence, followed by a dropout layer, LSTM layer, and a linear layer with an output size of 2 (benign/impostor), followed by softmax. Hyper-parameter tuning was performed using randomized search. The chosen set of parameters is described below:

Best results for the LSTM network were obtained using the following: learning rate 0.002, batch size: 32, weight decay: 0, hidden size: 64, embedding length: 100, drop-out: 0.2, bidirectional: False, number of layers: 1.

LSTM with Attention Architecture. Our LSTM with Attention architecture uses the LSTM architecture mentioned above and integrates the attention mechanism on top of the LSTM architecture. Hyper-parameter tuning was performed using randomized search. The chosen set of parameters is described below.

Best results for the LSTM with Attention network were obtained using the following: learning rate 0.002, batch size: 32, weight decay: 0, hidden size: 64, embedding length: 100, dropout: 0.2, bidirectional: False, number of layers: 1 (Fig. 2).

One-dimensional Convolutional Neural Network Architecture. Our 1D CNN architecture consists of a layer of word embedding where each word is a state in the sequence, followed by three consecutive convolutional blocks (convolutional layer, ReLU, and max pooling), a dropout layer, and a linear layer with an output size of 2 (benign/impostor), followed by softmax. Hyper-parameter tuning was performed using randomized search. The chosen set of parameters is described below.

Best results for the 1D CNN network were obtained using the following: learning rate 0.002, batch size: 32, weight decay: 0.0001, dropout: 0.5, stride: 1, padding: 0 (Fig. 3).

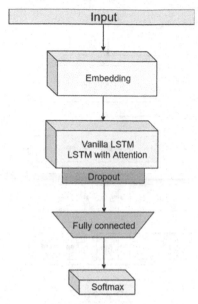

Fig. 2. LSTM/LSTM with Attention architecture.

4.3 Results

We tested different techniques to detect impostor activity for mouse devices by training different global models designed to distinguish between impostor activity and benign activity. The results are summarized in confusion matrices presented in Tables 1, 2, and 3, and their associated ROC graphs presented in Figs. 4, 5, and 6.

LSTM Results. Using the mouse data, our LSTM model achieves approximately 0.86 AUC with 97% true negative rate (TNR) and 57% true positive rate (TPR). We can observe that the LSTM model is more benign-oriented and can be effective when high TNR is needed, at the expense of the TPR. To improve our LSTM results, we also tried to use deep LSTM (stacking several LSTM layers). Stacking two to three LSTM layers improved results on benign users by 1–2%. Another approach we tried was using bidirectional LSTM; however, we did not see any significant improvement in the results.

LSTM with Attention Results. Using the mouse data, our LSTM with Attention model achieves 0.88 AUC with 98% true negative rate (TNR) and 63% true positive rate (TPR). We can observe that this model is also more benign oriented and can be effective when high TNR is needed, at the expense of the TPR. Stacking several layers of LSTM with Attention did not improve the results.

CNN Results. Using the mouse data, the one-dimensional CNN model achieves approximately 0.84 AUC with 98% true negative (TNR) and 56% true positive (TPR). We can observe that this model is also more benign-oriented and can be effective when high TNR is needed at the expense of the TPR.

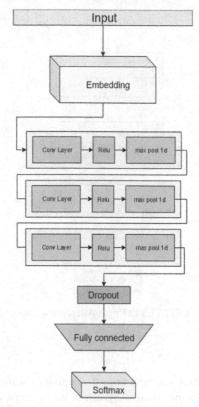

Fig. 3. One-dimensional Convolutional Neural Network Architecture.

Table 1. LSTM predicted results vs. actual labels on real web application users' data and impostors' data.

Predicted Results vs. Real Labels		Real Labels	
		Benign	Impostors
Predicted Label	Impostors	3%	**57%**
	Benign	**97%**	43%

The top performing algorithm in our experiments was the LSTM with Attention. Since keeping the FPR as low as possible is essential when focusing on commercial uses for continuous authentication, we compare our global model results with our previous user-based work [23], which used HMM with Linear Regression, while focusing on low FPR.

When focusing low FPR of up to 2%, the LSTM with Attention gains an advantage of up to 6% more TPR over the HMM with Linear Regression.

Table 2. LSTM **with Attention** predicted results vs. actual labels on real web application users' data and impostors' data.

Predicted Results vs. Real Labels		Real Labels	
		Benign	Impostors
Predicted Label	Impostors	2%	**63%**
	Benign	**98%**	37%

Table 3. 1D CNN predicted results vs. actual labels on real web application users' data and impostors' data.

Predicted Results vs. Real Labels		Real Labels	
		Benign	Impostors
Predicted Label	Impostors	2%	**56%**
	Benign	**98%**	44%

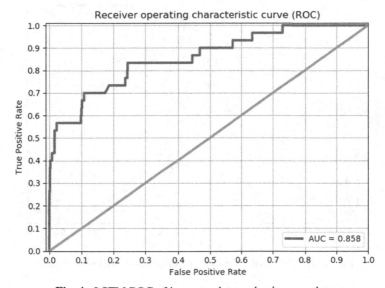

Fig. 4. LSTM ROC of impostor data vs. benign user data.

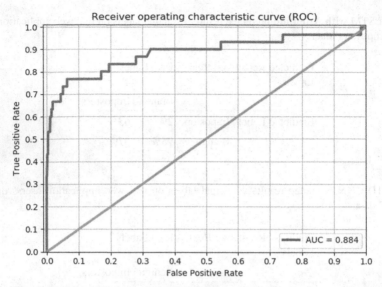

Fig. 5. LSTM **with Attention** ROC of impostor data vs. benign user data.

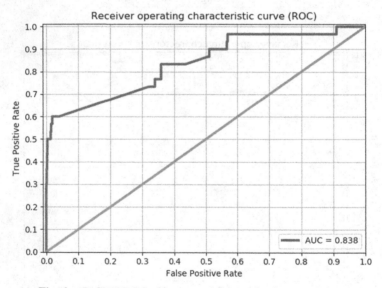

Fig. 6. 1D CNN ROC of impostors' data vs. benign users' data.

5   Conclusion

We presented a deep learning approach to verify user authenticity using the traversed paths of web elements, as we proposed in our previous work [23]. Instead of learning common features based on the users' pointing device movement (e.g., speed, angle), our method uses sequences of hovered or pressed web elements. Our previous work [23] introduced a model-per-user approach using HMM and Linear Regression. In our current work, we present various deep learning mechanisms that use a single global model.

We tested our current solutions using mouse data from IBM, containing data from daily internet tasks for more than 2000 real anonymous users, and showed that our different mechanisms were capable of successfully distinguish between impostors and benign users.

Among the deep learning methods that we tested; LSTM with Attention performed best with AUC of 0.884.

Although the overall AUC score of the HMM from our previous work was slightly higher (AUC of 0.908), the LSTM with Attention showed better results when focusing on the low FPR areas of the ROC curve with and improvement of up to 6% more TPR over the HMM, which is the desired case for most commercial usages of real-time authentication systems with high traffic that cannot tolerate high number of false alarms.

In addition, the LSTM with Attention has the major advantage of using one global model per web application instead of a model per user, which in a highly preferable in terms of memory consumption, storage, and implementation in high volume, real-time systems.

One limitation of this work is that due to insufficient touch data, we were only able to test our new methods on mouse data. Possible future work might focus on a touch dynamics dataset collected from mobile users who browse the web using their mobile devices.

References

1. Yampolskiy, R.V., Govindaraju, V.: Behavioural biometrics: a survey and classification. Int. J. Biometrics 1(1), 81–113 (2008)
2. Revett, K., Jahankhani, H., de Magalhães, S.T., Santos, H.M.D.: A survey of user authentication based on mouse dynamics. In: Jahankhani, H., Revett, K., Palmer-Brown, D. (eds.) ICGeS 2008. CCIS, vol. 12, pp. 210–219. Springer, Heidelberg (2008). https://doi.org/10. 1007/978-3-540-69403-8_25
3. Jorgensen, Z., Yu, T.: On mouse dynamics as a behavioral biometric for authentication. In: Proceedings of the 6th ACM Symposium on Information, Computer and Communications Security, pp. 476–482, March 2011
4. Levi, M., Allouche, Y., Kontorovich, A.: Advanced analytics for connected car cybersecurity. In: 2018 IEEE 87th Vehicular Technology Conference (VTC Spring), pp. 1–7. IEEE, June 2018
5. Bergadano, F., Gunetti, D., Picardi, C.: User authentication through keystroke dynamics. ACM Trans. Inf. Syst. Security (TISSEC) 5(4), 367–397 (2002)
6. Lau, E., Liu, X., Xiao, C., Yu, X.: Enhanced user authentication through keystroke biometrics. Comput. Network Secur. 6 (2004)
7. Gunetti, D., Picardi, Claudia: Keystroke analysis of free text. ACM Trans. Inf. Syst. Secur. (TISSEC) 8(3), 312–347 (2005)
8. Ahmed, A.A., Traore, I.: Biometric recognition based on free-text keystroke dynamics. IEEE Trans. Cybernetics 44(4), 458–472 (2013)
9. Monaco, J.V., Bakelman, N., Cha, S. H., Tappert, C.C.: Recent advances in the development of a long-text-input keystroke biometric authentication system for arbitrary text input. In: 2013 European Intelligence and Security Informatics Conference, pp. 60–66. IEEE, August 2013

10. Ahmed, A.A.E., Traore, I.: A new biometric technology based on mouse dynamics. IEEE Trans. Depend. Secure Comput. **4**(3), 165–179 (2007)
11. Awad, A., Ahmed, E., Traore, I.: Anomaly intrusion detection based on biometrics. In: Proceedings of the IEEE (2005)
12. Feher, C., Elovici, Y., Moskovitch, R., Rokach, L., Schclar, A.: User identity verification via mouse dynamics. Inf. Sci. **201**, 19–36 (2012)
13. Pusara, M., Brodley, C.E.: User re-authentication via mouse movements. In: Proceedings of the 2004 ACM Workshop on Visualization and Data Mining for Computer Security, pp. 1–8, October 2004
14. Shen, C., Cai, Z., Guan, X., Du, Y., Maxion, R.A.: User authentication through mouse dynamics. IEEE Trans. Inf. Foren. Secur. **8**(1), 16–30 (2012)
15. Zheng, N., Paloski, A., Wang, H.: An efficient user verification system via mouse movements. In: Proceedings of the 18th ACM Conference on Computer and Communications Security, pp. 139–150, October 2011
16. Shen, C., Cai, Z., Guan, X.: Continuous authentication for mouse dynamics: a pattern-growth approach. In: IEEE/IFIP International Conference on Dependable Systems and Networks (DSN 2012), pp. 1–12. IEEE (2012)
17. Kimon, L.B., Mirsky, Y., Rokach, L., Shapira, B.: Utilizing sequences of touch gestures for user verification on mobile devices. In: Phung, D., Tseng, V.S., Webb, G.I., Ho, B., Ganji, M., Rashidi, L. (eds.) PAKDD 2018. LNCS (LNAI), vol. 10939, pp. 816–828. Springer, Cham (2018). https://doi.org/10.1007/978-3-319-93040-4_64
18. Frank, M., Biedert, R., Ma, E., Martinovic, I., Song, D.: Touchalytics: On the applicability of touchscreen input as a behavioral biometric for continuous authentication. IEEE Trans. Inf. Foren. Secur. **8**(1), 136–148 (2012)
19. Feng, T., Liu, Z., Kwon, K.A., Shi, W., Carbunar, B., Jiang, Y., Nguyen, N.: Continuous mobile authentication using touchscreen gestures. In: 2012 IEEE Conference on Technologies for Homeland Security (HST), pp. 451–456. IEEE, November 2012
20. Zhang, H., Patel, V.M., Fathy, M., Chellappa, R.: Touch gesture-based active user authentication using dictionaries. In: 2015 IEEE Winter Conference on Applications of Computer Vision, pp. 207–214. IEEE, January 2015
21. Patel, V.M., Chellappa, R., Chandra, D., Barbello, B.: Continuous user authentication on mobile devices: recent progress and remaining challenges. IEEE Signal Process. Mag. **33**(4), 49–61 (2016)
22. Feng, T., Yang, J., Yan, Z., Tapia, E.M., Shi, W.: Tips: context-aware implicit user identification using touch screen in uncontrolled environments. In: Proceedings of the 15th Workshop on Mobile Computing Systems and Applications, pp. 1–6, February 2014
23. Levi, M., Hazan, I.: User profiling using sequential mining over web elements. In: 2019 IEEE 10th International Conference on Biometrics Theory, Applications and Systems (BTAS), Tampa, FL, USA, pp. 1–6 (2019). https://doi.org/10.1109/btas46853.2019.9186005
24. Graves, A., Mohamed, A.R., Hinton, G.: Speech recognition with deep recurrent neural networks. In: 2013 IEEE International Conference on Acoustics, Speech and Signal Processing, pp. 6645–6649. IEEE, May 2013
25. Sak, H., Senior, A.W., Beaufays, F.: Long short-term memory recurrent neural network architectures for large scale acoustic modeling (2014)
26. Chen, T., Xu, R., He, Y., Wang, X.: Improving sentiment analysis via sentence type classification using BiLSTM-CRF and CNN. Expert Syst. Appl. **72**, 221–230 (2017)
27. Antal, M., Egyed-Zsigmond, E.: Intrusion detection using mouse dynamics. IET Biometrics **8**(5), 285–294 (2019)

28. Hinbarji, Z., Albatal, R., Gurrin, C.: Dynamic user authentication based on mouse movements curves. In: He, X., Luo, S., Tao, D., Xu, C., Yang, J., Hasan, M.A. (eds.) MMM 2015. LNCS, vol. 8936, pp. 111–122. Springer, Cham (2015). https://doi.org/10.1007/978-3-319-14442-9_10
29. Tan, Y.X.M., Binder, A., Roy, A.: Insights from curve fitting models in mouse dynamics authentication systems. In: 2017 IEEE Conference on Application, Information and Network Security (AINS), pp. 42–47. IEEE, November 2017
30. Yang, Y., Guo, B., Wang, Z., Li, M., Yu, Z., Zhou, X.: BehaveSense: Continuous authentication for security-sensitive mobile apps using behavioral biometrics. Ad Hoc Netw. **84**, 9–18 (2019)
31. Jain, A., Kanhangad, V.: Exploring orientation and accelerometer sensor data for personal authentication in smartphones using touchscreen gestures. Pattern Recogn. Lett. **68**, 351–360 (2015)
32. Ngyuen, T., Voris, J.: Touchscreen biometrics across multiple devices. In: SOUPS (2017)
33. Paszke, A., et al.: Automatic differentiation in pytorch (2017)
34. Kingma, D.P., Ba, J.: Adam: a method for stochastic optimization. arXiv preprint arXiv:1412.6980 (2014)

An Interoperable Architecture for Usable Password-Less Authentication

Matthew Casey[1], Mark Manulis[2], Christopher J. P. Newton[2], Robin Savage[3], and Helen Treharne[2(✉)]

[1] Pervasive Intelligence Ltd., Fleet, UK
m.casey@pervasive-intelligence.co.uk
[2] Surrey Centre for Cyber Security, University of Surrey, Surrey, UK
{m.manulis,c.newton,h.treharne}@surrey.ac.uk
[3] SSP Ltd., Halifax, UK
robin.savage@ssp-worldwide.com

Abstract. Passwords are the de facto standard for authentication despite their significant weaknesses. While businesses are currently focused on implementing multi-factor authentication to provide greater security, user adoption is still low. An alternative, WebAuthn, uses cryptographic key pairs to provide password-less authentication. WebAuthn has been standardised and is resilient to phishing attacks. However, its adoption is also very low; the barriers to adoption include usability and resilience of keys. We propose a novel architecture for password-less authentication designed to improve usability and deployability. Our architecture is based on the WebAuthn standards and supports registration and login to web-services. We support a WebAuthn authenticator that generates and uses the key pairs on the client device by providing resilience for these key pairs by using a backup key store in the cloud. We also propose a WebAuthn authenticator using a key store in the cloud so that password-less authentication can be used interoperably between devices. We also assess the properties of these architectures against identified threats and how they can form the basis for improving usability and lowering the technical barriers to adoption of password-less authentication.

Keywords: Authentication · Password-less · Crypto-hardware · Key management · Security · WebAuthn

1 Introduction

Passwords are the de facto standard for authentication from e-commerce to online banking, yet they are a weak form of authentication [29]. To strengthen them, current advice [15, 27] focuses on making passwords more complex (but not too complex), avoiding password re-use (cf. [17]) and expiry, reducing the number of passwords we use and using password managers, for example LastPass [22]. These measures are designed to balance security with usability, where usability

© Springer Nature Switzerland AG 2020
A. Saracino and P. Mori (Eds.): ETAA 2020, LNCS 12515, pp. 16–32, 2020.
https://doi.org/10.1007/978-3-030-64455-0_2

is crucial in ensuring that we achieve acceptable levels of security. For the general population, however, only a minority of people appear to know how to protect themselves online [2], and hackers take advantage of this with 65% of malicious groups using phishing as their prime attack vector [32]. In simple terms therefore, passwords are easy to use but offer far lower levels of security than we need, especially for accounts that require stronger security, such as a user's prime email account or for online banking. The weaknesses of passwords make it desirable to replace them with stronger, password-less techniques which cannot so readily be subject to phishing attacks. In this paper we explore why password-less technologies are not being widely adopted and propose an architecture which can be used to unify existing password-less technologies and standards to make them interoperable in order to overcome their limitations and to help drive adoption.

Contributions: in this paper we review the barriers to adoption of password-less authentication technologies and propose how these barriers might be overcome. Our approach is to take advantage of the usability of password-less technologies, but to overcome issues of deployment to make them available for the general population through a unified architecture that provides an interoperable approach to password-less authentication adhering to the published standards [5]. We outline how the architecture can be designed, such that with strong security, trust and usability, we can help drive adoption.

In Sect. 3 we describe password-less authentication solutions and the user and business barriers to adoption. In Sect. 4 we propose how the technical barriers can be overcome through architectures that can be used to unify current and future standards-based password-less solutions. These architectures are described in Sects. 4.1 and 4.2 and we consider the trust assumptions and threats related to these architectures in Sect. 4.3. In Sect. 5 we consider how the architectures might be used by users and how this will affect how the systems are designed. Finally in Sect. 6 we conclude with the required next steps.

2   Background

To strengthen password authentication, *multi-factor authentication* (MFA) or (its more common subset) *two-factor authentication* (2FA) has been used, alongside password blacklists and throttling with lockouts [15,27]. Yet while these methods can improve security and, in particular, studies have found 2FA to offer acceptable levels of usability (cf. [31]), even here these extra measures can still be attacked because they rely on something that we know (or write down).

For example, some systems still use the far weaker *two-step verification* which requires the user to provide two pieces of information that they know, such as a password and memorable data, both of which can be compromised in the same way through phishing (cf. [28]). To correctly implement MFA, systems should require that a user provide information from two or more independent factors: 1) something they know, 2) something they have or 3) something they are [15]. However, even here, 2FA in particular can be compromised, for example weaknesses arise when users combine both independent factors into a single device (logging in from a phone which also receives the text message), or when the second factor is intercepted (text messages can be re-directed by compromising the telecommunications provider [21]).

While MFA provides stronger security compared to passwords alone, a bigger problem however is the lack of uptake of this and similar technologies. For example, in 2018 Google reported that less than 10% of users were using 2FA for their Google accounts [25].

For businesses, one of the drivers causing adoption of stronger authentication is the increasing cost of data breaches, with a global average cost per breach of $3.92m [18], a rise in cost by 12% over 6 years, and with one survey reporting that 94% of businesses cite that data breaches in the previous 12 months have influenced their security policies [33]. With malicious attacks causing 51% of data breaches in 2019 [18], businesses need stronger protection. In general, 58% of organisations believe that 2FA is the most likely access control tool which will be used to protect their systems [33], while 49% believe it is single sign-on and 47% biometric authentication. This shows that stronger access controls are being adopted, with one survey in 2019 [34] reporting 60% of organisations using 2FA or password-less technologies, and a further 29% looking at adoption or expansion of these technologies. However, 26% also cite complex implementation challenges, 26% customer friction and 10% expense as barriers to adoption.

3   Adoption of Password-Less Authentication

It is clear that both users and businesses struggle with the adoption of stronger authentication. If additional steps are implemented, such as basic forms of 2FA, user adoption is low because of perceived usability issues or a lack of understanding. For businesses, while the roll-out of stronger authentication is seen as beneficial, there is concern about implementation complexity. Here then, there is a clear need for stronger authentication, but the barriers to adoption are currently high for users, even if the majority of businesses are moving towards adoption. Microsoft have been promoting password-less authentication both for business (Windows Hello for Business [23]) and other users (Microsoft Authenticator App [24]) and these can work well in a Microsoft environment. Instead of promoting 2FA based on text messages and one-time passwords, or proprietary solutions, in this paper we discuss how a greater emphasis should be placed on password-less solutions using public key cryptography, which offer far better levels of security (thwarting phishing attacks [26]), usability and reduced management costs [37].

Password-less authentication [5,12] allows WebAuthn users to login to web applications using a cryptographic key pair. Once registered with their public key, to log in, the web application issues a challenge which must be signed using the user's private key that is then verified by the web application using the corresponding public key. This challenge-response protocol [5] is resistant to phishing because no credentials are ever exchanged, and instead relies upon the private key being kept secret (and here it is typically unknown and inaccessible to the user). Even if the encrypted challenge-response communication were intercepted, it cannot be used in a replay attack because a different challenge would be issued. Also, if a hacker were able to, say, clone the device which is holding the private key, an incremental usage counter can be used to reduce the likelihood that the clone could be used successfully to login. As a potentially usable and secure technology which offers far greater protection than passwords, why has adoption been slow and why has it not supplanted techniques which use passwords? Password-less authentication should be better for both users and businesses. There is clearly an uptake by industry, [10], but there are still barriers to overcome, including preconceptions, knowledge of techniques, expense and deployment (cf. [6]).

Password-less authentication was recently standardised in the W3C WebAuthn recommendation [5] and it is this proposal that we focus on here. WebAuthn is supported in all major web browsers and this gives businesses confidence to develop solutions which will work with any of them. Figure 1 represents the data flows which support registration and login to a web application using WebAuthn. In the W3C documentation login is referred to as the authentication ceremony. In this paper since we use the word authentication in several contexts, we use the term login instead of the WebAuthn authentication term. In the figure we show an authenticator app separate from the authenticator itself, in some cases this may be a single entity. The WebAuthn protocol requires a user to authenticate with the authenticator, this might be using biometrics, a PIN, or a passphrase. The web application, known as a relying party, can decide what security level it will accept for this authentication. We now outline the protocols used for registration and login.

When a user wishes to register an account with a relying party they connect to it (1). The relying party sends the user a challenge (2) which is passed to the authenticator (3). The user needs to authenticate themselves (4) and the authenticator generates a new signing key pair against an identifier for the relying party (5). The identifier, public key and signed challenge are then sent back to the relying party for verification (6) and storage against the newly created account (7).

At a later time when the user wishes to login (1), the relying party sends a challenge to the user (2) and it is passed to the authenticator (3). The user needs to authenticate themselves (4) and then the authenticator signs the challenge using the same private key (5) and sends it back (6). Login is successful if the challenge signature is validated against the public key for the user (7).

WebAuthn defines the protocols and data structures necessary to support registration and login to web applications. In particular it defines the interface for a WebAuthn authenticator which is used to generate the necessary key pairs (on registration) and sign the challenges when a user wishes to login to a relying party. This standard grew out of the work of the FIDO Alliance on the Fast Identity Online protocol and Client to Authenticator Protocol (current versions are FIDO2 [12] and CTAP2 [7]) and many systems base their current implementations on these standards.

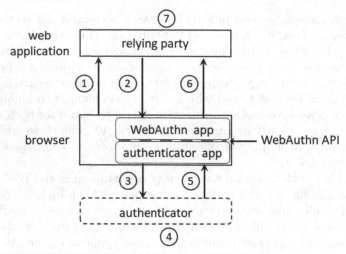

Fig. 1. Data flows in WebAuthn

	Registration	Login
(1)	user registers	user requests access
(2)	server sends challenge data	server sends challenge data
(3)	challenge passed to authenticator	challenge passed to authenticator
(4)	user verification	user verification
(5)	authenticator generates key pair	authenticator signs the challenge
(6)	public key and attestation sent to server	response sent to server
(7)	server validates response	server validates response

When built into a device, an authenticator (a *platform authenticator*) is typi-cally just used to protect private keys and other secrets used on that device only. This protection is achieved by, for example, using biometric access to apps, like that provided by Apple's Face ID. Other authenticators are designed to allow the associated keys to be used on any compatible computer via, for example, USB or NFC, and these are known as *roaming authenticators*. These devices are used to hold (or re-generate) key pairs for signing and offer portability between devices, but have limited capacity.

Both platform and roaming authenticators have the same problem: if a device with a platform authenticator or a roaming authenticator is lost or damaged, the data they hold is lost and hence so is a user's access to their registered relying parties. At the moment users of roaming authenticators would need to purchase them in pairs and create backup access by registering both of them with a relying party. This would mitigate the problem of loss or damage, but does not get over their limited capacity. Platform authenticators do not have the same capacity problem, but even when private keys are backed up to the cloud where they are typically encrypted so that they can only be decrypted on the corresponding phone [3]. So, while either type of authenticator offers strong security and improved usability over passwords their different capabilities are confusing, and this prevents adoption.

This highlights that usability is only one aspect which affects adoption of password-less authentication. Bonneau et al. [6] developed a wider, subjective framework for the comparison of password and password-less authentication methods and their properties. Crucially, this included deployability and security, as well as usability. They concluded broadly that usability and security can be improved through measures such as single sign-on (reducing the need for multiple passwords), but that of the technologies surveyed, most were an improvement in security relative to passwords. However, they also highlighted that every alternative was harder to deploy in some way. Specifically, they were less accessible, more expensive, less compatible with browsers or servers, less mature or proprietary. This is backed up by a study on secure communications tools, which found that usability is not the prime barrier to adoption, but that interoperability, low quality, lack of trust and misunderstanding were also factors [1]. Password-less solutions offer far greater security only if such technologies are actually used, therefore how they are implemented and deployed is just as crucial.

3.1 Adoption Challenges

From this we can summarise the barriers to adoption of password-less authentication faced by users and businesses as follows (building on [6]):

User Adoption Barriers:

Knowledge: With perhaps only 15% of people having sufficient knowledge of how to protect themselves online [2], and the majority of people using passwords, shifting to stronger authentication will take persuasion. Although when mandated by a service provider, people do learn how to adopt new authentication technologies.

Capabilities: There are over 70 FIDO2-certified authenticators [13] available on the market. They each offer different capabilities, such as the ability to roam between devices, and the number of keys that they can hold. They also differ in levels of protection, from no hardware-based protection (Level 1) over to uncertified (Level 2) and certified (Level 3) use of trusted tamper-resistant hardware [4,20,35]. A transparent comparison of capabilities would help, but a unified set of capabilities which meet minimum usability and security requirements would further promote adoption.

Expense: Hardware authenticators have an associated cost (for example, the latest generation of Yubikeys start at $45 per authenticator and Google Titan from $25) While crypto-hardware currently only tends to be built into more expensive devices (Google Pixel 3 from $399 and iPhone from $449). Adoption can therefore be expensive.

Privacy and trust: How do users know that their information is secure and that their privacy is not being compromised? Transparent design and associated information is needed to demonstrate trust in the underlying security.

Availabillty: While WebAuthn is supported by all major web browsers, service providers must adopt WebAuthn in their web applications for it to be available to users. Without this developer support, user adoption is not possible.

Registration and use: When a user has chosen a solution they must be able to deploy password-less access as easily as using a password. Studies on the deployment of Yubikeys (for 2FA) have shown that simple changes to registration instructions can improve adoption [11], so clear guidance is needed.

Resilience: If a roaming hardware authenticator, host computer or phone is lost, key pairs are lost with the device. This reliance on a single device to hold key pairs provides tangible physical security, but is inconvenient.

Service Provider Adoption Barriers:

Security and trust: Which solutions offer the best security for the needs of the business? For example, 2FA is currently the predominant technology being rolled out, perhaps because of its maturity and availability [33,34]. Businesses must be able to select a trusted solution which complies with the levels of security and certification they need (for example, FIPS 140-2 [30]).

Implementation complexity: Some businesses already consider the adoption of stronger authentication mechanisms potentially too complex [34] and these perceptions and the actual complexity of solutions must be overcome.

Roll-out and support: Roll-out of new technologies takes effort in design, implementation, marketing and support, as well as the direct cost for the service. Which solution presents the best value for the available budget? Does the solution reduce on-going support costs? For example, anecdotal evidence for the higher education sector in the UK suggests that Microsoft's Azure MFA has been adopted because of its lower cost.

Interoperability: When deploying password-less authentication to staff within a business, the authentication mechanism, such as a hardware authenticator, can be mandated to reduce complexity. When deploying to consumers, there is little choice over what types of password-less authenticator are used. Interoperable solutions are therefore required with adherence to standards [5,12].

3.2 Overcoming Adoption Barriers

These barriers to adoption lead us to the following aims in designing solutions to promote the adoption of password-less authentication:

- To unify technologies using standards to take advantage of crypto-hardware in a way which provides a minimum set of capabilities for all, therefore reducing confusion over which solution is right for users and businesses.
- To enable secure interoperability between solutions to provide backup and portability of key pairs to improve usability and mitigate against loss.

– To implement security by design and formally verify protocols to instil trust.
– To widely disseminate guidance on password-less technologies, their benefits and use to reduce preconceptions and increase adoption.

In this paper we focus on the first two aspects in order to propose cloud architectures for password-less authentication and we are mindful of the associated adoption challenges when designing them.

4 General Cloud Architectures for Password-Less Authentication

To achieve adoption by business, any approach that is proposed to support password-less authentication must conform, as far as possible, with existing standards, in particular WebAuthn and accepted hardware solutions [35,38]. We do not want to reinvent solutions, especially since a number are well established, rather we want to define a unified framework to support password-less authentication which is interoperable to present a unified user experience. We propose a cloud service approach that works for three use cases:

Use case 1 provides more resilience and reliability for devices that use a platform authenticator (e.g. a biometric reader, a Trusted Platform Module (TPM) [35] or an Intel Software Guard Extensions (SGX) [20] enclave) or a roaming authenticator (e.g. Yubikey) to provide a WebAuthn authenticator. While a local hardware authenticator may offer high levels of security and privacy, if the authenticator can only be used on a single device (i.e. platform authenticator), this restricts users to only using password-less access on that device. While a roaming authenticator offers portability, albeit with limited capacity, if the device is lost then access to relying parties is lost. Our first use case, outlined in Sect. 4.1, provides the same level of security as existing solutions, where the authenticator is local to the device and moreover a cloud service makes the key pairs available to other devices a user wishes to use and alleviates the limitation of key capacity and loss/failure of devices.

Our approach supports two further uses cases where the main functionality of the authenticator is provided by the cloud service application. Section 4.2 provides more details of the architecture that supports these two use cases.

Use case 2 is where a user device has a platform authenticator or roaming authenticator that can be used to authenticate to the cloud service. The cloud service uses a cloud authenticator to generate and manage key pairs that are used to access relying parties. This may be because the authenticator hardware is not WebAuthn compatible or because of limited capacity in the authenticator hardware. This can be considered as the hybrid use case.

Use case 3 is where a user device does not have a platform authenticator or access to a roaming authenticator. This use case is more akin to a password manager, but is now a secure key pair manager, where similar weaknesses of authenticating to the cloud service application are exhibited, but the vulnerabilities that can be introduced by password managers are avoided [8].

Note also that a user may have more than one use case across their devices - for example a user may posses a roaming authenticator that is compatible with one device (use case one), but a second device with is not compatible with the hardware (use case three). Our architecture allows the strongest possible authentication to be used on each device.

One important point to note is that in all cases the cloud service uses a hardware based security module (SM) that handles the keys and encrypts them for storage. An SM could be realised for example using a TPM or, with suitable enclave software, for example, SGX.

4.1   Cloud Service for Backup and Resilience

We propose that users' keys are stored in the cloud using a cloud service. Figure 2 shows a user device and the cloud service. The user device has a local authenticator, either a platform or a roaming authenticator (in what follows we will use the term local authenticator to cover both of these possibilities). The components of the cloud service are an application, a security module that is responsible for managing the keys and a key store that stores encrypted keys and associated data. Thus, even if an attacker gained access to the encrypted keys they would be unusable. This cloud service can be used to backup the keys from the authenticator but can also be used to support the migration of the keys to new devices. This key migration protocol already exists for TPMs. The benefit of this is that it adds resilience and avoids the necessity of registering a new device with each of the relying parties that the user accesses when a user changes device.

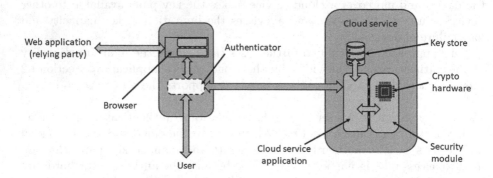

Fig. 2. Using a key store as backup.

When a user registers with a relying party a key pair is generated by the local authenticator and the private key can then be backed-up to the cloud service by setting up a secure channel between the local authenticator and the cloud SM. To set up the secure channel the user needs to authenticate to the cloud service. Since the device has access to a local authenticator this can also be done using WebAuthn and hence provides strong authentication.

When a user wishes to access a relying party they simply use the local authenticator and do not need to use the cloud service. For this use case we do not consider the situation where the number of encrypted keys in the key store is greater than the storage capacity of the local authenticator. This model could be extended to allow encrypted keys to be swapped in an out as required. However, our second use case provides the ability to handle extra keys when the local authenticator has limited storage.

4.2   Cloud Service as Authenticator

For users whose local authenticator has limited WebAuthn key storage, or those without a local authenticator at all we propose a cloud service application that acts as the WebAuthn authenticator (see Fig. 3). When the cloud service acts as the authenticator the key pairs are generated, used to sign challenges and protected by the crypto-hardware inside the SM.

As discussed earlier, this architecture supports two use cases. Firstly, where a user device has access to local authenticator and authentication to the cloud service can be done using WebAuthn. Secondly, when a user device does not have access to a local authenticator and authentication to the cloud service is be acheived by using a master password together with some form of software authenticator (for example, Google Authenticator). Once authenticated, the WebAuthn protocol works as usual.

When a user first registers with a relying party, the WebAuthn protocol issues a challenge which is relayed to the cloud service through the interface using TLS 1.2 [19] or above. The cloud service then uses its SM to generate a new key pair associated with the relying party, signs the challenge and returns the signature, public key and attestation information. When the user next logs into the relying party, a challenge is issued and again signed by the cloud service.

4.3   Basic Trust Assumptions and Threats

In this section we examine the trust assumptions and threats related to each use case.

Backup and Resilience Service: To understand how this service can resist attack, we have listed our trust assumptions and identified possible threats and their mitigation.

1. We assume that the cloud service application together with the cloud service provider are architected in such a way as to ensure resilience in the case of hardware/software failures via replication/clustering etc.

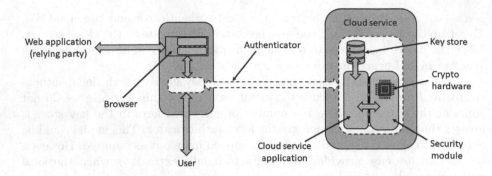

Fig. 3. WebAuthn configuration using a cloud service with SM

2. We do not assume that the communication channels between the different parts of the system are secure by default and so TLS 1.2 or above should be used when the user's device connects to the cloud service. In addition, once a user has authenticated to the cloud service application a secure channel should be established between the local authenticator on the user's device and the cloud service's SM to further secure the keys and data being transferred.
3. The cloud service application is trusted for integrity and availability of associated data and, where necessary, encrypted keys. In addition it is assumed to correctly pass information between the SM, a user's device and a relying party for (i) exchange of WebAuthn challenge and response messages and (ii) migration of keys.
4. We assume that the SM can be trusted and that includes the integrity and confidentiality of the keys generated and processed by the SM. Should the SM be compromised an attacker would be able to access all plaintext data and monitor its operations. User devices must therefore attest to the correct operation of the SM prior to any actions being performed. In addition, each user's data within the key store should be encrypted at rest, preferably using a key derived from the user's password provided this password was set up when registering with the cloud application service (although this would remove any possibility of password reset). The system design should ensure that these credentials are only be available within the SM once a user has authenticated and has established a secure channel.
5. We assume that a user's device is operating correctly. Our confidence in this assumption can be reinforced if the device can perform local attestation to confirm the state of its system before the SM establishes a secure channel for communication. This is in addition to the attestation used to confirm the state of the SM to the user.
6. We assume that the user's device correctly authenticates with the cloud service. The use of the local authenticator for WebAuthn authentication to the cloud service means that the cloud service application can rely of this authentication. Where a local authenticator is not available, authentication must be via a password with a second factor.

Cloud Authentication Service: The same assumptions listed above are made about this service, but when there is no local authenticator some of the mitigations are no longer possible, in particular those for items 5 and 6. Authentication to the cloud service can use a strong password and a second factor, such as the use of a software authenticator or a time-based one-timed password. However, attestation of the user's device will not be possible. There is clearly a trade off between the ability to use any device and the extra security provided by just restricting access to devices with local authenticators.

In addition since the cloud service is used to generate and use key pairs for specific relying parties, user privacy may be compromised if a malicious cloud service records user logins. This possibility can be mitigated by using, for example, the hash of the relying party's identifier rather than the relying party's identifier itself when using the cloud authentication service.

5   Using Our Password-Less Authentication Architectures Across Multiple Devices

Our approach must support users with multiple devices, since many users have more than one device which are likely to have different security capabilities, for example a phone, tablet and laptop. Thus the combination of devices can be categorised as follows:

Combination 1. Multiple devices all of which use local authenticators (either platform or roaming) supporting use case 1,

Combination 2. Multiple devices none of which use local authenticators (either platform or roaming), i.e. supporting use case 3,

Combination 3. Multiple devices some of which can use local authenticators (either platform or roaming), others with no available local authenticator, which is the most heterogrenous combination of capabilities supporting use cases 1, 2 and 3.

The different combination types have their own security implications that will influence the overall implementation of our approach but clearly the architectures presented in Sects. 4.1 and 4.2 may be used simultaneously by multiple devices.

The aspects we need to consider are when (i) users register new devices with the cloud service, (ii) register with a relying party, (iii) access a relying party and (iv) a user a loses a device.

5.1   Registration and Authentication of a User Device with the Cloud Service

When a user registers their device with the cloud service using their local authenticator a WebAuthn key pair is generated which can be used to give them access. The user would also need to provide an alternative means of authentication to use in case their device becomes lost or damaged. This would ideally be another device with a local authenticator, but the user may need to fall back on using a password and a second factor not associated with their WebAuthn device. Once a device with a local authenticator is registered it can be used to vouch for any further registrations of devices with local authenticators to ensure that they are associated with the same user.

Users without any devices with a local authenticator would need to register with the cloud service using a password and second factor as there is no device to register in this case; this is analogous to registering with a password manager. The mechanism used to register with the cloud service determines what a user would also need to do when subsequently authenticating to the cloud service. The use of multiple devices does not introduce security complexity for this aspect.

Recall, that once a device with a local authenticator is registered, it can then be automatically authenticated to the cloud service as necessary. If a device does not have a local authenticator, it would either need to do this each time or this can be made less of a problem by allowing a user to stay authenticated from a particular device for some time (using a token for example).

5.2   Registering with a Relying Party

We have already described how a single device with or without a local authenticator registers with a relying party. We now consider each combination and highlight what needs to be considered.

For combination 1, a device uses its local authenticator to register a user with a relying party. Then we anticipate that at pre-defined intervals a user's local keys are backed up to the cloud service. If the user has more than one device with a local authenticator then the keys would be synchronised across all devices so that the same relying parties can be seamlessly visited from any of them using the same key pair. If a local authenticator cannot store all of the keys then swapping of keys in and out of this local authenticator may be possible. If a local authenticator cannot synchronise then the associated user device would be required to utilise the cloud authenticator (combination 3).

For combination 2 the use of multiple devices introduces no further complications, the user logs in to the cloud service and is then able to register with relying parties and the keys are stored in the cloud. Once authenticated to the cloud service, the keys can then be available to the user from any of their devices. There are no capacity issues in this case.

For combination 3 those devices with access to a local authenticator could behave in the same way as combination 1 or they could just use the local authenticator to support authentication to the cloud service. In this case the ability to use the cloud authenticator would remove any capacity issues. Those without access to a local authenticator would need to authenticate to the cloud service using the registered password and second factor and would use the cloud authenticator to register with relying parties. The policies for sharing keys across devices would need to be carefully considered. In the case of devices in combination 3 not having a local authenticator you would expect that all keys be shared, as is the case in a password manager. In the case of a device which uses local authenticator for authentication, it would also be natural to share the keys with devices with no local authentication but accepting that there is some downgrade in the security. In the case of a device which has a local authenticator and we consider the sharing of its keys with devices that have a local authenticator only used for authentication with the cloud service, and with devices that have no local authenticator, then implementation policies may need to be introduced to restrict this sharing. For example, if the device with a local authenticator which stores its keys locally is used to access a bank account, then it may be appropriate to restrict other devices with weaker security capabilities from accessing it.

5.3 Logging on to a Relying Party

We have already described how a single device with and without a local authenticator accesses a relying party. Since the controlling of access to the keys and policies is determined when registering with a relying party, no further issues are introduced when accessing it in any of the combinations.

5.4 Loss of a Device and Revocation

For a user with a single device with a local authenticator their keys will be regularly backed up so that should their device become unusable/lost/stolen and need to be replaced they can register a new device with a local authenticator using the two factor authentication previously set up. Once the new device is registered the WebAuthn data will be downloaded and can be used. All of the user's previous relying party registrations can still be used. As above, if there are any capacity issues with downloading the keys then, as above, the device would not use the local authenticator to store the keys for the relying party but rather use the cloud key store. If the replacement device did not have a local authenticator, the keys would simply remain in the cloud and be accessed from there. If a device with no local authenticator was to be replaced by another then the replacement would similarly either download the keys or retrieve them from the key store.

An implementation would also need to consider the revocation of keys in the case of a lost or stolen device. If the device had no local authenticator (and hence did not store any WebAuthn private keys) then only its two-factor authentication would need to be deactivated on the cloud service to prevent anyone from access the cloud service on user's behalf. If the device was equipped with a local authenticator then any WebAuthn private keys that were simultaneously stored on the device and the cloud store must be revoked. The user would first use these private keys in the cloud authenticator to login to relevant relying parties and ask them to deactivate corresponding WebAuthn public keys, before deleting these private keys from the cloud store and deactivating cloud service access for the lost device.

6   Conclusion and Future Work

This paper proposes a cloud approach that works for three use cases. The first use case increased the resilience of devices that have a platform or a roaming authenticator to provide a WebAuthn authenticator and also strong authentication to the cloud service application. The second and third use cases moved the main authenticator functionality from a user's device to the cloud service application and this is where the innovation in our approach lies; the two use cases differ only in the use of a local authenticator if available to authenticate with the cloud service. It provides the opportunity for a variety of devices to utilise our cloud approach with differing levels of security depending on how authentication to the cloud service application is achieved. The issues of authenticating to a cloud service is not unique to our approach, but are challenges that would apply to any cloud based system. Our motivation for this research was to minimise the friction of an authentication approach in order to make secure password-less authentication more feasible for users with less technical experience and who cannot afford to upgrade or supplement their existing hardware. Therefore, we proposed an approach that would be applicable to a range of users whose devices and hardware have different capabilities.

The next step in this research is to focus on the development of the proposed cloud authenticator and its protocols and it will be important to take recent work by Chen et al. [9] and by Fryman et al. [14] into account. This will require definition of WebAuthn specific binding to ensure inter-operability. Once the architecture has been fully developed with its corresponding security protocols then a formal analysis will need to be conducted to verify its security. Such analyses can expose threats which can then be mitigated. Formal analysis has already been conducted for WebAuthn [16] and our experience of formally analysing direct anonymous attestation protocols will also be relevant [36]. Furthermore, a reference implementation of the architecture will also serve to promote discussion with industry. It will also be important to examine the socio-technical aspects of the architecture to re-visit the barriers to user adoption because reflecting these concerns in architecture design is particularly important.

Acknowledgments. This research was funded by EPSRC through the DICE project, EP/N028295/1. The authors would like to thank the reviewers for reviewing this paper and for their helpful comments.

References

1. Abu-Salma, R., Sasse, M.A., Bonneau, J., Danilova, A., Naiakshina, A., Smith, M.: Obstacles to the adoption of secure communication tools. In: IEEE S&P 2017, pp. 137–153, May 2017. https://doi.org/10.1109/SP.2017.65
2. Ames, A., Stannard, J., Stellmacher, D.: UK cyber security survey 2019. https://www.ipsos.com/ipsos-mori/en-uk/uk-cyber-security-survey-2019/ (2019)
3. Apple Inc.: Storing keys in the secure enclave — apple developer documentation. https://developer.apple.com/documentation/security/certificate_key_and_trust_services/keys/storing_keys_in_the_secure_enclave/ (2020)
4. Arm Limited: Trustzone - Arm developer. https://developer.arm.com/ip-products/security-ip/trustzone/ (2019)
5. Balfanz, D., et al.: Web authentication: an API for accessing public key credentials level 1, March 2019, https://www.w3.org/TR/2019/REC-webauthn-1-20190304/

6. Bonneau, J., Herley, C., Oorschot, P.C., Stajano, F.: The quest to replace passwords: a framework for comparative evaluation of web authentication schemes. In: 2012 IEEE S&P, pp. 553–567, May 2012. https://doi.org/10.1109/SP.2012.44
7. Brand, C., et al.: Client to authenticator protocol (CTAP), January 2019. https://fidoalliance.org/specs/fido-v2.0-ps-20190130/fido-client-to-authenticator-protocol-v2.0-ps-20190130.html
8. Carr, M., Shahandashti, S.: Revisiting security vulnerabilities in commercial password managers. In: International Conference on ICT Systems Security and Privacy Protection, IFIP SEC 2020, February 2020. https://sec2020.um.si/
9. Chen, S., Barbosa, M., Boldyreva, A., Warinschi, B.: Provable security analysis of fido2. Cryptology ePrint Archive, Report 2020/756 (2020). https://eprint.iacr.org/2020/756
10. Cimpanu, C.: Microsoft: 150 million people are using passwordless logins each month. https://www.zdnet.com/article/microsoft-150-million-people-are-using-passwordless-logins-each-month/ (2020)
11. Das, S., Russo, G., Dingman, A.C., Dev, J., Kenny, O., Camp, L.J.: A qualitative study on usability and acceptability of Yubico security key. In: Proceedings of the 7th Workshop on Socio-Technical Aspects in Security and Trust, pp. 28–39. STAST 2017, Association for Computing Machinery (2018). https://doi.org/10.1145/3167996.3167997
12. FIDO Alliance: FIDO2: Moving the world beyond passwords using WebAuthn & CTAP. https://fidoalliance.org/fido2/ (2019)
13. FIDO Alliance: Certified products. https://fidoalliance.org/certification/fido-certified-products/ (2020)
14. Frymann, N., Gardham, D., Kiefer, F., Lundberg, E., Manulis, M., Nilsson, D.: Asynchronous Remote Key Generation: An analysis of Yubico's proposal for W3C WebAuthn. In: ACM CCS 2020. ACM (2020), https://dx.doi.org/10.1145/3372297.3417292
15. Grassi, P.A., et al.: NIST special publication 800–63B: Digital identity guidelines: authentication and lifecycle management, June 2017. https://pages.nist.gov/800-63-3/sp800-63b.html
16. Guirat, I.B., Halpin, H.: Formal verification of the W3C web authentication protocol. In: 5th Annual Symposium and Bootcamp on Hot Topics in the Science of Security. HoTSoS 2018, Association for Computing Machinery (2018). https://doi.org/10.1145/3190619.3190640
17. Hussain, T., Atta, K., Bawany, N., Qamar, T.: Passwords and user behavior. J. Comput. **13**, 692–704 (2018). https://doi.org/10.17706/jcp.13.6.692-704
18. IBM Security: Cost of a data breach report 2019. https://databreachcalculator.mybluemix.net/ (2019)
19. IETF: The transport layer security (TLS) protocol. https://tools.ietf.org/html/rfc5246 (2008)
20. Intel: Intel® software guard extensions. https://software.intel.com/en-us/sgx/ (2020)
21. Jacobs, F.: How Russia works on intercepting messaging apps. https://www.bellingcat.com/news/2016/04/30/russia-telegram-hack/ (2016)
22. LastPass: LastPass technical whitepaper. https://support.logmeininc.com/lastpass
23. Microsoft: Passwords-less protection. https://query.prod.cms.rt.microsoft.com/cms/api/am/binary/RE2KEup
24. Microsoft: Enable passwordless sign-in with the microsoft authenticator app. https://docs.microsoft.com/en-us/azure/active-directory/authentication/howto-authentication-passwordless-phone (2019)

25. Milka, G.: Anatomy of account takeover. In: Enigma 2018 (Enigma 2018). USENIX Association, Janunary 2018. https://www.usenix.org/node/208154
26. Mirian, A., DeBlasio, J., Savage, S., Voelker, G.M., Thomas, K.: Hack for hire: exploring the emerging market for account hijacking. In: WWW 2019. p. 1279–1289. ACM (2019). https://doi.org/10.1145/3308558.3313489
27. National Cyber Security Centre: Password administration for system owners. https://www.ncsc.gov.uk/collection/passwords/updating-your-approach/ (2018)
28. National Cyber Security Centre: Setting up two-factor authentication (2FA). https://www.ncsc.gov.uk/guidance/setting-two-factor-authentication-2fa/ (2018)
29. National Cyber Security Centre: Passwords, passwords everywhere. https://www.ncsc.gov.uk/blog-post/passwords-passwords-everywhere/ (2019)
30. National Institute of Standards and Technology: FIPS 140–2: Security requirements for cryptographic modules, June 2001. https://csrc.nist.gov/publications/detail/fips/140/2/final
31. Reese, K., Smith, T., Dutson, J., Armknecht, J., Cameron, J., Seamons, K.: A usability study of five two-factor authentication methods. In: Fifteenth Symposium on Usable Privacy and Security (SOUPS 2019). USENIX Association, Santa Clara, CA, August 2019. https://www.usenix.org/conference/soups2019/presentation/reese
32. Symantec: Internet security threat report (ISTR) 2019. https://www.symantec.com/content/dam/symantec/docs/reports/istr-24-2019-en.pdf (2019)
33. Thales: 2019 Thales access management index. https://safenet.gemalto.com/identity-access-management-index/ (2019)
34. ThumbSignIn, One World Identity, Gluu: Customer authentication practices 2019. https://thumbsignin.com/customer-authentication-report-2019/ (2019)
35. Trusted Computing Group: TPM 2.0 library specification. https://trustedcomputinggroup.org/resource/tpm-library-specification/ (2016)
36. Wesemeyer, S., Newton, C., Treharne, H., Chen, L., Sasse, R., Whitefield, J.: Formal analysis and implementation of a TPM 2.0-based direct anonymous attestation scheme. AsiaCCS 2020 (to appear) (2020). https://ethz.ch/content/dam/ethz/special-interest/infk/inst-infsec/information-security-group-dam/research/publications/pub2020/eccdaaimp-asiaccs20.pdf
37. World Economic Forum: Passwordless authentication: The next breakthrough in secure digital transformation. http://www3.weforum.org/docs/WEF_Passwordless_Authentication.pdf (2020)
38. Yubico: Yubico — YubiKey strong two factor authentication. https://www.yubico.com/ (2020)

auth.js: Advanced Authentication for the Web

Neophytos Christou$^{(\boxtimes)}$ and Elias Athanasopoulos

Department of Computer Science, University of Cyprus,
P.O. Box 20537, 1678 Nicosia, Cyprus
{nchris23,eliasathan}@cs.ucy.ac.cy

Abstract. Several research works attempt to replace simple authentication schemes, where the cryptographic digest of a plaintext password is stored at the server. Those proposals are based on more elaborate schemes, such as PAKE-based protocols. However, in practice, only a very limited amount of applications in the web use such schemes. The reason for this limited deployment is perhaps their complexity as far as the cryptography involved is concerned. Today, even the most successful web applications use text-based passwords, which are simply hashed and stored at the server. This has broad implications for both the service and the user. Essentially, the users are forced to reveal their plain passwords for both registering and authenticating with a service.

In this paper, we attempt to make it easier for any web service to a) enable easily advanced authentication schemes, and b) switch from one scheme to another. More precisely, we design and realize auth.js, a framework that allows a web application to offer advanced authentication that leverages sophisticated techniques compared to typical cryptographically hashed text-based passwords. In fact, auth.js can be easily enabled in all web applications and supports traditional passwords – however, once enabled, switching to a more elaborate scheme is straight forward. auth.js leverages advanced cryptographic primitives, which can be used for implementing strong authentication, such as PAKE and similar solutions, by ensuring that all cryptographic primitives are trusted and executed using the browser's engine. For this, we extend Mozilla Crypto with more cryptographic primitives, such as scrypt and the edwards25519 elliptic curve. Finally, we evaluate auth.js with real web applications, such as WordPress.

1 Introduction

Authentication is vital for the majority of on-line web applications. Through the process of authentication, services can distinguish their users and offer dynamically generated and personalised content. Unfortunately, the authentication process is often an attractive target for attackers. The goal of attackers is to impersonate users by stealing their credentials and therefore have access to their data. Notice that, beyond accessing sensitive data, the attacker can also *generate* information on behalf of the compromised user [6,21].

© Springer Nature Switzerland AG 2020
A. Saracino and P. Mori (Eds.): ETAA 2020, LNCS 12515, pp. 33–49, 2020.
https://doi.org/10.1007/978-3-030-64455-0_3

Several attacks exist depending on the way authentication is implemented. In the case of text-based passwords, it is common to salt, cryptographically hash, and store them at the server. The mechanics of the password protection, which is based on storing the password hashed at the server, coerces the user to *reveal* their plain password to the server each time they log in, which is very likely to already be used in other services, as well. A malicious server could then use the user's plain password to try to take control of another account of the same user in another service. This can be dramatically augmented due to password reuse [14], where users recycle passwords among different services. Other solutions that combat password reuse, like password managers that auto-generate strong passwords do exist, but unfortunately such solutions have not been thoroughly adopted [8]. Furthermore, the majority of other authentication schemes, like SSO services such as OAuth [15], still make use of plaintext passwords. These services do reduce password reuse, since users can authenticate to many services through a single SSO provider. However, they are still vulnerable to password reuse attacks. If a user registers to a malicious website by reusing the same password as the one they use for their SSO provider, the attacker could then use the password to authenticate as the user at all the other services in which the user is registered with their SSO provider.

On the other hand, advances in cryptography have developed all necessary tools for realizing protocols that do more than simply sending a string to be salted and hashed. For instance, several protocols for Password Authentication Key Agreement (PAKE) [10] permit a password to act as a seed for generating cryptographic keys. Regardless of the actual implementation, such schemes allow users to send a secret to the server for authenticating instead of the password in plain. The secret is cryptographically connected with the password and, therefore, even non-trusted servers must perform cracking attacks for revealing a user's password.

Despite the availability of such protocols, services continue to base their authentication on hashing plain passwords. An exception to this rule is Keybase [1], a service which offers cryptographic functions to users (for instance encrypted chat, filesystem and version control). Keybase assumes that the password (or *passphrase*, as they call it) of the user serves as a seed for generating a pair of keys that belong to an elliptic curve [11]. The private key is generated on the fly by the browser and allows the user to sign a message that is validated using the public key stored at the Keybase server. Thus, the password of the user is never revealed to Keybase, while complex handling of cryptographic keys is not an issue; the keys can be re-generated from the passphrase every time the user logs in (from any device).

Unfortunately, Keybase implements all this functionality, including the cryptographic operations, using its own code and does not use the browser's engine to do so. A web site may advertise that it supports a Keybase-like authentication process, where the password of the user is never revealed to the server, in order to convince users to register with it. However, unless the cryptographic primitives are executed in a secure context, it is unclear whether the aforementioned web site implements the authentication algorithm correctly or deliberately violates it in order to read the user's password.

In this paper, we build a framework for allowing any web site to offer advanced authentication, where plain passwords are used but are never exposed to any server. In particular, we design, implement and evaluate auth.js, an authentication framework with a JavaScript interface, which allows developers to enable any PAKE-like protocol in their apps. As a proof-of-concept, we use auth.js to enable Keybase-like authentication to WordPress with just a few code modifications. auth.js can be used through JavaScript, however, all cryptographic primitives are enforced by the browser engine, which we assume trusted. For this, we extend Mozilla Crypto with more cryptographic primitives, such as scrypt and the edwards25519 elliptic curve.

1.1 Contributions

To summarize, this paper contributes:

- we extend Mozilla Crypto with more cryptographic primitives, such as scrypt and the edwards25519 elliptic curve – although this is a solely engineering task, we consider it important for enabling new cryptographic capabilities for web applications;
- we design and realize auth.js, a framework that allows a web application to offer advanced authentication that leverages sophisticated techniques compared to typical cryptographically hashed text-based passwords;
- auth.js can be easily enabled in all web applications and supports traditional passwords – however, once enabled, switching to a more elaborate scheme is straight forward;
- we evaluate auth.js with real web applications, such as WordPress. Enabling auth.js in WordPress requires modifying about 50 LoCs of the main authentication code and adding 50 LoCs for enabling password recovery and signature validation.

2 Background

In this section, we briefly discuss some common authentication schemes supported by most web applications. auth.js can easily support all mentioned schemes, as well as more elaborate ones, such as PAKE protocols [10].

2.1 Conventional Password Authentication

The most common authentication scheme used in the web is text-based passwords. A general overview of how this scheme works is the following. Firstly, when a user registers a new account, they send their password over a (usually encrypted) channel to the web server. The web server uses a cryptographic hash function to compute the hash of the user's password and stores the hash, along with other information about the user, such as their username.

When the client wants to authenticate itself to the server, the user is prompted for their password and the password is sent back to the server. At the server, the hash of the password is computed again and compared against the stored hash. If the two hashes match, the authentication is successful and the user is logged in. For storing different cryptographic digests for identical passwords, the server often concatenates a random, non secret, *salt* to the plain password before hashing it.

2.2 Public Key Authentication

An alternative method is public-key authentication. This form is often combined with keys that are derived from a password, in order to simulate the typical text-based password experience. For this authentication scheme, the client does not send their password to the server that it wants to register to. Instead, it generates a key pair consisting of a public key, which is sent to the server, and a private key, which the client stores locally.

For authentication, the client informs the server that it wants to authenticate. The server then sends a message to the client and the client uses their stored private key to sign the message, in order to prove ownership of the private key. The signed message is sent back to the server, and the server verifies the signature using the stored public key of the user. If the verification is successful, the user is logged in.

2.3 Keybase Authentication

Keybase [1] is a service which offers to its users the ability to prove their identity on social media platforms by mapping their profiles to generated encryption keys. It also offers end-to-end encrypted messaging between its users, an encrypted cloud storage system and other services. Keybase uses a public key authentication system which works as follows. When a new user tries to sign up [3], they firstly type in a password. However, the password is not directly submitted to the server. Keybase uses its signup API call to generate a random salt value and an `scrypt` hash is generated using the password and the salt. Some bytes of the generated hash value are interpreted as an EdDSA private key, which is then used as a seed to another function to generate the corresponding EdDSA public key. This public key is sent to the Keybase server and is stored as the user's credential. At the login phase [2], the EdDSA private key is recomputed similarly to the signup phase. In order to prove ownership of the key, the client recomputes the private key by prompting the user to re-type their password. Using this key, the client creates a signature which is verified by the server using the stored public key of the user.

3 Architecture

In this section we provide an overview of the architecture of `auth.js`, as well as the steps needed to be taken by the web application programmer in order to use the framework. We also provide an example of a use case where a server chooses to use an advanced authentication scheme based on public-key cryptography, and specifically based on the authentication scheme of Keybase described in Sect. 2, to register and authenticate its users. This scheme is referenced as scrypt_seed_ed25519_keypair by the auth.js API. The cryptographic primitives required to be performed for authentication and registration are handled on the client side by the auth.js framework, which uses the client's browser engine to ensure that the cryptographic operations are performed in a secure context.

3.1 Overview

auth.js provides simple API calls for the programmer that wants to use advanced authentication techniques in their web application, without needing to worry about the underlying implementation. This is especially important for the various cryptographic elements, which may be leveraged during authentication. First, the programmer does not need to re-implement any cryptographic primitives and, second, all primitives are enforced by the web browser, which we consider trusted.

When a client requests a web application, the web server will direct the client to retrieve a copy of auth.js. The library can be provided to the client either by the web server directly, or via a trusted third party such as a Content Distribution Network, as seen in Fig. 1. Ideally, a user can even pre-install auth.js, eliminating any need to retrieve it through the web for each authentication. After retrieving the library, the client is able to start the registration or authentication process. In particular, our library provides two API calls, **authenticate** and **register** that, when called, will use the client's browser Web Crypto API to perform the correct cryptographic operations depending on the chosen authentication scheme. For example, in the case of the scrypt_seed_ed25519_keypair scheme, the library will use the implemented scrypt hash function and the Ed25519 key generation to create a key pair using the user's password. For authentication, it will use the generated private key to sign a nonce sent by the server using the Ed25519 signature scheme, to prove ownership of the private key.

Our library currently supports traditional plain password authentication, as well as the more advanced public key authentication scheme based on the Keybase authentication. It can be extended to support any authentication scheme, as long as the browser supports the corresponding cryptographic primitives.

3.2 auth.js API

Usage. Our JavaScript library provides an easy-to-use API that can be used by the web application programmer with minimal effort. The library will be used as follows:

- The server that wants to use our library includes auth.js in the web application's source.

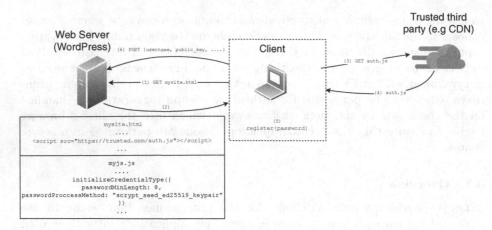

Fig. 1. Overview of the architecture of `auth.js`. The client requests the web application from the server (1). The server responds by sending the html file, which directs the client to retrieve `auth.js` from a trusted third party, as well as with a JavaScript file in which the authentication options are initialized (2). The client then retrieves `auth.js` from the trusted source (3 and 4). The client's browser prompts the user for a password and the register API call from `auth.js` is used to generate the correct credential (5). In this case the generated credential is the user's public key, which is generated based on the password which the user provided. Finally, the credential is sent to the server (6), where it will be verified.

- The desired authentication options must be initialized by the web programmer using the `initializeCredentialType` API call in the main web application (e.g. in the JavaScript file served by the web server), as depicted in Listing 1.2. This call takes as an argument a JSON object describing the authentication options. The library currently supports two options. First, the `passwordMinLength` option allows the server to choose the minimum password length it can accept. The second option, `passwordProcessMethod`, enforces the use of one of the supported authentication schemes. The currently supported schemes are `plain`, which is the traditional text-based password and `scrypt_seed_ed25519_keypair`. If the `initializeCredentialType` call is not used, the library will use the default values of no minimum password length and the `plain` authentication scheme.
- After initializing the options, the `authenticate` and `register` calls can be used. Those calls are placed in the web application's JavaScript source by the web programmer, to be called when the user tries to perform a authentication or registration action. The `register` function takes as an argument the password which the user typed and returns the corresponding credential based on the chosen authentication scheme, to be sent to the server. The `authenticate` function also takes as an argument the user's password and, in the case where an advanced public-key based authentication scheme is used, the optional message argument, which is the nonce that should be signed

using the user's private key. The function generates the private key based on the password, signs the message if needed, and returns the signed message. In the case of the plain authentication scheme, the two functions simply return the user's password.

- The web application sends the generated credential to the server. If the authentication or registration is successful, the user can continue using the web application as usual.

Example. In the following example, we depict how a server chooses to use the scrypt_seed_ed25519_keypair authentication scheme, with a minimum of 8 characters for the password. The web application HTML code directs the user to retrieve auth.js from a trusted source, as seen in Listing 1.1. The API calls of auth.js, register and authenticate, are then used to generate the correct credentials that the web application can now send to the server.

```
1  <html>
2  <head>
3  ...
4  <script type = "text/javascript" src = "https://trusted.com
       /auth.js"></script>
5  <script type = "text/javascript" src = "myjs.js"></script>
6  ...
7  </head>
8  <body>
9  /* Registration and login form */
10 </body>
11 </html>
```

Listing 1.1. Web application html file. The client is directed to get auth.js from a trusted source.

```
1   initializeCredentialType({
2       passwordMinLength: 8,
3       passwordProccessMethod: "scrypt_seed_ed25519_keypair",
4   });
5       let password = document.getElementById("password");
6           /* On registration action */
7       let credential = register(password);
8           /* On login action */
9       let message = document.getElementById("nonce");
10      let credential = authenticate(password, message);
11  /* Send credential and other necessary information to the
        server */
```

Listing 1.2. Web application JavaScript file. The minimum password length and authentication scheme are initialized. The register and authenticate API calls are called when a user tries to register to or authenticate with the server. auth.js generates the correct credential based on the user's password, and the credential is then sent to the server along with other necessary information, such as the user's username

4   Implementation

Since modern web browsers do not yet provide support for the cryptographic primitives needed for offering advanced cryptographic capabilities, we extended Mozilla's Network Security Services, which is the set of cryptographic libraries used by Mozilla, to support the use of the scrypt cryptographic hash function, the creation of Ed25519 public and private keys and the use of the Ed25519 signature scheme. Firefox's Web Crypto API also needed to be extended, so as to enable the option to make use of the new cryptographic primitives through the browser. By adding those capabilities, the client does not need to rely on untrusted external sources to perform the aforementioned cryptographic operations, since their own browser's engine executes the cryptographic primitives in a secure context.

4.1   Extending Mozilla's Network Security Services

Adding the scrypt Cryptographic Hash Function. We added a new cryptographic hash function based on the implementation of scrypt taken from Tarsnap [5] into the NSS. The new function is added in NSS similarly to other existing cryptographic hash functions, such as the implementation of SHA256. An example of how the new scrypt works, along with the existing SHA256, is depicted in Listing 1.3.

```
1  void
2  SHA256_End(SHA256Context *ctx, unsigned char *digest,
3             unsigned int *digestLen, unsigned int
      maxDigestLen)
4  {
5      unsigned int inBuf = ctx->sizeLo & 0x3f;
6      unsigned int padLen = (inBuf < 56) ? (56 - inBuf) : (56
      + 64 - inBuf);
7      ...
8      /* SHA256 implementation */
9  }
10 void
11 SCRYPT_End(SCRYPTContext *ctx, unsigned char *digest,
12            unsigned int *digestLen, unsigned int
      maxDigestLen)
13 {
14     /* Set scrypt parameters */
15     _crypto_scrypt (...);
16 }
```

Listing 1.3. sha512.c in Mozilla's NSS implementation, which contains the implementation of existing hash functions. SCRYPT_End calls the _crypto_scrypt function (part of the Tarsnap scrypt implementation) to perform the hashing.

Adding the Ed25519 EdDSA Signature Scheme. In a similar fashion, we added support for the Ed25519 signature scheme. In particular, we added the functionality to create a public-private key pair based on a given seed, as well as the signing functionality of the scheme. For this cryptographic primitive, we used parts of the SUPERCOP benchmarking tool's implementation of Ed25519 [4].

4.2 Extending Mozilla's Web Crypto API

Apart from extending the NSS library, we also needed to extend Mozilla's Web Crypto API, in order to enable the use of the newly added cryptographic primitives through JavaScript API calls. Similarly to the NSS extension, we located the files containing the calls to other cryptographic primitives and extended them to also provide calls to the newly added operations. With this addition, the client's browser can use the Web Crypto API to perform password hashing using the scrypt hash function, as shown in Listing 1.4, generate Ed25519 keys and sign messages using those keys.

```
1 const encoder = new TextEncoder();
2 //Get scrypt hash of password
3 const passwordEncoded = encoder.encode(password);
4 const hashScrypt = crypto.subtle.digest("SCRYPT",
    passwordEncoded);
```

Listing 1.4. scrypt hash function called from Firefox using Mozilla's Web Crypto API.

4.3 WordPress

WordPress is one of the most popular open-source web management systems. It is written in PHP and is widely used for building various websites, ranging from simple blog spots to professional websites. Since it is open-source, we modified the source code to incorporate our authentication and registration system, by extending the current WordPress functionality.

The current default login and registration system of WordPress works as follows. When users wish to register to the website, they provide their user name and email. The user then receives an email with what is essentially link to a reset password form, where they can set their first password. After the user chooses a password, it is sent to the server, where it is salted and hashed with the MD5 hash function and stored.

At the login phase, the user fills in their user name or email and their password in the login form, which is submitted to the server. There, the hash of the submitted password is checked against the stored hashed password and, if they match, the user is logged in.

A web developer that wishes to use auth.js in a WordPress site can do so by making minor tweaks to the WordPress source code. The number of changes needed to be made depend on the authentication scheme that is chosen to be used. Simply adding auth.js in a WordPress website that wishes to continue using its current authentication system is as simple as adding a few lines of code, while switching to the public key authentication scheme requires some extra steps, such as the addition of a few more functions using the hooks provided by WordPress, in order to extend the functionality of the authentication system. Both of the aforementioned additions are demonstrated below.

Using `auth.js` with the Current WordPress Authentication System.
A web developer can choose to add `auth.js` to a WordPress website without wishing to change the default authentication scheme. To do so, the following steps are required:

- Include `auth.js` in the list of the scripts which are loaded along the log in and reset password pages. Note that as discussed in Sect. 3, this could also be done by loading the file from a trusted third party, such as a CDN.
- Modify the log in and reset password form to make `auth.js` intervene before the form submission, in order to change the typed user password to the corresponding credential for the chosen authentication method. Even though no modification will be made on the password field when the `plain` (default) authentication scheme is chosen, adding this will make it easier to switch between authentication schemes in case the web developer wishes to change to a more advanced authentication scheme in the future.

Adding the `auth.js` file can easily be done using the `login_enqueue_scripts` hook provided by WordPress, as shown in Listing 1.5. This should be added in the `wp-login.php` file, which handles the login, reset password and registration forms.

```
1    add_action( 'login_enqueue_scripts', 'enqueue_authjs' )
     ;
2
3    function enqueue_authjs( $page ) {
4            wp_enqueue_script( 'auth', home_url() . '/wp-
     includes/js/auth.js', null, null, true );
5    }
6    do_action( 'login_enqueue_scripts' );
```

Listing 1.5. Using the `login_enqueue_scripts` hook to enqueue auth.js.

To modify the reset password form, a script that temporarily stops the form submission must be added. We demonstrate how this can be done using JQuery in Listing 1.6. The minimum password length and authentication scheme must be initialized using the `initializeCredentialType` call. Before eventually submitting the form, the script uses the `auth.js` API to generate the correct credential and change the credential value which will be submitted. Similarly to the reset password form, a script can be added to change the submitted password value on the login form. In the case of the `plain` authentication scheme, the typed password length is checked and the password is submitted as is.

Both the reset password and log in form scripts can be saved in the site's resources in the `wp-includes/js` folder and enqueued in the same way the `auth.js` file is enqueued, by including them in a JavaScript file in the website resources and then using the `login_enqueue_scripts` hook in the `wp-login.php` file.

Using auth.js with the Public Key Authentication Scheme. In order to switch to the more advanced public key authentication scheme, the following additional steps must be made, apart from the steps described above:

- Whenever the `initializeCredentialType` is used to set the options for the credential generation, use `scrypt_seed_ed25519_keypair` as the value for the `passwordProccessMethod` field.
- Modify the login form to include a random token that will be utilized as a nonce and get signed with the user's private key in order to perform authentication.
- Add the same nonce as a cookie that will be submitted along with the form, in order for the server to have the original value of the nonce and be able to verify the signature.
- Modify the default authentication check of WordPress to make it verify the submitted signed nonce using the stored public key.

```
1  jQuery("#resetpassform").on("submit", function (e) {
2      e.preventDefault(); //Stop form submission
3      let self = jQuery(this);
4      initializeCredentialType({
5        passwordMinLength: 8,
6        passwordProccessMethod: "plain",
7      });
8      let password = jQuery("#pass1").val();
9      let public_key = register(password); //Generate the
       credential using auth.js
10     public_key.then( (pk) => {
11         console.log(pk);
12         jQuery("#pass1").val(pk); //Set the new credential
       value to be submitted
13         jQuery("#pass2").val(pk);
14         jQuery("#resetpassform").off("submit");
15         self.submit();//Submit the form
16     })
17  });
```

Listing 1.6. JavaScript code that uses `auth.js` API to generate the credential and submit the reset password form

To use the public key authentication scheme in the log in and reset password forms, the `passwordProccessMethod` field seen in Listing 1.6 needs to be changed to `scrypt_seed_ed25519_keypair`. When this authentication scheme is chosen, the `register` API call of `auth.js` will use the browser's Web Crypto API and perform the necessary cryptographic operations to change the value of the typed password to the corresponding Ed25519 public key, which is generated using the `scrypt` hash of the password as a seed. The log in script will use the authenticate API call to sign the nonce placed in the login form using the private key corresponding to the public key mentioned earlier. The submitted value will be the public key concatenated with the generated signature. Note that the server must have a way to get the original value of the cookie, in order to be able to verify the signature.

Next, the nonce that will be utilized as a message and get signed using the user's private key needs to be added. A simple way to do so is to generate a nonce on the server and attach this nonce in a hidden field in the login form and also add the same value as a cookie. This way, the server does not need to keep the state of each session, since the original value of the nonce before it was signed can be retrieved from the cookie. This addition is demonstrated in Listing 1.7 and should again be made in the wp-login.php file.

```
1 # Create nonce and set it as a cookie
2 $token = bin2hex(openssl_random_pseudo_bytes(16));
3 setcookie("nonce-message", $token, time() + 60 * 60 * 24);
4 ...
5 # Add the nonce as a hidden field in the login form
6 <input type="hidden" id="nonce-message" name="nonce-message
      " value="<?= $token ?>" />
```

Listing 1.7. Add a nonce as a cookie, as well as in the log in form as a hidden field

```
1 function wp_authenticate_username_password( $user,
     $username, $password ) {
2
3     if ( ! wp_check_password( $password, $user->user_pass,
     $user->ID ) ) {
4         return new WP_Error(
5             'incorrect_password',
6             sprintf(
7                 /* translators: %s:    User name . */
8                 __( '<strong>ERROR</strong>: The password
     you entered for the username %s is incorrect. ' ) ,
9                 '<strong>' . $username . '</strong>'
10                ...
11     }
12 ...
13 }
```

Listing 1.8. wp_authenticate_username_password, one of the default authentication functions used in WordPress

Finally, the authentication check in the WordPress server side needs to be modified. To do this, the authenticate hook can be used to add a new function to authenticate the user. This hook should be added in the default-filters.php file, in the wp-includes folder. We added the new user authentication function, called authjs_authenticate, in the user.php file. authjs_authenticate functions similarly to the default authentication functions[1] used by WordPress, except that, for checking the user's credentials, it does not call the default `wp_authenticate_email_password` function. Instead, it calls a new function called `check_public_key`. The differences between the two functions can be seen in Listings 1.8 and 1.9.

```
function authjs_authenticate( $user, $username, $password )
    {
...

    if ( !check_public_key( $password, $user->user_pass ,
    $user->ID ) ) {
        return new WP_Error(
            'incorrect_public_key',
            sprintf(
                __( '<strong>ERROR</strong>: Wrong public
    key' ),
        }
}
```

Listing 1.9. The `authjs_authenticate` function which is used in place of the default authentication function of WordPress

The `check_public_key` function is added in the `pluggable.php` file. Listing 1.10 shows how `check_public_key` verifies that the submitted signature is correct. In particular, it parses the received credentials to get the public key and signature values and checks if the hash of the public key submitted by the user matches the stored public key hash. Then, it uses the submitted signature along with the Ed25519 public key and the original nonce value to verify the signature. We implemented this check as an external Python script, which uses the PyNaCl library to verify that the given signature is correct. After the signature is verified, the user is successfully logged in.

```
        // Get the original value of the nonce from the
    cookie, so we can verify the signature
        $message = $_COOKIE["nonce-message"];
        $public_key = substr($credentials, 0, 64);
        $signature = substr($credentials, 64);
        // Check if the user sent the correct public key
        $check = hash_equals( $stored_pk, md5( $public_key
    ) );
        /* Run python script to verify signature */
        ...
        return apply_filters( 'check_password', $check,
    $credentials, $stored_pk, $user_id );
```

Listing 1.10. The `check_public_key` function that verifies the submitted signature using the user's stored public key

---

[1] To be precise, WordPress has three default authentication methods: one using username and password, one using email and password and one using a cookie.

5   Evaluation

In this section we evaluate the performance of auth.js and particularly the overhead that the public key authentication system adds over the traditional password authentication method.

5.1   Setup

For the following measurements, we used two Linux machines running Ubuntu 18.04 LTS. The first machine run a dummy server with minimal functionality. The second machine run a fork of Mozilla Firefox Nightly 73.0a1, compiled with the disable optimizations and enable debug options.

5.2   Average Time for Posting Credentials on the Server and Getting a Reply

We measured the average time for generating and posting a user's credentials using the two authentication methods, traditional password authentication and public key authentication, from the machine running Firefox to the machine running the dummy server. For checking the password, the dummy server simply checked if the posted password matched the user's stored password in its database. For checking the posted signature, the server run the Python script mentioned in Sect. 4. Table 1 presents the average time for 1,000 repetitions.

Table 1. Average time for posting key pairs and signatures.

Credential posted	Average time
Password	260 ms
Signature	328 ms

5.3   Average Time for Key Pair and Signature Generation

We measured the performance of auth.js for creating Ed25519 key pairs and signing messages using the private key of the pair. We split the measurement in 3 parts: the time for only generating key pairs with a given password, the time for only signing a given message with a given key pair, and the time for both generating a key pair using a given password and signing a given message with the generated private key. Table 2 presents the average time for these three measurements for 10 thousand repetitions.

Table 2. Average time for generating key pairs and signatures.

	Average time
Generate key pair	30.9 ms
Sign message	29.5 ms
Generate key pair + sign message	59.3 ms

6 Related Work

6.1 Advanced Authentication Schemes

Apart from the public key authentication scheme we presented, various more authentication methods exist. PAKE protocols such as SRP [22] allow clients to authenticate themselves to a server and exchange a secret securely, without needing to send their actual password. Even though certain PAKE protocols have seen some adoption, many of them have not been successfully deployed yet. Other password-based authentication mechanisms which are based on PAKE protocols, such as [23], are also starting to get proposed. `auth.js` can serve as a single framework from which such protocols can be deployed. As long as the cryptographic primitives needed for a protocol are implemented in the client's browser, `auth.js` can securely enforce their usage, assuming of course that the browser is not compromised. A web programmer who wishes to use another scheme for authenticating users can do so simply by changing the `passwordProccessMethod` field in their forms to the authentication scheme of their choosing and transparently switch to a new authentication method, assuming that the server also supports the use of a chosen protocol. The authentication scheme mentioned in this paper is based on the authentication scheme used by Keybase [1]. The major difference is that Keybase uses its own source code to perform the cryptographic operations, while `auth.js` uses the cryptographic primitives that are built in the user's browser, ensuring that the operations will be performed securely.

6.2 Cryptographic Primitives

In the recent years, many improvements have been made and many new cryptographic primitives have been introduced, which are not yet implemented by the major web browsers. For our work, we added the scrypt [18] hash function as well as the Curve25519 elliptic curve [11] to Mozilla Firefox and specifically in the Web Crypto API, in order to use them for our authentication scheme. We expect that those cryptographic primitives, as well as more primitives such as the bcrypt [19], Argon2 [12] and blake2 [9] hash functions or new elliptic curves such as the FourQ curve [13] will eventually be implemented in the major web browsers and will be available to use. As more and more cryptographic primitives are added, `auth.js` can be modified to support the usage of these primitives to create new authentication schemes. Other projects have also explored the extension of the Web Crypto API functionality to add support for other operations, such as document signing [16]. New types of cryptographic primitives are also starting to get implemented. For example, Microsoft's SEAL [20] provides an API that can be used to perform homomorphic encryption.

6.3   Cryptography Frameworks

Other frameworks have also tried making advanced cryptography more accessible and easier to use. For example, Let's Encrypt [7,17] makes it easy to obtain a TLS certificate without the need of human intervention. Keybase is another web service that offers advanced cryptography to simple users, such as an advanced authentication scheme, end-to-end encryption, public identity verification and encrypted storage.

7   Conclusion

In this paper we designed, implemented and evaluated `auth.js`, a framework that allows web developers to integrate any authentication scheme in their applications. `auth.js` allows a developer to express the authentication policy in JavaScript and realize complex schemes, that leverage modern cryptographic primitives, in the browser environment. Moreover, the framework makes sure that cryptographic operations are not implemented in JavaScript, but are instead carried out using the browser's internal engine, which is considered trusted. For this, we extended Mozilla Crypto with the `scrypt` hash function and the edwards25519 elliptic curve in order to easily implement the authentication used in Keybase. In the same fashion, `auth.js` can support other cryptographic-based authentication schemes, such as PAKE. Enabling `auth.js` in existing web application is trivial and, once the framework is in place, switching from one authentication to another is straight forward. For demonstrating this, we enabled `auth.js` in a popular open-source web application, namely WordPress. Our modifications do not exceed 50 LoCs for the main authentication code in WordPress and require additionally 50 LoCs for enabling password recovery and signature validation.

Acknowledgments. We thank the anonymous reviewers for helping us to improve the final version of this paper. This work was supported by the European Union's Horizon 2020 research and innovation programme under grant agreements No. 786669 (ReAct), No. 830929 (CyberSec4Europe), and No. 826278 (SERUMS), and by the RESTART programmes of the research, technological development and innovation of the Research Promotion Foundation, under grant agreement ENTERPRISES/0916/0063 (PER-SONAS).

References

1. Keybase.io. https://keybase.io/
2. Keybase.io Login API Documentation. https://keybase.io/docs/api/1.0/call/login

3. Keybase.io Signup API Documentation. https://keybase.io/docs/api/1.0/call/signup
4. Supercop Benchmarking Tool. https://bench.cr.yp.to/supercop.html
5. Tarsnap Scrypt 1.3.0. https://www.tarsnap.com/scrypt/scrypt-1.3.0.tgz
6. Abu-Nimeh, S., Chen, T., Alzubi, O.: Malicious and spam posts in online social networks. Computer **44**(9), 23–28 (2011)
7. Aertsen, M., et al.: How to bring HTTPS to the masses? Measuring issuance in the first year of let's encrypt (2017)
8. Alkaldi, N., Renaud, K.: Why do people adopt, or reject, smartphone password managers? (January 2016)
9. Aumasson, J.P., Neves, S., Wilcox-O'Hearn, Z., Winnerlein, C.: BLAKE2: simpler, smaller, fast as MD5. In: Jacobson, M., Locasto, M., Mohassel, P., Safavi-Naini, R. (eds.) Applied Cryptography and Network Security. ACNS 2013. Lecture Notes in Computer Science, vol. 7954. Springer, Heidelberg (2013). https://doi.org/10.1007/978-3-642-38980-1_8
10. Bellovin, S.M., Merritt, M.: Encrypted key exchange: password-based protocols secure against dictionary attacks. In: Proceedings 1992 IEEE Computer Society Symposium on Research in Security and Privacy, pp. 72–84. IEEE (1992)
11. Bernstein, D.J., Duif, N., Lange, T., Schwabe, P., Yang, B.-Y.: High-speed high-security signatures. In: Preneel, B., Takagi, T. (eds.) CHES 2011. LNCS, vol. 6917, pp. 124–142. Springer, Heidelberg (2011). https://doi.org/10.1007/978-3-642-23951-9_9
12. Biryukov, A., Dinu, D., Khovratovich, D.: Argon2: new generation of memory-hard functions for password hashing and other applications. In: 2016 IEEE European Symposium on Security and Privacy (EuroS P), pp. 292–302 (2016)
13. Costello, C., Longa, P.: FourQ: four-dimensional decompositions on a Q-curve over the Mersenne Prime. In: Iwata, T., Cheon, J.H. (eds.) ASIACRYPT 2015. LNCS, vol. 9452, pp. 214–235. Springer, Heidelberg (2015). https://doi.org/10.1007/978-3-662-48797-6_10
14. Gaw, S., Felten, E.W.: Password management strategies for online accounts. In: Proceedings of the Symposium on Usable Privacy and Security, SOUPS (2006)
15. Hardt, D.E.: The OAuth 2.0 authorization framework. Internet Requests for Comments (October 2012)
16. Hofstede, N., Bleeken, N.V.D.: Using the W3C WebCrypto API for document signing (2013)
17. Manousis, A., Ragsdale, R., Draffin, B., Agrawal, A., Sekar, V.: Shedding light on the adoption of let's encrypt. CoRR, abs/1611.00469 (2016)
18. Percival, C.: Stronger key derivation via sequential memory-hard functions (2009)
19. Provos, N., Mazieres, D.: A future-adaptable password scheme. In: USENIX Annual Technical Conference, FREENIX Track, pp. 81–91 (1999)
20. Microsoft SEAL (release 3.4): Microsoft Research, Redmond, WA (October 2019). https://github.com/Microsoft/SEAL
21. Thomas, K., Grier, C., Song, D., Paxson, V.: Suspended accounts in retrospect: an analysis of twitter spam. In: Proceedings of the 2011 ACM SIGCOMM Conference on Internet Measurement Conference, IMC 2011, pp. 243–258. Association for Computing Machinery, New York (2011)
22. Wu, T.D., et al.: The secure remote password protocol. In: NDSS, vol. 98, pp. 97–111. Citeseer (1998)
23. Zhang, Z., Wang, Y., Yang, K.: Strong authentication without temper-resistant hardware and application to federated identities (January 2020)

Automated and Secure Integration of the OpenID Connect iGov Profile in Mobile Native Applications

Amir Sharif[1,2]([envelope]) [ORCID], Roberto Carbone[1] [ORCID], Giada Sciarretta[1] [ORCID],
and Silvio Ranise[1,3] [ORCID]

[1] Fondazione Bruno Kessler, Trento, Italy
{asharif,carbone,giada.sciarretta,ranise}@fbk.eu
[2] DIBRIS, University of Genova, Genova, Italy
[3] Department of Mathematics, University of Trento, Trento, Italy

Abstract. Electronic identification schemes have been built to simplify citizens access to online public administration services and reduce password fatigue via a single sign-on experience. To provide a precise specification for government and public service domains on how to protect the user's identity information and activity from unintentional exposure, the OAuth working group together with the OpenID Connect foundation have published the International Government Assurance Profile (iGov) document. As the specification contains high-level concepts and brings together a lot of insights from already published documents to increase the baseline security and structure deployments, it may be unclear or misleading for mobile application developers. This is mainly due to the fact that firstly, they are not usually security experts and secondly, the aforementioned documents are not mostly designed for the native applications that can affect the implementation security based on the differences between the native and web environment. The aforementioned source of uncertainty for inexperienced developers can lead to various threats that can expose user's resources. To avoid these problems, we demystify the iGov profile for non-security experts by extracting the wealth information from the iGov specifications, and we apply the best current practices for native applications within the iGov profile to conceptualize the flow for native applications. Furthermore, we provide a wizard-based approach to automatically integrate the secure code for the iGov profile in Android native applications.

Keywords: Identity management · OAuth 2.0 · OIDC · iGov · Android security

---

Partially supported by the innovation activity 19184 "API Assistant" of the Digital Infrastructure action line of the EIT Digital, and by the joint laboratory "DigiMat Lab" between FBK and the Italian National Mint and Printing House (IPZS).

A. Saracino and P. Mori (Eds.): ETAA 2020, LNCS 12515, pp. 50–70, 2020.
https://doi.org/10.1007/978-3-030-64455-0_4

1   Introduction

Infrastructures for digital Identity Management (IdM) are key enablers for secure and trusted access to e-government services. A Single Sign-On (SSO) protocol enables users to login to an IdM provider (hereafter, IdMP) once and gain access to several client applications without requiring users to authenticate for each one of them. This is helpful both for usability and security. Historically, one of the most widely adopted standard in this context is SAML 2.0 [3]. Among the profiles defined in the SAML standard, the most used is the web browser SSO profile [14].

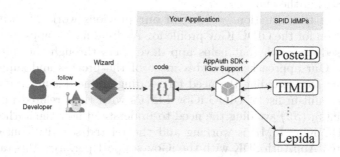

Fig. 1. Proposed Approach to support iGov (SPID scenario).

Recently, because of the increasing access to Internet via mobile, e-government projects are considering to transition from SAML to OpenID Connect [24] (hereafter, OIDC) to ease the integration of mobile applications (hereafter, app) with their digital IdM infrastructures. To enhance authentication transactions based on common requirements for the public domain, the OAuth working group and the OIDC foundation published the International Government Assurance profile (hereafter, iGov) drafts for OAuth 2.0 (hereafter, OAuth) and OIDC [9,10]. In addition, to help app developers within the implementation process, they have also released an SDK library called AppAuth [22]. It is a client SDK for native apps that implements the security and usability best practices identified in the OAuth for native apps [4] specification.

Despite the main aim of these specifications and the released SDK is to help app developers to secure the implementation of IdM solutions, many available apps are poorly implemented nonetheless [16,28]. Although IdMPs try to help developers to mitigate security issues by providing documentations, if developers are not security experts and do not understand security critical code, their IdM solutions may be exposed to serious security vulnerabilities. Furthermore, in the iGov scenario, the situation would be even worse as many local administrative agencies (e.g., municipalities) are small entities with limited resources, that may not accomplish all the development life cycle phases, such as the security testing, to avoid vulnerability proliferation. So, given the lack of competences and the difficulty in understanding the security-related implications, the transition from SAML to iGov in the e-government projects is not without troubles.

The Italian digital identity framework SPID [2] is an example of e-government framework that is facing the transition from SAML to OIDC iGov [1]. In the near future, as described in the new draft specification, SPID IdMPs (9 in the current federation, such as PosteID, TIMiD, and intesaID) will support also the OIDC iGov profile. The effort of this transition is substantial in the mobile scenario, as app developers should: (*P1*) refer to the iGov IdMP documentation, the related OIDC RFCs, and the OAuth for native Apps specification; (*P2*) understand the full document and its security-related topics that most of the time are abstract and hard to digest; (*P3*) write pieces of code to implement the login with the iGov IdMP within the app.

To alleviate this situation, we extend our previous work [25] with secure code integration for the OIDC iGov profile for Android native apps by providing a wizard-based approach that helps app developers through the implementation process. Our approach automates most of the process and supports app developers by: (*S1*) avoiding the need for reading online documentations since it provides a built-in list of OIDC iGov IdMPs with their related information (e.g., endpoints); (*S2*) avoiding the need to understand how the authentication with an OIDC iGov IdMP is working and the related security considerations (the integrated AppAuth SDK with the iGov support performs this task effortlessly and securely); (*S3*) automatically integrating the code to incorporate the OIDC iGov profile within the app and enabling the communication with OIDC iGov IdMPs. Notice that *S1–S3* solve *P1–P3* respectively. Figure 1 shows our approach for the SPID Scenario. To summarize, our main contributions are:

- We demystify the iGov profile specification to extract the wealth information, summarize it in plain English as it is hard to digest by non-security experts, and apply the best current practices for native apps within iGov profile to conceptualize the flow for native apps.
- We identify the security best practices for the iGov profile for native apps by deriving them from revisiting the iGov profile as an extension of OIDC for native apps that is explained later in the paper.
- We extend our wizard-based approach to allow app developers to integrate in their app the OIDC iGov profile for native apps effortlessly and in a secure manner.

Paper Structure. In Sect. 2, we introduce the main concepts of the OIDC flow and the best current practice for native apps. The OIDC iGov profile for native apps is then summarized and compared with the OIDC flow in Sect. 3. The extended wizard-based approach to support the OIDC iGov profile together with its architecture and security analysis are explained in Sect. 4. Related work is provided in Sect. 5, and finally, we sum up the main results and provide some insights for future work in Sect. 6. Table 1 provides a list of abbreviations that are used in the paper.

2 A Biased Introduction to OIDC for Native Apps

In Fig. 2, we propose a simplified relationship among OAuth, OIDC, iGov profiles, and SPID OIDC documentations. The actual situation is even more complex as these documents refer to many other specifications that either bring new functionalities (e.g., the OAuth Dynamic Client Registration [11]) or an extension to improve their security (e.g., the Proof Key for Code Exchange [23]). As shown in Fig. 2, OIDC [24] is an authentication layer developed on top of the OAuth Authorization Framework [8] and is the current de-facto standard for providing SSO login. A common scenario in OIDC involves a user, called Resource Owner (RO), who wants to authenticate on a client app (C), without having to share her credentials with C. Indeed, RO authenticates by using her User Agent (UA) with a trusted OIDC server, called Authorization Server (AS), which issues a token to C carrying information about the authentication process and basic attributes about RO. OIDC targets clients of all types, but the focus of this paper is on native apps. In Sect. 2.1, we detail the OIDC flow for native apps and in Sect. 2.2 we present the best current practices (BCPs) for this scenario.

Table 1. List of abbreviations.

Abbreviation	Concept	Abbreviation	Concept
IdM	Identity management	IdMP	IdM provider
app	Mobile native application	SSO	Single sign-on
OIDC	OpenID Connect	BCP	Best current practice
C	Client	RO	Resource Owner
AS	Authorization Server	UA	User Agent
PSI	Program structure interface	$PKCE$	Proof Key for Code Exchange

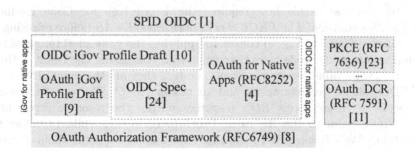

Fig. 2. The relationship among OAuth, OIDC, iGov profiles and SPID.

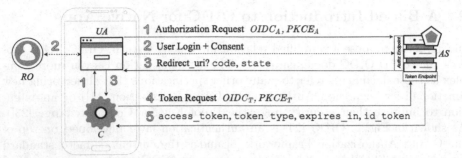

1. *C* initiates the flow by directing the *RO*'s *UA* to the authorization endpoint including the $OIDC_A$ and $PKCE_A$ parameters.
2. *AS* authenticates *RO* by displaying the login and consent form in *UA*.
3. Assuming the access grant acceptance by the *RO*, *AS* redirects *UA* back to *C* with an authorization code and the `state` parameter.
4. *C* sends the $OIDC_T$ and $PKCE_T$ parameters to *AS* asking for the OIDC tokens.
5. *AS* executes the PKCE checks. If they are successful, it releases two OIDC tokens: `access_token` of type `token_type` (usually `Bearer`) with an expiration indicated in the parameter `expires_in`, and `id_token`, a signed JWT that contains basic attributes about *RO*.

Fig. 3. OIDC authorization code flow with PKCE for native apps.

2.1 OpenID Connect for Native Apps

As the OIDC specification [24] is not specifically designed for the native scenario, we extracted the information for OIDC for native apps by starting from the OIDC specification and integrating the BCPs set out in the OAuth for native Apps specification [4]. Indeed, the OAuth working group has released this document to address the lack of details on how to implement in a secure and usable way the SSO login in case the role of *C* is played by a native app. They suggest which flow, user agent and redirection mechanism shall be used. The OIDC flow for native apps is shown in Fig. 3 together with an explanation of each step. We list the query parameters of the authorization and token requests in Table 2.

To avoid authorization `code` interception—that may lead to un-authorized access to user data—this flow requires the Proof Key for Code Exchange (*PKCE*) [23] extension. The *PKCE* checks performed by *AS* before releasing the OIDC tokens (Step 5 of Fig. 3) consist in applying the `code_challenge_method` transformation to the `code_verifier` value and comparing the result with the `code_challenge` value received in Step 1. Only if they are the same, *AS* releases two OIDC tokens (`access_token` and `id_token`) to *C*. The `access_token` is used by *C* to either access *RO*'s resources within the resource server or to request *RO*'s claim to the *AS* using *UserInfo* endpoint, while `id_token` is a signed JSON Web Token (JWT) [13] that contains basic claims about *RO* used by *C* to authenticate *RO*.

Table 2. OIDC query parameters of authorization code flow with PKCE for native apps.

Tag	Query parameter	Value	Description
$OIDC_A$	response_type	code	Determines the authorization flow to be used
	scope	oidc	A space-separated string of the scopes being requested and the oidc must be present when OIDC is supported
	client_id	string	The unique identifier of the native app
	state	string	A random string generated by the app used for maintaining state between the request and the callback
	redirect_uri	string	The URL to return to after the successful authentication
$PKCE_A$	code_challenge	string	A string generated by applying code_challenge_method to the code_verifier value
	code_challenge_method	plain or S256	Transformation method used to calculate code_challenge
$OIDC_T$	grant_type	authorization_code	Determines the way C gets the OIDC-Core tokens
	code	string	The authorization code received in Step 3 from AS
$PKCE_T$	code_verifier	string	A high-entropy cryptographic random string

2.2 Best Current Practices for Native Apps

As mentioned in Sect. 2.1, the OAuth working group has released "OAuth 2.0 for Native Apps" [4], which extends the OAuth Authorization Framework (as shown in Fig. 2) providing a set of BCPs for native apps. The key points related to BCPs are summarized in Table 3, and discussed below.

As shown in Fig. 3, the suggested flow is the *Authorization Code* flow together with the *PKCE* extension [23]. The OAuth working group introduced *PKCE* to avoid the authorization code interception on public clients and consequently stealing of a valid access_token to access the user data. The *PKCE* avoids the aforementioned attack by adding the three parameters (code_challenge, code_challenge_method, and code_verifier) described in Table 2. BCPs sug-

Table 3. BCPs for native apps.

Concept	Best practice
Flow	Authorization Code w/o client secret
PKCE	If Custom URI, then PKCE mandatory
UA	External (possibly "in-app browser" tabs)
Redirection	HTTPS or Custom URI

gest avoiding the use of the *Implicit* flow support as this flow returns OIDC tokens (`access_token` and `id_token`) directly in the authorization response (Step 3 of Fig. 3) and cannot be secured by *PKCE*, which makes it vulnerable to the token leakage.

The User Agent (*UA*) shown in Fig. 3 is an external browser. In the Android environment, two kinds of *UA* are supported: *embedded* (e.g., Web View) and *external* (e.g., OS browsers, in-app browser tabs and native apps). For security reasons, developers should avoid the usage of *embedded UA*, due to the full control of the app on the user data (a malicious *C* app could, for example, steal the *RO*'s password). Indeed, BCPs recommend the usage of the *external UA*, in particular an external browser supporting "in-App browser tabs" [4]. The suggestion of using in-App browser tabs is mainly due to usability reasons: these tabs allow developer to pre-start and pre-fetch content for faster loading, and they can be customized for matching the application theme. The customization helps users to feel they have not left the app, and this helps to provide a sense of familiarity and security that is less available when lunching external browsers.

For the redirection of the authorization `code` to the *C* app, there are three methods that can be used within native apps: (*i*) app-declared *Custom URI* scheme, (*ii*) app-claimed *HTTPS URI* scheme, and (*iii*) *Loopback URI* redirection [4]. Among the aforementioned methods, the app-claimed *HTTPS URI* redirection (known as *App Link*) is recommended wherever it is supported by the OS, because it provides a way to guarantee the identity of native apps: after an app installation, the OS checks whether the app has the right to claim a specific URL, in this way checking the app identity [15]. Otherwise, the *Custom URI* scheme is recommended due to its wider adaptability with different Android OS versions and for security reasons, it must be used alongside with *PKCE*. Indeed, when *PKCE* is not used, if a malicious application registers the same *Custom URI* as the legitimate app, it can fool the user to open the malicious instead of benign app and this leads to code interception attacks.

3   OIDC iGov Profile for Native Apps

As shown in Fig. 2, based on the security requirements raised in different real world scenarios (fintech, identity assurance, governmental services, and so on), several profiles have been proposed on top of the OIDC specification [24] to satisfy the needed level of security and privacy.

Different national identity frameworks are in the process of adopting the OIDC iGov profile [10], among them, we consider the Italian digital identity framework SPID [2]. Similarly to OIDC [24], the OIDC iGov profile was designed without keeping in mind the native scenario. Therefore, in the following description we integrate the BCPs for native apps [4] (see Sect. 2.2) within the OIDC iGov profile to conceptualize the flow for native apps. In addition, as our focus is on authentication, in the rest of the paper we refer to the OIDC iGov profile directly with "iGov".

In Sect. 3.1, we explain the two client registration methods (namely, *static* and *dynamic*) supported by the iGov profile. In Sect. 3.2, we describe three iGov flows for native scenario by detailing the client authentication methods. We compare these three flows with the OIDC flow for native apps (Fig. 3) to incrementally explicit the changes that app developers must consider (e.g., mandatory parameters in authorization/token request). Finally, Sect. 3.3 discusses the main security and privacy considerations of these flows.

3.1   Client Registration

The OAuth iGov profile [9], which OIDC iGov profile is based on, specifies two client registration methods:

Static Client Registration: app developers obtain a single `client_id` for a native app from the identity management provider (IdMP) during the client registration phase at the IdMP app portal.

Dynamic Client Registration: app developers obtain a different `client_id` for each instance of the native app. IdMPs may implement the Dynamic Client Registration (DCR) endpoint as either an OAuth protected or publicly accessible resource [11]. While in the former case, the protected DCR endpoint may require an initial `access_token` that is obtained beforehand during the registration phase by developers, in the latter case, it is publicly accessible to developers.[1] Considering the protected DCR scenario, in the following we describe the general DCR flow and explain how the parameters are customized for the native scenario in iGov:

a. The C app initiates the flow by setting the `authorization` header with the previously obtained `access_token` and sending the client registration request to the DCR endpoint to register a new C app with the IdMP. This request contains the following parameters:

`application_type`: defines the application type. In the case the parameter is not present, IdMP sets the value into web. Thus, in the context of native apps, it must be set to `native`.

`jwks`: C's JSON Web Key Set [12] document. It contains the signing key(s) IdMP uses to validate signatures from C. It must be set to provide support for the `private_key_jwt` authentication.

`token_endpoint_auth_method`: defines which client authentication method should be used in the token endpoint. While its default value is set into `client_secret_basic`, in iGov following DCR, it must be set to `private_key_jwt`.

`response_type` (Optional): defines the `response_type` that C restricts itself to using. As the default value is set to `code`, we do not need to specify this parameter in the DCR request.

`grant_type` (Optional): defines the `grant_type` that C restricts itself to using. As the default value sets into `authorization_code`, we do not need to specify this parameter in DCR request.

---

[1] In the case of publicly accessible DCR endpoint, requests may be constrained through various techniques (e.g., rate limited) to prevent DoS attacks.

redirect_uri: the URL to return to after the registration.

b. The DCR endpoint processes the request and releases a new client_id.

While the static client registration is the recommended method for the public clients that do not have a back-end to store the secrets securely, the dynamic client registration is recommended wherever a back-end is existing. Based on the two aforementioned client registration methods, the iGov profile recommends different ways to authenticate the native app at the token endpoint during the iGov flow (see Table 4); we provide more detail in the corresponding section below.

3.2   Client Authentication

In the following, we firstly explain the two iGov flows for native apps by detailing the client authentication method with regard to their corresponding client registration methods, and then we describe how these flows are combined in the SPID iGov flow.

iGov Following Static Client Registration. As it is shown in Table 4, in case of static client registration, C must be considered as a public client, i.e. not capable of storing a client secret securely, and thus the only (mandatory) option is the usage of *PKCE*.

Compared to the flow of Fig. 3, the iGov flow following the static client registration shows the following two differences in the authentication request (Step 1): (i) nonce is added as mandatory parameter. Being present in the authorization request, this string will be returned in the id_token to mitigate replay attacks; and (ii) code_challenge_method=S256. This means that the challenge value will be always calculated performing a SHA256 hash of the code_verifier string.

iGov Following Dynamic Client Registration. In this scenario as a consequence of DCR, C is considered as an entity that is able to securely handle the client credentials (public/private key) that are created on the user's device. In this case, as shown in Table 4, the client authentication is based on the private_key_jwt method as preliminary specified in the token_endpoint_auth_method parameter exchanged during the DCR (to obtain the client_id). The private_key_jwt method requires C to send a JWT signed with its private key when requesting

Table 4. iGov and SPID scenarios.

	Client registration method	Client authentication method	
		PKCE	Private key JWT
iGov	Static CR	✓	×
	Dynamic CR	Opt	✓
SPID	Dynamic CR	✓	✓

access tokens. Thus, a token request will contain the following parameters: (i) `client_assertion` is a single JWT that is signed by using the private key of the C app and its structure is detailed in Table 5; and (ii) `client_assertion_type` defines the type of assertion that is used by the C app.

In addition, DCR may use *PKCE* even if it is not mandatory.

The iGov flow following the DCR encompasses three differences compared to the flow of Fig. 3:

- In the authentication request (Step 1), beside the addition of the `nonce` parameter, the $PKCE_A$ parameters may be removed.
- In the token request (Step 4), if the C app uses the *PKCE* parameters, then the $PKCE_T$ parameters are provided together with the parameters required for the `private_key_jwt` client authentication method, which are `client_assertion` and `client_assertion_type`. Otherwise, in the token request, only the `private_key_jwt` client authentication parameters are present.
- In Step 5, if the PKCE is not present, then IdMP only verifies the `client_assertion` value. Otherwise, IdMP must perform both PKCE and `client_assertion` checks.

iGov Flow in SPID. As shown in Fig. 2, SPID integrates the iGov profile with BCPs for native apps and consequently combines both the client authentication methods `private_key_jwt` and *PKCE* as depicted in Table 4.

Compared with the iGov flow illustrated in Fig. 3, the iGov flow in SPID encompasses the following differences. In the authentication request (Step 1):

- `prompt`, `nonce`, `acr_values`, and `claim` are added as mandatory parameters;
- `code_challenge_method=S256`;
- all the $OIDC_A$ and $PKCE_A$ parameters (see Table 2) together with the new mandatory parameters are all wrapped into a JWT parameter, called `request` (for details see Table 6). This parameter can be optionally signed by the C app private key.

Table 5. `client_assertion` JWT Structure.

Key	Value	Description
iss	String	`client_id` of the C app creating the request
sub	String	`client_id` of the C app creating the request
aud	String	the URL of the IdMP's token endpoint
iat	String	the issue time of the C request
exp	String	the C request expiration time
jti	String	a unique 128 bits identifier generated by the C per request

In addition, it contains the following changes in the token request/response: (i) in the token request (Step 4), together with the $PKCE_T$ parameters, the parameters required for the `private_key_jwt` client authentication method are added; and (*ii*) in Step 5, IdMP together with the PKCE checks also verifies the `client_assertion` value.

The `request`, `acr_values`, `prompt`, and `claim` are optional parameters of the OIDC that provide the following benefits: `request` enables the authentication request to be passed in a single, self-contained parameter and provides message integrity as it can be signed. The `acr_values` parameter enables IdMPs to request strong authentication methods to harden intrusion attempts against users by mandating additional authentication factors. The `prompt` parameter defines how the re-authentication must be performed, for example if its value is set to "Consent", the consent screen is displayed every time C app requests authorization of scopes of access, even if all scopes were previously granted. Finally, `claim` provides a way to explicitly define the user claims that the C app is asking for.

Table 6. Request object JWT structure definition.

Key	Values	Description
$OIDC_A$	$OIDC_A$	Mandatory OIDC parameters as defined in Table 2
$PKCE_A$	$PKCE_A$	PKCE parameters as defined in Table 2 with `code_challenge_method=S256`
nonce	String	A unique value used to verify the integrity of the `id_token` and mitigate replay attacks
prompt	Login/Consent/Login Consent	Specifies whether IdMP prompts the RO for reauthentication and consent
acr_values	SPID L1/L2/L3	Enables the IdMPs to request strong authentication methods
claim	JSON obj	Provides a way to explicitly define the user claims that the C app is asking for

3.3 Security and Privacy Considerations

The iGov profile is designed on top of the OIDC specification to provide a higher level of security in the governmental domains. The main considerations concerning the increased security achieved in iGov can be summarized as follows.

1. the iGov profile enforces the usage of the *Authorization Code* flow (similar to OIDC flow for native apps in Fig. 3) to avoid security issues raised by the improper flow selection. Indeed, as explained in Sect. 2.2 the usage of the *Implicit* grant and other response types—that cause an IdMP to issue access tokens directly in the authorization response—are vulnerable to token leakage and replay attacks [17].
2. the iGov profile supports *PKCE* to mitigate code injection attacks. As shown in Table 4, *PKCE* is mandatory for static client registration and optional for DCR where the client authentication is performed with `private_key_jwt`.

In addition:

3. the iGov profile mandates IdMP to accept authorization request with the `request`, `claim`, and `nonce` parameters, while their support is instead optional in the OIDC specification.
4. the iGov profile enforces
   - the use of the `nonce` parameter to mitigate replay attacks;
   - `code_challenge_method=S256`. Thus, the `challenge` parameter cannot assume directly the `code_verifier` value, but it will be equal to a SHA256 hash of the `code_verifier` value.
5. the iGov profile following DCR provides an additional security layer by releasing separate credentials for each C instance. The main advantage is that the attacker will compromise just one C app instead of all Cs that may share the same credentials (as it is possible when using static client registration).

The iGov flow in SPID inherits all the advantages described before. In addition, SPID enforces the usage of the level of assurance (`acr_values`) and `request` parameters.

Even if the described designed choices enhance the security of the iGov profile, we suggest to take also into account the security measures pointed out in the OAuth Security Best Current Practice [17] and the RFC6819 [18].

Regarding privacy issues, the iGov profile defines techniques to avoid user tracking and enforce data minimization. To avoid user tracking by the means of the `sub` value (that is the identifier of the end-user) the iGov profile suggests the use of pairwise identifiers that allow an OIDC IdMP to represent a single user with a different subject identifier (`sub`) for every C the user connects to. It is worth mentioning that the use of this technique does not avoid clients from correlating data based on other identifiable attributes, such as document and phone numbers. To support data minimization, the iGov profile introduces the following mechanisms:

1. By using the `claim` parameter: IdMP only returns information on the subject that C specifically asks for, and does not add extra information about the subject. For example, if C only needs a single government document number, IdMP must not send the information related to other documents to C.
2. The returned user claims as response to a *UserInfo* request must match the `scope` and claims requested to avoid that IdMP over-expose a user's information. In addition, IdMP can also establish a binding of the user claims to different levels of assurance by considering both the `scope` and `acr_values` parameters. For example, high sensitive user data (such as social security number) should not be returned in case of mismatch with the `acr_values` parameter.

While the user tracking avoidance technique must be supported by all iGov providers, the data minimization is optional. The iGov flow in SPID, by making both `acr_values` and `claim` parameters mandatory, enforces also data minimization.

4 Wizard-Based Approach

Based on the rational reconstruction of the iGov profile (cf. Sect. 3), we extend
the wizard-based approach for Android native apps in [25] to support the iGov
profile with the two client authentication methods following static and dynamic
registration and the extensions required in SPID to provide a secure and compliant code integration within governmental apps. Indeed, the main goal of this
work is to help public administrations with automatically code integration of
iGov flows to develop services that can be easily and securely accessed via
national identity infrastructures.

Our wizard-based approach encompasses two processes: (*i*) *DB Population*,
where security experts populate the database by inserting information for the
supported IdMPs (such as endpoints, the supported scenario, profile and the
redirection scheme); and (*ii*) *Wizard Questions*, where app developers (even
with little or no experience) select one of the supported IdMPs and follow the
instructions of the wizard providing the missing information concerning their
own apps.

In Sect. 4.1 and 4.2, we detail the *DB Population* and *Wizard Questions*
processes, respectively. We describe how our wizard-based approach customize
the wizard questions based on the client registration methods supported by an
iGov provider. Finally, in Sect. 4.3 we describe the architecture of our plugin and
summarize the security analysis of the code that is automatically integrated in
a demo app to communicate with an iGov provider based on the client authentication method following static client registration.

4.1 DB Population

We explain which information should be provided by security experts for each
new iGov *IdMP*.

1. *IdMP*.Redirect specifies the redirection mechanisms supported by the
   IdMP and can assume the following values: HTTPS if only HTTPS URI redirection is supported; CustomURI if only Custom URI Scheme is supported;
   and both if both of them are supported.
2. *IdMP*.Acr_Values_necessity specifies whether the level of assurance
   parameter acr_values is mandatory for the *IdMP*, and can assume the val-
   ues Yes | No.
3. *IdMP*.Acr_Values specifies the supported level of assurance (i.e. the values
   of the acr_values parameter), and can assume LoA1 | LoA2 | LoA3.
4. *IdMP*.Discovery specifies the discovery URL, where the *IdMP* publishes
   its metadata (such as endpoints and scopes supported).
5. *IdMP*.Scenario specifies the supported scenarios, and can assume the following values: SSO if only Single Sign-On Login is supported; AD if only Access
   Delegation is supported; and both if both of them are supported.
6. *IdMP*.Client_Registration_Methods specifies the supported client regis-
   tration method and assumes the values Static CR | Dynamic CR | both.

7. $IdMP$.Profile specifies the supported profile and assumes the values Core | iGov.

Among the information stored in the DB, Acr_Values_necessity, Redirect, and Client_Registration are used by the wizard to customize the questions for the app developer (as described in Sect. 4.2), while the discovery URL is used to properly configure the AppAuth SDK that is integrated within our plugin to enforce BCPs (defined in Sect. 2.2).

The following changes apply to the DB population process in case $IdMP$ is a SPID provider: (i) Since in SPID the usage of acr_values is mandatory, $IdMP$.Acr_Values_necessity is always equal to Yes; (ii) as SPID introduces the prompt parameter, the database should store its possible values. $IdMP$.Prompt can assume the values Login | Consent | Login Consent; and (iii) $IdMP$.Profile assumes the new value SPID. While in the general IdMP scenario security experts are in charge of the IdMP DB population, the solution we envisage for SPID is to delegate this task to the Italian institution responsible for coordinating the implementation process of SPID, namely Agenzia per l'Italia digitale (AGID).

Listing 1.1. Wizard Questions for iGov Scenario.

// General IdMPs Selection   1
1. *Please, select IdMP among the list of supported Providers*   2
if the $IdMP$.Profile=iGov then   3
The wizard reads the endpoints for the selected iGov Provider from the IdMPs   4
    DB, fills the AppAuth conf file, and populates the questions within the
    plugin GUI.
// Implementation Selection   5
If the $IdMP$.Client_Registration_Method=both then   6
2. *Please, select the implementation methodology:* either [2.1] *iGov following*   7
    Static CR, or [2.2] *iGov following* Dynamic CR
Otherwise, ignore the question and go to Configuration.   8
// Configuration   9
3. *Please, enter the configuration information: Scopes and the Name of the*   10
    Button you create
If [2.1] or $IdMP$.Client_Registration_Method= Static CR then *Enter*   11
    ClientID
If $IdMP$.Acr_Values_necessity=Yes then *Enter Acr_Values*   12
The provided info are used by the wizard to update the AppAuth conf file and   13
    initialize the login button.
// Redirection   14
If $IdMP$.Redirect=both then   15
4. *Choose the preferred Redirection Method:* either [4.1] *HTTPS scheme, or*   16
    [4.2] *CustomURI scheme*
If [4.1] or $IdMP$.Redirect=HTTPS then *Enter your valid domain URL:*   17
    scheme, host, and path
If [4.2] or $IdMP$.Redirect=CustomURI then *Enter the Custom URI of your*   18
    app
The provided info are used by the wizard to complete the AppAuth conf file   19
    and fill the Intent filter in the Android manifest.

4.2 Wizard Questions

In Listing 1.1, we show which are the questions asked to a C app developer
by the wizard (in *italic*) to support the iGov scenario. In addition, Listing 1.1
explains how the questions are customized according to the information provided
in the *DB Population* process. According to the choices of the app developer, the
wizard automatically integrates the code incorporating the security and privacy
considerations (discussed in Sect. 3.3) within the app.

Concerning the iGov flow in SPID, namely in case $IdMP$.Profile=SPID,
the code integration scheme for the wizard is similar to Listing 1.1, apart from
the following main differences: (i) the *"Implementation Selection"* question (cf.
Line 7) is omitted, as SPID combines both Static and Dynamic client registration; (ii) the *"Configuration"* questions (cf. Line 10) are slightly different, as
the SPID profile contains two additional parameters (prompt and claim) and
acr_values appears as mandatory; (iii) in SPID, the developer must provide
the configuration info for all the SPID providers (9 in the current federation), in
a way that the end-user can choose the one he/she has already registered with.

4.3 Implementation and Security Analysis

To assess the practical value of our approach, we extend the mIDAssistant plugin [25] to support app developers with secure and compliant code integration of
the iGov flows as discussed in Sect. 3. The mIDAssistant plugin has been developed using the Intellij Idea environment,[2] it can be integrated in Android Studio
and leverages the AppAuth library [22] as the main building block to guarantee
the enforcement of BCPs. While the iGov profile following static client registration is already implemented in the plugin, the iGov profile following dynamic
client registration and the extensions required in SPID are in progress. In the
following, we explain the workflow of the mIDAssistant plugin and an evaluation
of the code integrated by the plugin in terms of security.

mIDAssistant Plugin. Assuming that an app developer creates a C app with an
iGov activity beforehand, as shown in Fig. 4, the mIDAssistant plugin workflow
contains three main steps, namely: (i) interacting with the plugin front-end, (ii)
processing the obtained information from the plugin front-end in the core, and
(iii) integrating the customized AppAuth code within the developer's app. In
Step (i), developers run the mIDAssistant plugin and interact with the plugin
front-end to compile wizard questions as explained in Listing 1.1. This step
provides client configuration info and the Programming Structure Interface (PSI)
as an output. The aforementioned outputs are needed for the code integration
process within the plugin core. After that, in Step (ii), the plugin utilizes the code
templates together with the inputs from the previous step (client configuration
info and PSI) to initialize the code injector/handler within the plugin core.
While PSI is used in the plugin core by the code injector/handler to find the
specific file element for the code integration process, the client configuration

---

[2] https://www.jetbrains.com/idea/.

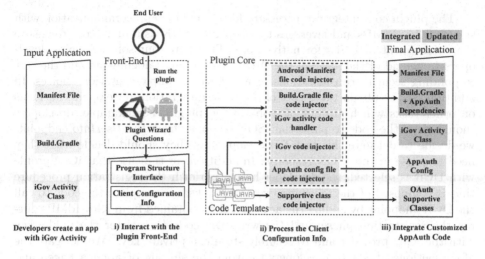

Fig. 4. mIDAssistant plugin workflow.

info is used to instantiate the customized code. It is worth mentioning that the code templates are mostly obtained from the AppAuth[3] repository. In the following, we explain the functionality of each code injector/handler component within the plugin core. In case developers choose the HTTPS redirection scheme within the wizard GUI, the *Android Manifest file code injector* extracts the HTTPS redirection scheme value from the client configuration info to initialize the customized code to handle the HTTPS redirection. The *Build. Gradle file code injector* initializes the customized code to add the AppAuth SDK dependencies. In addition, in case of custom uri selection by developers, it handles the custom uri redirection by obtaining its relevant value from the client configuration info. The *AppAuth config file code injector* initializes a JSON structure by extracting the values from the client configuration info. This step is necessary to enable the app communication with specific iGov IdMPs. The *iGov code injector* and *iGov activity code handler* initialize the customized code to add the main iGov functionality within the iGov activity class. They accomplish the aforementioned task by obtaining the relevant values and code from the client configuration info and code templates, respectively. While *iGov activity code handler* adds the initialization code for the iGov button within the `OnCreate` method in the iGov activity class, the *iGov code injector* provides the main functionalities in the above mentioned class for the iGov button. In contrast to previous code injectors, the *Supportive class code injector* initializes the customized code only from code templates (Fig. 4) which provides necessary iGov functionality, such as read/validate the application configuration JSON file. Finally, in Step (*iii*), the code injector/handler incorporates the customized code into the app to update Build.Gradle, Android Manifest, and iGov activity class files. It also integrates the newly created JSON config and supportive classes files.

---

[3] https://github.com/openid/AppAuth-Android.

The plugin core integrates necessary files to enable app communication with specific iGov IdMPs and leverages the AppAuth SDK as a main core to ensure the enforcement of BCPs for native apps. Therefore, our solution helps developers to get rid of the maze of the OIDC/iGov related documents and the corresponding security considerations to avoid wrong implementation choices. In addition, as the plugin takes care of the iGov integration, developers can focus on other tasks which are out of scope of the plugin. For example, developers should write the code to parse the JSON response from the *UserInfo* endpoint; we decide to delegate this task to developers as they should decide what they need to parse in the JSON response. In addition, in the case that iGov profile with DCR is selected, the developer has to perform the registration procedure that is composed of the following two main tasks: (*i*) complete the code to call the DCR endpoint by adding the `access_token` obtained from iGov IdMPs during the registration phase; and (*ii*) write the code to register the public key with the iGov provider and to securely store the private key.[4] We delegate the aforementioned tasks to developers to avoid the sharing of `access_token` and public/private keys of developers with the plugin. Indeed, if we obtain these values within the plugin, developers have to fully trust us that we do not misuse the obtained values. It is worth mentioning that the plugin helps the developer also with these tasks by adding comments into the places where the developer must complete the code.

Besides the advantages provided by our solution, there are two main limitations: there is a need for (*i*) integrating new BCPs within the plugin whenever new threat models and security considerations have been published; and (*ii*) keeping the IdMP DB up-to-date. The possible solutions for problem (*i*) can either involve experts from the OAuth working group or have dedicated security experts (in the OAuth/OIDC field), who are capable to analyze the new RFCs and integrate it with the plugin. Problem (*ii*) is easier to handle as we need to periodically inspect the provider's website to detect potential changes and integrate them within the plugin DB through a plugin update release.

To increase the trust in the correctness of the plugin, we are going to make its code open-source.[5] This provides a way to perform a code-review process by the experts in this field. In addition, as detailed in the paragraph below, we have used both open-source and commercial static code analysis tools to perform the security source-code analysis on the code integrated by the plugin.

Security Analysis. In this section, we summarize the results of the security analysis performed on the code integrated by the mIDAssistant plugin. In our security analysis procedure, we consider the AppAuth SDK source code secure based on the following assumptions: AppAuth is an open source project primarily developed by the Google Identity Platform team and endorsed by the OIDC foundation since 2016; and it is used within Google's own client-side authenti-

---

[4] The client authentication method following dynamic client registration is a work in progress.

[5] https://github.com/stfbk/mIDAssistant_iGov.

cation stack in Android and reviewed by the Google's internal security team for vulnerabilities.[6] Given that, we verify only the security of the integrated code within the developer's app by using both open-source and commercial source code analysis tools.

In the first phase, we perform a security analysis on the integrated plugin code by utilizing two open-source tools, namely: Super[7] and MobSF.[8] The security analysis results reveal two possible security issues: (i) weak cryptography algorithm; and (ii) security information disclosure. With a further analysis, we discover that both results are not security issues in our case. Indeed, the detected weak algorithm is used to create a hash of the configuration file that the SDK uses to detect the change in the configuration file to clear the authorization state. The second item is not a security issue, as the MobSF tool marks all the plain strings with a certain length as possible secret keys. In the second phase, we perform the source code analysis by utilizing a commercial tool called Approver.[9] The security report of the tool contains the following issues: (i) insufficient code obfuscation; and (ii) undesired access to private data. Although all the reported findings are security issues in general, they are considered out of scope of our plugin work. Indeed, the main goal of our plugin is to help app developers with integration of iGov flows within their app, therefore, we delegate the tasks for performing code obfuscation, and encrypting the information in preferences to developers.

5   Related Work

Many tools have been proposed to help app developers to implement secure code, whether just after the development cycle, such as Chex [19] and Role-Cast [26], or during the implementation phase, such as Android Lint Tool [6], FixDroid [20], and App Link Assistant [7]. Although the aforementioned tools are helpful to solve specific app quality and security problems, just App Link Assistant provides a wizard-based approach to help developers with proper configuration of App Link within their apps, the other tools have nothing to do with IdM implementation problems. Compared to App Link Assistant tool, our wizard-based approach assists developers in the whole implementation process, including App Link proper configuration. In the context of iGov profile, there are some governmental solutions, such as US Governmental portal [27], NHS Login [21], Dutch Government Assurance Profile [5] and recently MiTRE provides an enterprise mission tailored OIDC profile that is derived from the OIDC iGov profile [29]. However, most of these works are providing a general description of the iGov profile (e.g., describing parameters in the authentication/token

---

[6] The internal review was not published by Google, this information was obtained from a conversation with the main developer of AppAuth SDK.

[7] https://github.com/SUPERAndroidAnalyzer/super.

[8] https://github.com/MobSF/Mobile-Security-Framework-MobSF.

[9] https://www.talos-sec.com.

request) and they miss a documentation to help developers with the implementation (e.g., example apps). The US Governmental Portal [27] is the only one that also provides example apps for the iGov following static client registration. However, developers still need to write the code to integrate the solution within their app, and the dynamic client registration is not supported. Compared to US Governmental Portal [27], our wizard-based approach assists developers with automatic and secure code integration of iGov following static client registration.

6   Conclusion and Future Work

In this paper, we have demystified the iGov profile for native apps. As the iGov profile was designed without keeping in mind the native scenario, we have identified BCPs for the considered profile and enforced them in the mIDAssistant plugin by using the AppAuth SDK to automatically integrate code in native mobile apps. This dramatically simplifies the development of apps that use national infrastructures for digital identities complying with the iGov profile even for developers with little or no experience in security. In particular, we have considered the iGov profile recently proposed for SPID (the Italian national digital identity) and help public administrations with limited resources to integrate compliant iGov solutions withing their governmental apps that demands heterogeneous skills and capacities in cybersecurity.

As future work, we plan to add the code exchange on the app backend to secure cases that need to use the private key during the authorization request; complete the implementation of iGov following dynamic client registration and SPID; and extend the plugin to support multi-platform development environments, such as Xamarin [30] that is used to develop cross-platform applications (e.g., Android, iOS, and Windows).

References

1. AGID: Linee Guida OpenID connect in SPID (2019). https://docs.italia.it/AgID/documenti-in-consultazione/lg-openidconnect-spid-docs/it/bozza/
2. AGID: Sistema Pubblico di Identità Digitale (2019). https://www.spid.gov.it/
3. Cantor, S.: SAML version 2.0 Errata 05, March 18, 2015 (2012)
4. Denniss, W., Bradley, J.: OAuth 2.0 for Native Apps (RFC8252). Internet Engineering Task Force (IETF) (2017)
5. Geonovum: Dutch government assurance profile for OAuth 2.0 (2020). https://geonovum.github.io/KP-APIs-OAuthNL/
6. Google: Android Lint (2016). https://developer.android.com/studio/write/lint
7. Google: App Link Assistant tool (2017). https://developer.android.com/studio/write/app-link-indexing
8. Hardt, D.: The OAuth 2.0 Authorization Framework (RFC6749). Internet Engineering Task Force (IETF) (2012)
9. Internet-Draft: International Government Assurance Profile (iGov) for OAuth 2.0 (2018)

10. Internet-Draft: International Government Assurance Profile (iGov) for OpenID Connect 1.0 (2018)
11. Jones, M., Bradley, J., Machulak, M., Hunt, P.: OAuth 2.0 Dynamic Client Registration Protocol (RFC7591). Internet Engineering Task Force (IETF) (2015)
12. Jones, M.: JSON Web Key (RFC7517). Internet Engineering Task Force (IETF) (2015)
13. Jones, M., Bradley, J., Sakimura, N.: Json Web Token (RFC7519). Internet Engineering Task Force (IETF) (2015)
14. Lewis, K.D., Lewis, J.E.: Web single sign-on authentication using SAML. Int. J. Comput. Sci. Issues **2**, 41–48 (2009)
15. Liu, F., Wang, C., Pico, A., Yao, D., Wang, G.: Measuring the insecurity of mobile deep links of Android. In: 26th USENIX Security Symposium (USENIX Security 2017), Vancouver, BC, Canada, August 16–18, 2017, pp. 953–969 (2017)
16. Liu, X., Liu, J., Wang, W., Zhu, S.: Android single sign-on security: issues, taxonomy and directions. Future Gener. Comput. Syst. **89**, 402–420 (2018). https://doi.org/10.1016/j.future.2018.06.049
17. Lodderstedt, T., Bradley, J., Labunets, A., Fett, D.: OAuth 2.0 security best current practice (draft-ietf-OAuth-security-topics-16). Internet Engineering Task Force (IETF) (2020)
18. Lodderstedt, T., McGloin, M., Hunt, P.: OAuth 2.0 threat model and security considerations (RFC6819). Internet Engineering Task Force (IETF) (2013)
19. Lu, L., Li, Z., Wu, Z., Lee, W., Jiang, G.: Chex: statically vetting android apps for component hijacking vulnerabilities. In: Proceedings of the ACM SIGSAG Conference on Computer and Communications Security, CCS 2012, Raleigh, NC, USA, October 16–18, 2012, pp. 229–240 (2012). https://doi.org/10.1145/2382196.2382223
20. Nguyen, D.C., Wermke, D., Acar, Y., Backes, M., Weir, C., Fahl, S.: A stitch in time: supporting Android developers in writing secure code. In: Proceedings of the ACM SIGSAC Conference on Computer and Communications Security, CCS 2017, Dallas, TX, USA, October 30–November 3, 2017, pp. 1065–1077 (2017). https://doi.org/10.1145/3133956.3133977
21. NHS: United Kingdom national health service login (2020). https://www.nhs.uk/using-the-nhs/nhs-services/nhs-login/
22. OIDF: AppAuth Mobile Client SDK (2016). https://github.com/openid/AppAuth-Android
23. Sakimura, N., Bradley, J., Agarwal, N.: Proof key for code exchange by OAuth public clients (RFC7636). Internet Engineering Task Force (IETF) (2015)
24. Sakimura, N., Bradley, J., Jones, M., De Medeiros, B., Mortimore, C.: OpenID Connect Core 1.0 incorporating errata set 1. The OpenID Foundation, Specification 335 (2014)
25. Sharif, A., Carbone, R., Ranise, S., Sciarretta, G.: A wizard-based approach for secure code generation of single sign-on and access delegation solutions for mobile native apps. In: Proceedings of the 16th International Joint Conference on e-Business and Telecommunications, ICETE 2019 - Volume 2: SECRYPT, Prague, Czech Republic, July 26–28, 2019, pp. 268–275 (2019). https://doi.org/10.5220/0007930502680275
26. Son, S., McKinley, K.S., Shmatikov, V.: RoleCast: finding missing security checks when you do not know what checks are. In: Proceedings of the 26th ACM International Conference on Object Oriented Programming Systems Languages and Applications, OOPSLA 2011, Portland, OR, USA, October 2011, vol. 46, pp. 1069–1084 (2011). https://doi.org/10.1145/2048066.2048146

27. US General Service Administration: Login.gov (2020). https://login.gov
28. Wang, H., et al.: Vulnerability assessment of OAuth implementations in Android applications. In: Proceedings of the 31st Annual Computer Security Applications Conference, ACSAC 2015, Los Angles, CA, USA, December 7–11, 2015, pp. 61–70 (2015). https://doi.org/10.1145/2818000.2818024
29. Westman, R., et al.: Enterprise mission tailored OpenID connect (OIDC) profile. Tech. rep., MITRE (2020)
30. Xamarin: Xamarin tools for cross platform app development (2015). https://releases.xamarin.com

Micro-Id-Gym: A Flexible Tool for Pentesting Identity Management Protocols in the Wild and in the Laboratory

Andrea Bisegna[1,2]([✉]) [iD], Roberto Carbone[1] [iD], Giulio Pellizzari[3] [iD], and Silvio Ranise[1,4] [iD]

[1] Security & Trust, Fondazione Bruno Kessler, Trento, Italy
{a.bisegna,carbone,ranise}@fbk.eu
[2] DIBRIS, University of Genova, Genova, Italy
[3] DISI, University of Trento, Trento, Italy
giulio.pellizzari@studenti.unitn.it
[4] Department of Mathematics, University of Trento, Trento, Italy

Abstract. Identity Management (IdM) solutions are increasingly important for digital infrastructures of both enterprises and public administrations. Their security is a mandatory pre-requisite for building trust in current and future digital ecosystems. Unfortunately, not only their secure deployment but even their usage are non-trivial activities that require a good level of security awareness. In order to test whether known exploits can be reproduced in different environments, better understand their effects and facilitate the discovery of new vulnerabilities, we need to have a reliable testbed. For this, we present Micro-Id-Gym which abstractly supports two main activities: the creation of sandboxes with an IdM protocol deployment and the pentesting of IdM protocol deployments in the wild or in the laboratory (on the created sandboxes).

Keywords: Security protocols · Penetration testing · OAuth

1 Introduction

Identity Management (IdM) solutions are increasingly important for building trust in current and future digital ecosystems. The design and implementation of the IdM protocols underlying the most widely adopted IdM solutions is notoriously error-prone, as witnessed by several vulnerabilities reported in the last few years [3].

The activities for a pentester, especially in digital identity scenarios, require a deep knowledge of the protocols and the related implementation aspects. The lack of compliance with the IdM protocols defined in the standards or a missing check of the value of an HTTP messages can lead also to major security

© Springer Nature Switzerland AG 2020
A. Saracino and P. Mori (Eds.): ETAA 2020, LNCS 12515, pp. 71–89, 2020.
https://doi.org/10.1007/978-3-030-64455-0_5

problems. Then considering also the problem of compliance with the Payment Services Directive 2 (PSD2) [1] regulations, the activities for a pentester increase significantly. Thus it is non-trivial for a pentester to have the skills and technical knowledge to perform all the pentesting activities required to ensure proper security posture for IdM protocols.

Several tools for automatic pentesting exist, but they usually target specific vulnerabilities, and few of them are able to spot all the relevant vulnerabilities for IdM protocols. In addition, in case a vulnerability has been detected, the burden of finding adequate mitigation measures is completely left on the tester who must also collect information about the identified problem and related fixes. Typically, such information is distributed in several sources ranging from the official standards and related security considerations to scientific papers addressing specific novel vulnerabilities.

Another issue with IdM protocols is the fact that in many cases it is not possible to perform a pentesting in the wild in the production environment due to several attacks with high impact like DoS or identity theft with serious legal implications. Therefore it is desirable to reproduce the production solution in a controlled environment. Unfortunately, the steps to reproduce the production environment are complicated and it is not always possible to create the right conditions to be able to spot the same vulnerabilities as in the production environment.

For this, we propose Micro-Id-Gym, offering on the one hand (in the laboratory) an easy way to configure the production environment in a sandbox where pentesters can develop hands-on experiences on how IdM solutions work, performing attacks with high impacts and better understand the underlying security issues. On the other hand (in the wild) a set of pentesting tools for the automatic security analysis of IdM protocols are provided. In [4] we have provided a high level overview of the main idea behind Micro-Id-Gym where the main focus was on the educational purposes. In this paper we are focusing on real environments describing the architecture and the main technical details of Micro-Id-Gym. We make the following four main contributions:

- We have provided a flexible environment for pentesting IdM protocols, which provides a set of deployments (by using container-based micro-services) and exploits the possibility to federate and set-up a local network among them.
- We have provided pentesting tools for the automatic security analysis of IdM protocols. To ease this phase, the penetration testing tools communicates with an application (MSC Drawer) that animates a message sequence chart (MSC) of the IdM protocols under consideration.
- We have assessed the penetration testing tools by analyzing a deployed service for PSD2 in the wild: the MSC Drawer has been extremely helpful to quickly show the differences between the expected MSC and the one obtained by analyzing the service. Then, we performed a finer-grained security analysis by reporting other relevant issues.

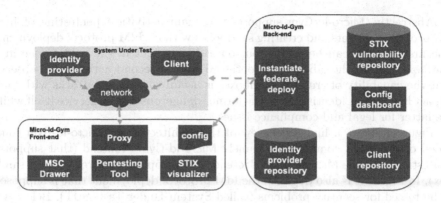

Fig. 1. Overview of Micro-Id-Gym.

- We have assessed the environment for pentesting and the MSC Drawer in the laboratory experience: we used Micro-Id-Gym to create the proper experience, by considering vulnerable scenarios, and assessed the effectiveness of MSC Drawer to help in finding vulnerabilities.

Plan of the Paper. In Sect. 2 we give an overview of Micro-Id-Gym. Then, we provide more details of Micro-Id-Gym components in Sect. 3. To evaluate the effectiveness of Micro-Id-Gym, Sect. 4 reports the use of Micro-Id-Gym in the wild. Section 5 presents the results of a user study involving bachelor and master degree students in the laboratory. We conclude and overview future work in Sect. 6.

2 Overview of Micro-Id-Gym

To assist system administrators and testers in the deployment and pentesting of IdM protocol instances we propose Micro-Id-Gym. In this section we provide an overview of the tool before giving the details of the various components in the rest of the paper.

The IdM protocols are designed specifically for the transfer of authentication information and consist of a series of messages in a preset sequence designed to protect data as it travels through networks or between servers. All the IdM protocols provide standards for security to simplify access management, help in compliance, and create a uniform system for handling interactions between users and systems. For IdM protocols we refer to the web protocols where a Client (C) relies on a trusted third-party server called Identity Provider (IdP) for user authentication. Security Assertion Markup Language Single Sign-On v2.0 (hereafter SAML) [8] and OAuth 2.0 (OAuth) [6]/OpenID Connect (OIDC) [10] are two of the most known protocols providing this authentication pattern despite the fact that different names may be used to refer to the aforementioned entities. In the case of SAML, C takes the name of Service Provider (SP).

Abstractly, Micro-Id-Gym supports two main activities: pentesting of IdM protocol deployments and creating sandboxes with an IdM protocol deployment. The first activity can be carried out on a deployment in the wild or one in a sandbox—say, in the laboratory—obtained by the second activity. We observe that the capability of creating sandboxes is useful to perform attacks with high impact like DoS or identity theft, the former dangerous for the service itself while the latter for legal and compliance issues.

Figure 1 shows a high level view of the architecture of Micro-Id-Gym composed of two main components, namely Micro-Id-Gym Frontend (that supports pentesting) and the Micro-Id-Gym Backend (that supports the creation of a sandbox). In Fig. 1, it is also depicted the IdM protocol deployment that is supposed to be tested for security problems (called System Under Test, SUT). Below, we provide an overview of the two main components.

2.1 Micro-Id-Gym Backend

The Micro-Id-Gym Backend is used to recreate locally a sandbox as an instance of an IdP and a C and it can be done by uploading the own proprietary sandbox or by composing a new sandbox choosing the instances of IdPs and Cs provided by the tool as depicted in Fig. 1 in the IdP and C repositories. All the provided instances have been collected so far during our experience of using Micro-Id-Gym and they satisfy the requirements to be compatible with Micro-Id-Gym namely to have an instance of the IdP, at least one for the C and to use SAML or OAuth/OIDC as IdM protocols. The backend is also in charge to instantiate the selected instances, to federate each other, to exchange the required metadata, to perform the deployment of the sandbox and to set up the local network.

The process of creating a sandbox is straightforward: from the Dashboard the user picks Cs and an IdP from a set of available IdM protocol instances (Cs and IdPs repositories in Fig. 1) and sets the URLs and ports. Once the sandbox has been selected, the tool automatically connects the chosen instances and run them in the SUT which includes the entities of IdP and Cs properly instantiated, federated and deployed.

The Micro-Id-Gym Backend provides also Cyber Threat Intelligence (CTI) information useful for assessing vulnerabilities and threats related to the chosen instances. These data follow the Structured Threat Information Expression (STIX) format proposed by OASIS CTI TC.[1] This information is very useful since it immediately makes the pentester aware of possible specific attacks of that protocol known in the literature.

2.2 Micro-Id-Gym Frontend

The Micro-Id-Gym Frontend consists of tools to support user pentesting activities on the SUT, namely a Proxy, a set of Pentesting Tools, and two tools called

---

[1] https://www.oasis-open.org/committees/cti/.

MSC Drawer and MSC STIX Visualizer. As already mentioned, the SUT can be a sandbox or any IdM protocol available on Internet.

Proxy. It is a web proxy tool used to intercept the traffic between the user agent (i.e. a web browser) and the SUT. It provides a set of APIs used by the pentesting tools to inspect, modify, replay and drop the intercepted messages.

Pentesting Tool. It supports a user to perform pentesting of an IdM protocol deployment, by providing instruments to automatically detect security issues. The tools perform both passive and active tests. Passive tests analyze the HTTP messages exchanged between the browser and the servers, while active tests also intercept and modify those messages. An example of a passive test can be to check whether the format of the exchanged messages is compliant to what prescribed by the standard. Instead, an example of an active test can be the modification at run time of a parameter referred as required by the standard. With these tests, it is possible to detect vulnerabilities specifically due to an incorrect implementation of the IdM protocols. For instance, in case of a SAML implementation, the Pentesting Tool can identify a vulnerability leading to man-in-the-middle attack due to an incorrect implementation of the `RelayState` parameter, an identifier for the resource at the SP that the IdP will redirect the user to after successful login. All the security issues identified by the tools are reported in a table, including the suggestions to mitigate them.

MSC Drawer. The messages intercepted by the Proxy are then passed to the MSC Drawer which represents their flow as a MSC. The MSC Drawer provides a graphical overview of the authentication flow and allows easier inspection of the exchanged messages. For each HTTP message, the pentester can dive into headers, parameters, and body. Usually the standards for IdM protocols prescribe which are the mandatory/optional messages and their format, and the endpoints to invoke. Still, they usually do not prescribe anything about what happens between two subsequent requests to an endpoint. The messages of the standard can be thus interleaved with other "spurious" messages. For spurious messages we mean any HTTP traffic between two subsequent invocations prescribed by the standard (e.g., advertisements and images). Thus, being able to extract information about the standard is an extremely time consuming task for a pentester. Available state-of-the-art web proxy tools provide searching features, but it is still difficult to grasp the main messages, by selecting the relevant information referring to the standard, among the spurious messages.

MSC STIX Visualizer. It provides a graph of CTI information taken from the STIX vulnerability repository related to the intercepted authentication flow, currently only for SAML. Using the MSC Drawer UI the pentester can choose the granularity of CTI information he wants to look for. For instance, in case of a SUT using the SAML protocol, the pentester can look for CTI information regarding the `RelayState` parameter or, more generally, for CTI information related to a SAML IdP. The combination of these features with the pentesting tools makes the process of vulnerability identification and cyber risk assessment easier.

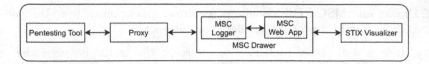

Fig. 2. Micro-Id-Gym Frontend.

Usage of the Micro-Id-Gym Frontend. The tools of the Micro-Id-Gym Frontend are used for the analysis of the HTTP messages generated during the authentication flow. The first step towards this process is to perform the authentication on the SUT. The messages exchanged during this process are displayed in the MSC Drawer. This is useful because at first glance the pentester can recognize whether the SUT follows the expected flow or not. The second step is to execute the automated tests provided by the Pentesting Tools. These automated tests verify if the SUT suffers the vulnerabilities tested by the tools. If a test was successful, the result will report the discovered vulnerability, otherwise, no alert will be reported.

Thanks to the vulnerability results, the pentester can identify where it is exposed, thus he knows where it has to be patched. Furthermore, using the CTI information provided by MSC STIX Visualizer, the pentester can assess how the vulnerability can be exploited and how severe it is.

3   The Components of Micro-Id-Gym

In this section we provide more details about components of the Micro-Id-Gym Frontend and the Micro-Id-Gym Backend.

3.1   The Components of Micro-Id-Gym Frontend

As depicted in Fig. 2, the Micro-Id-Gym Frontend is composed by Pentesting Tool, MSC Drawer (consisting of MSC Logger and MSC WebApp), MSC STIX Visualizer and a Proxy.

Proxy. It is a web proxy tool that intercepts the HTTP traffic between a browser and the servers of the SUT. It offers functionalities for inspecting, collecting, and modifying the HTTP messages, which are leveraged by the Pentesting Tool and MSC Drawer.

MSC Drawer. It is a tool for drawing MSC and allows the pentesters to quickly select the relevant messages, being able to spot a potential gap w.r.t. what prescribed by the standard and it is extremely helpful to save time, being more effective. IdM protocols are often expressed as a MSC with the advantage to immediately detect any incorrectness in the messages of the MSC and consequently identify any flaws. We evaluated some of these claims by performing a classroom experience, described in Sect. 5.

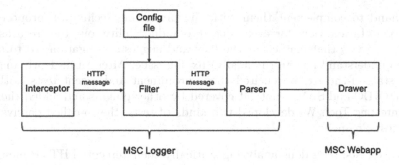

Fig. 3. MSC Drawer components.

The Fig. 3 depicts the main components of the MSC Drawer. The MSC Logger is a Proxy's plugin reponsible to capture a selection of the HTTP messages, to filter and parse them according to the specific configuration, and send them through API to the MSC WebApp, a web application exposing a set of Restful API and responsible to draw a MSC.

As depicted in Fig. 3, the MSC Logger has the following functionalities:

- Configuration: it allows to set a password not allowing to overwrite a MSC already drawn and setup the URL of the MSC WebApp (the configuration information can be also provided through a configuration file, generated through the Dashboard of the Micro-Id-Gym Backend);
- Interceptor: it collects all the intercepted HTTP messages;
- Filter: it allows to add filters in terms of keywords of the HTTP messages that will be collected and reported in the MSC. The keywords can refer to Host, Request Headers, Request Parameters, Response Headers and Response Body; and
- Parser: it allows to add rules for mapping keywords or sequence of keywords in new terms in order to further improve the readability of the MSC. For instance, in a training context, it is possible to provide a MSC closer to the abstract view of the protocol under test (e.g., by mapping the actual URL of a Client with the label C).

Pre-configured filtering and parsing rules are currently available for SAML and OIDC/OAuth. In addition, the penstester can add custom rules.

To allow the MSC Drawer to create the MSC, the pentester has to navigate with the browser following the steps of the protocol and the corresponding MSC is dinamically generated in another browser at the URL set in the Dashboard. Directly in the MSC, the pentester can dive into the messages, and thanks to the interaction with the MSC STIX Visualizer he can check the available CTI information related to the parameters of the HTTP message.

Pentesting Tool. It provides a set of tools to perform automatic pentesting of IdM protocol. Our idea is on the one hand to integrate in our tool (most of) the existing open source tools for automatic pentesting of IdM protocol, on the other hand to complement them with the pentesting techniques proposed in this paper. In addition, for every detected vulnerability, our tool returns the HTTP messages that may cause the flaw and suggests mitigations so to allow users to understand how to (manually) fix the issue. After an in-depth analysis of the state-of-the-art, we elicited those prominent and recent tests both for OAuth/OIDC and SAML, not yet covered by other plugins and added them in the Pentesting Tool. We developed two kinds of tests, the so-called passive and active tests, namely:

– Passive tests: tests done analyzing statically the intercepted HTTP messages without any interaction/modification of the HTTP messages during execution of the IdM protocol.
– Active tests: tests that need an interaction during the execution of the IdM protocol. After the initial execution, the user actions are stored and automatically re-executed while intercepting/changing the content of the messages before sending them to the C and IdP.

By using both active and passive tests, Pentesting Tool performs the following test categories: (i) Compliance with a given standard in terms of format of the messages, and mandatory fields, (ii) General security checks, performed on any collected HTTP message, and (iii) Specific tests for C and IdP roles. We decided to detail each test about OAuth/OIDC in Sect. 4 and not provide details regards the test for SAML because the scenario that we analyzed in this paper is based on OAuth/OIDC. The list of the SAML tests is available at the complementary material page.[2]

Table 1. Collection of security tests targeting *any* role.

Security Test	Prot.	P/A	Description	Mitigation
Use of HTTPS	-	P	Check if all HTTP messages communicates over a secure channel	Change conf. of the web server and forward unsecured HTTP messages to HTTPS
Clickjaking prevention	-	P	Check if all the HTTP messages has the header X-FRAME-OPTIONS set as DENY or SAME-ORIGIN	Set DENY or SAME-ORIGIN the header X-FRAME-OPTIONS

The set of pentesting tests is far from being complete. We started from that, but we would like to include in our tool (most of) the existing open source tools for pentesting IdM protocol. Our goal is to cover as many vulnerabilities/attacks as possible.

We provide an excerpt of all the tests for OAuth/OIDC protocol we are currently supporting, and in detail the Table 2 reports the tests for IdP, and

---

[2] https://stfbk.github.io/complementary/ETAA2020.

Table 2. Collection of security tests targeting *IdP* role.

Security test	Prot.	P/A	Description	Mitigation
CSRF prevention	O	P	Checks whether state parameter is used	Introduce the state parameter in the flow
Check compliance with standard	O	P	Checks whether all the parameters reported as REQUIRED in the Standard are in the HTTP messages of the considered flow	Introduce the missing parameters in the flow
Adopted PKCE	O	P	Checks whether the implementation used the parameter Proof Key for code exchange (PKCE)	Introduce the PKCE parameter in the flow
Alteration state parameter	O	A	Changes in the Authorization Request the value of the state parameter	Sanitize the value of state parameter
Deletion state parameter	O	A	Deletes the value of the state parameter when sent to the AS with the Authorization Request	Sanitize the value of state parameter
Alteration code_challenge parameter	O	A	Changes the value of the code_challenge parameter when sent to the AS with the Authorization Request	Sanitize the value of code_challenge parameter
Deletion code_challenge parameter	O	A	Deletes the value of the code_challenge parameter when sent to the AS with the Authorization Request	Sanitize the value of code_challenge parameter
Alteration code_challenge_method parameter	O	A	Changes the value of the code_challenge_method parameter when sent to the AS with the Authorization request	Sanitize the value of code_challenge_method parameter
Deletion code_challenge_method parameter	O	A	Deletes the value of the code_challenge_method parameter when sent to the AS with the Authorization request	Sanitize the value of code_challenge_method parameter

Legenda: "P": Passive Test, "A": Active Test.   "-": any protocol

Table 1 for both IdP and C. For each test we set: *(i)* a name to identify the test (e.g., Use of HTTPS), *(ii)* the IdM protocol implemented in the environment where the test will be executed ("O" stands for OIDC), *(iii)* the type of test Passive (P) or Active (A), *(iv)* the description of the security test, and *(v)* the description of the mitigation.

3.2   The Components of Micro-Id-Gym Backend

The goal of the Micro-Id-Gym Backend is by construction to provide a test environment generator tailored to IdM protocols and deploy the environment in the SUT. Given a set of available IdM protocol implementations collected while using the tool for third parties, the SUT automatically sets-up a working environment in a local network. The main reason is to allow system administrators to recreate locally in the laboratory their production environments, being able to pentest them in sandboxes. As depicted in Fig. 4, the Micro-Id-Gym Backend is composed by a set of IdPs and Cs instances both for OAuth/OIDC and SAML, a STIX notes repository and a Dashboard. The set of available instances is indeed a work in progress, and can be easily extended/updated over the time. By design, the architecture allows continuous integration of newer and different implementations.

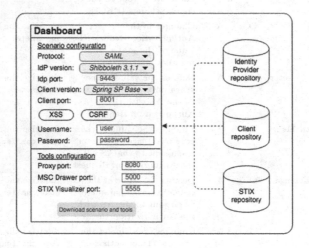

Fig. 4. Micro-Id-Gym Backend.

The component editor (i.e. the person in charge to configure the SUT) through a Dashboard can select the IdM protocols (currently either SAML or OAuth/OIDC), an IdP instance and one or more C instance(s) he wants the SUT to deploy, among the ones available. At the moment of the selection, the Dashboard consults the STIX notes repository and shows which known security issues the selected entities might suffer (e.g., XSS and CSRF in Fig. 4). The user can also insert customized credentials to authenticate on the IdP and configure the ports where C and IdP will run. Once the selection has been completed the SUT will *(i)* generate and deploy the sandbox, *(ii)* create a local network within the agents, *(iii)* perform the federation of the entities and *(iv)* set the credentials for each IdP instance.

Finally, the Dashboard can be used to configure some components of the Micro-Id-Gym Frontend. In particular, customized ports can be selected for the Proxy, the MSC Drawer and the MSC STIX Visualizer.

3.3   Implementation

In this section, we provide the technical details about the implementation of the Micro-Id-Gym.

All the instances are Docker-based and the currently available implementations are depicted in Table 3. For each instance, we report the version, the protocol running on that implementation and the technology used. The proxy we decided to adopt is the Community Edition of Burp Suite (hereafter Burp). This choice has been done because it provides a set of useful and easy-to-use APIs for the pentesting tools development.

Table 3. Collection of C and IdP instances.

Version	Prot.	Technology	Provider
Base	S	Spring SP	C
Supported c14n algorithm	S	Spring SP	C
DTD enabled	S	Spring SP	C
DTD disabled and c14nWithComments algorithm	S	Spring SP	C
RelayState validation enabled	S	Spring SP	C
RelayState validation disabled	S	Spring SP	C
Sample Webapp	O	KeyCloak	C
Simple Webapp	O	MitreID	C
3.3.x	S	Shibboleth IdP	IdP
3.2.x	S	Shibboleth IdP	IdP
3.3.3 with RelayState sanitization enabled	S	Shibboleth IdP	IdP
1.3.3 without redirect_uri validation	O	MitreID	IdP
1.3.3 with redirect_uri validation	O	MitreID	IdP
10.0.1 without redirect_uri validation	O	Keycloak	IdP
10.0.1 with redirect_uri validation	O	Keycloak	IdP

Legenda: "S": SAML, "O": OAuth/OIDC

A web application (hereafter webapp) developed in NodeJs provides the Dashboard for the configuration of the instances, the Proxy, and the Pentesting Tool. Through a form, the user can customize the ports where the services will run, insert custom credentials to authenticate at the IdP, and give a name to the environment he is creating. The form submission starts the generation of the needed files. A folder with the chosen environment name is created and the selected implementation is copied into it. Docker and Burp configuration files are then customized through a find-replace process. Targeted placeholders are substituted with the information inserted by the user. Finally, the steps to run the environment together with the location of the environment folder are displayed in the dashboard. The same information is also written in a Readme file added to the environment folder.

Following the provided instructions, the user has to run the frontend. Once opened the terminal and reached the folder where the customized environment is located, he finds three directories: `proxy`, `tools` and `sso`. The `proxy` folder contains Burp, part of the Pentesting Tool, and the JSON files used for the automatic configuration. The user can run the Proxy and load tools and configuration with `java -jar` command. The folder `tools` contains MSC Drawer and MSC STIX Visualizer. Both are developed in NodeJs and deployed as Docker containers. A `docker-compose` command automatically deploys and run them. The last folder, `sso`, contains the configured instances. As well as the tools, the instances are deployed and run through a `docker-compose` command.

For the interested reader, the Micro-Id-Gym tool is online[3] and a demo video is available at the complementary material page.

4   Micro-Id-Gym at Work in the Wild: Pentesting of a PSD2 Deployment

In the context of an European project we had to assess a PSD2 service provided by an important Italian identity provider. PSD2 is the second Payment Services Directive, designed by the countries of the European Union. Strong Customer Authentication (SCA) is one of the fundamental building blocks for building secure PSD2 deployments composed by Multi Factor Authentication and dynamic linking. The best solution to implement this scenario (such as proposed by many like the Berlin group) can be done by adopting OAuth which allows delegation to third parties to access resources. It could revolutionize the payments industry, affecting everything from the way we pay online, to what information we see when making a payment. Security of electronic payments is fundamental for ensuring the protection of users and all payment services offered electronically should be carried out in a secure manner, adopting technologies able to guarantee secure user authentication.

The involved scenario that we analyzed uses OAuth and OIDC as an IdM protocol. The OAuth protocol is an authorization standard allowing a user (resource owner, RO)—which interact with a user agent (UA), typically a web browser—is to delegate to a C the access to his resources stored on another web server controlled by an Authorization Server (AS). OIDC is an identity layer on top of the OAuth protocol that is used for authentication purposes. The aim of the user which interacts with UA is to get access to a service provided by C, leveraging AS as IdP. Figure 5 shows a MSC providing a simplified view of the OAuth Authorization Code flow. A brief description of the protocol is as follows:

1 C initiates the flow by directing RO's UA (typically a web browser) to the authorization endpoint. C includes its identifier (`client_id`), requested scope (`scope`), local state (`state`), and a redirection URI (`redirect_uri`) to which the AS will send UA back once access is granted (or denied).
2 The AS authenticates the RO (via the UA) and establishes whether the RO grants or denies the C's access request.

---

[3] https://github.com/stfbk/micro-id-gym/.

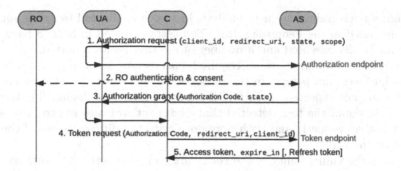

Fig. 5. OAuth authorization code flow (simplified view).

3 Assuming RO grants access, AS redirects UA back to C using the redirection URI provided earlier (in the request or during C registration). The redirection URI includes an authorization code and any local state provided by C earlier.

4 C requests an access token from AS's token endpoint by including the authorization code received in the previous step. When making the request, C authenticates with AS. C includes the redirection URI used to obtain the authorization code for verification.

5 AS authenticates C, validates the authorization code, and ensures that the redirection URI received matches the URI used to redirect C in step 3. If valid, AS responds back with an access token and, optionally, a refresh token.

The description of OAuth abstracts away several details that are crucial for security. A trust relationship between C and AS must be established before running the protocol by distributing appropriate meta-data between the two entities. The user must possess credentials to access AS. The configurations of auxiliary modules must be properly performed, and the format of the messages must be properly set and checked.

To perform the security assessment, we leveraged the Pentesting Tool component of Micro-Id-Gym, and we were able to identify some vulnerabilities and a misconfiguration of the OIDC protocol. In particular, we followed the following two steps:

- Being the SUT an OIDC implementation, we set the MSC Drawer on the OIDC mode, in such a way to collect all the relevant traffic concerning OIDC. We have been thus able to spot very quickly the differences between the expected OIDC flow and the one shown by the MSC Drawer in terms of the intercepted HTTP messages. Thanks to MSC Drawer we were able to identify two HTTP messages exchanged between entities not encrypted using Transport Layer Security (TLS). The usage of HTTPS protects against man-in-the-middle attacks, eavesdropping and tampering. Thus this provides a reasonable assurance that one is communicating with the intended website without interference from attackers.

- Then, a finer-grained security analysis has been conducted by using our plugin included in the Pentesting Tool. The tests reported in Sect. 3 have been automatically executed and a number of relevant issues reported.

About the compliance, some required parameters according to the OIDC standard were not present in the protocol. On the contrary, some parameters which are not expected in the OIDC standard have been included in the protocol. In detail the tool detected that redirect_uri and state parameters were not set properly and both were not verified in different steps of the process by the IdP.

Regards the vulnerability in the redirect_uri parameter, AS, authorization endpoint, and client redirection endpoint can be improperly configured and operate as open redirects. An open redirect is an endpoint using a parameter to automatically redirect a user-agent to the location specified by the parameter value without any validation. Open redirects can be used in phishing attacks, or by an attacker to get end-users to visit malicious sites by using the URI authority component of a familiar and trusted destination. In addition, if AS allows C to register only part of the redirection URI, an attacker can use an open redirect operated by C to construct a redirection URI that will pass the authorization server validation but will send the authorization code or access token to an endpoint under the control of the attacker [12].

Regards the state parameter, it is a recommended parameter in OAuth [2]. It is an opaque value used by C to maintain state between the request and callback. The AS includes this value when redirecting the user-agent back to the C. The state parameter is set by C in the Authorization Request, in step 1 in Fig. 5, and it is checked by C when C receives it in step 3. If the integrity of the state parameter field is not adequately protected, it may allow hackers to mount cross-site request forgery attacks (CSRF) [9]. To exploit these vulnerabilities an attacker causing the target browser to send the target site a request containing the attacker's own authorization code or access token. As a result, the target site might associate the attacker's protected resources with the target user's current session; possible undesirable effects could include saving user credit card details or other sensitive user data to an attacker-controlled location.

These results pointed out the need of tools, like Micro-Id-Gym, capable to support developers in order to properly implement, configure and test the OIDC implementations. Another interesting consideration emerges from our assessment. Some parameters were included in the protocol, meaning that we could detect them while checking the HTTP traffic. Yet, some of them were not used in end. For instance, the values of some parameters were not checked at all by the IdP. This highlights the need of active tests to check whether the parameters are indeed used properly.

All the discovered issues were notified to the company and fixed by their developers. In detail, about the HTTP messages exchanged not over TLS, the developers reviewed all the URL inside the application and modified the web server so that all messages will pass in HTTPS. Regards the missing sanitization of the `redirect_uri` parameter, the developers implemented a method inside the application to sanitize the parameter and do not allow any manipulation from an attacker. For the not adequately protection of the `state` parameter, the developers added some code to adequate protect the parameter. Lastly, about the redundant parameters not included in the protocol, the developers removed all of them from the flow.

5 Micro-Id-Gym at Work in the Lab: Evaluation of the Effectiveness

While in Sect. 4, we reported a use case where we used Micro-Id-Gym in the wild in this section, we evaluate it in the laboratory. We create a couple of scenarios of deployments for IdM protocol based on OIDC where some implementations have implemented the protocol correctly and others where there are some vulnerabilities to identify. In order to evaluate if and how the tool it is used effectively we have organized a structured user experience in a couple of workshops involving 8 bachelor and 30 master students from the Department of Information Engineering and Computer Science of the University of Trento, playing the role of inexperienced security testers. Bachelor students have quite a broad background on information security, because they attended (among others) the course *Introduction to Computer and Network Security*, that covered the OIDC protocol. Master students attended other courses about security, including the course *Security Testing* that covered, in particular, attacks to OIDC implementations.

In this lab we are focusing on the MSC Drawer component of Micro-Id-Gym. The goal of the study is to evaluate the effectiveness of understanding an OIDC execution trace, when visualized either by MSC Drawer or by OWASP Zap,[4] one of the most popular free security tools, by conducting an experimental user study. Below, we detail the settings of the experimentation (designed following the template and guidelines by Wohlin et al. [5]) and summarize the main results. The experimental setting starts with the definition of the research question: Do the usage of MSC *increase* the effectiveness to find the *correct* OIDC implementation by a security tester? The research question aims to evaluate whether MSC helps security tester to increase security effectiveness of OIDC implementations. By answering this research question (see Sect. 5.4), we will be able to assess the added value in adopting MSC Drawer instead of available state-of-the-art proxy tools.

5.1 Context

The *context* of this study consists of the *participants* involved in the experiment and the software *systems* whose deployment contains vulnerabilities.

---

[4] https://www.zaproxy.org/.

Participants. As far as the participants are concerned, we are aware that the expertise of students may be different from that of professionals. However, finding professionals available to conduct a demanding experiment as the one we designed is not easy. We mitigated this limitation by considering students with different levels of education and by making sure that participants had enough knowledge on OIDC protocols and its related vulnerabilities. All in all, the use of undergraduate students as a proxy of junior developers to draw conclusions is a common practice in empirical software engineering that is largely accepted and validated [7,11,13].

Systems. The systems used to conduct the experiment are two different deployments of the OIDC protocol:

- S_1 a defective OIDC implementation vulnerable to a missing sanitization of the `redirect_uri` parameter; and
- S_2 a defective OIDC implementation vulnerable to a not adequate protection of the `state` parameter.

The selected systems are comparable in terms of complexity of the operations required to detect the problem. It is important to note that these systems are representative of realistic OIDC implementations and both vulnerabilities and their related attacks are described in Sect. 4. To fit the time constraint of our experiment, only one vulnerability is present in each system.

5.2 Variables Selection

To measure the support of vulnerability detection and to conduct a corrective maintenance on OIDC implementations, we identified as the main factor of the experiment—that acts as an independent variable—the presence of the MSC during the execution of the task. In our experiment, the *base* treatment case TR_{zap} consists of using OWASP ZAP; and TR_{mig} consists of using MSC Drawer, that includes not only the list of the HTTP intercepted messages, but also generates a MSC of the intercepted traffic. Moreover, we instrumented the experimental settings to measure **Correctness** of each corrective tasks performed by participants.

5.3 Experiment Design and Procedure

We adopt a counter-balanced experimental design intended to fit two lab sessions. Participants are randomly assigned to four groups (despite they work alone), each one working in two labs on different systems with different treatments. The design allows for considering different combinations of *Systems* and *Treatments* in different order across *Labs* (see Table 4).

Before our experiment, participants were properly trained with lectures and exercises on OIDC protocol, on MSC Drawer and on OWASP ZAP, to provide/recall the required background. The purpose of training is to make participants confident about the kind of tasks they are going to perform and the

Table 4. Experimental design.

	Group A	Group B	Group C	Group D
Lab 1	S_1 with TR_{mig}	S_2 with TR_{zap}	S_2 with TR_{mig}	S_1 with TR_{zap}
Lab 2	S_2 with TR_{zap}	S_1 with TR_{mig}	S_1 with TR_{zap}	S_2 with TR_{mig}

environment they will have available. The experiment was carried out according to the following procedure. Participants had to *(i)* complete a pre-experiment profiling survey questionnaire, *(ii)* perform the detection task for the first lab, *(iii)* perform the detection task for the second lab, and *(iv)* complete a post-experiment survey questionnaire.

The pre-experiment profiling survey collects background knowledge about the participants, such as their previous experience with Proxy tool and their knowledge of OIDC protocol. Post-experiment survey questionnaire (reported in Appendix A) deals with the clarity of the tasks, cognitive effects of the treatments on the behavior of the participants and perceived usefulness of MSC Drawer.

5.4   Summary of Findings

We collected all the results and noticed that: *(i)* the distributions of correct/wrong answers when using MSC Drawer is respectively 262 and 80, *(ii)* the distributions of correct/wrong answers when using OWASP ZAP is respectively 222 and 120, *(iii)* 8 participants over 38 were able to detect correctly and completely the vulnerabilities when they were using MSC Drawer, and *(iv)* only 3 participants were able to detect correctly and completely the vulnerabilities when using OWASP ZAP.

The feedback questionnaire was positive and from the post-experiment survey we can learn that 87.5% of the students considers TR_{mig} more useful and 84.4% assessed that TR_{zap} is more complex to understand. In addition, all the students positively recommend our tool. Here we report some comments: "Very clear in the presentation of information.", "Simple to visualize the HTTP messages with directions.", "It is easier and faster to read all the information.".

Finally, looking at their subjective feedback, it seems that participants agree with our claim that MSC Drawer is highly beneficial in detecting vulnerabilities in OIDC implementations and it will help to increase the security awareness.

6   Conclusions and Future Work

We have described Micro-Id-Gym a flexible tool for pentesting IdM protocols easy to configure and in which users can develop hands-on experiences on how IdM protocols work, performing attacks with high impacts and better understand the underlying security issues. For ease of configuration and deployment, Micro-Id-Gym uses container-based micro-services and state-of-the-art penetration testing tools. We have improved Micro-Id-Gym by supporting new IdM protocols and a catalog of realistic scenarios in which different vulnerabilities and attacks can be re-created, analyzed, and mitigated. Secondary, we have analyzed a real use-case scenario involving a PSD2 service provided by an important Italian identity provider. Finally, we have validated the user experience and security awareness provided by our framework by using the results of a user-study experimentation involving students from university.

As future work, we plan to extend Micro-Id-Gym by *(i)* integrating new pen-testing tools, *(ii)* supporting other multi-party web applications, and *(iii)* supporting STIX also for OAuth/OIDC.

A   Post-questionnaire

The following table shows the content of the post-experiment survey questionnaire mentioned in Sect. 5. It deals with object clarity of the tasks, cognitive effects of the treatments on the behavior of the subjects and perceived usefulness of MSC Drawer. The first set of questions (Q1–Q6) needs to be answered twice (one answer for each performed lab) while the remaining set only needs to be answered once as it refers to the overall session (Table 5).

Table 5. Post-experiment survey questionnaire.

ID	Applies to	Question
Q1	Each lab	I had enough time to perform the tasks. (1–5)
Q2	Each lab	I experienced no difficulty in detecting the vulnerability. (1–5)
Q3	Each lab	Which operations (e.g., mouse over steps, open tab, search, ...) did you perform to understand whether the protocol was vulnerable to the mentioned vulnerability?
Q4	Each lab	Did you consult internet to find help to answer the questionnaire? If yes, which online queries did you search(e.g., keywords used)? Which content was helpful?
Q5	Overall	Which tool did you find more useful to answer the questions? (Report of Lab 1–2)
Q6	Overall	Which tool did you find more intuitive? For which tool was more difficult to find the proper information about the protocol in order to answer the questions? (Report of Lab 1–2)
Q7	Overall	Which tool would you use for your work? Motivate your answer (to the previous question). (open question)
Q8	Overall	Do you know any tool that performs similar tasks? (open question)
Q9	Overall	Do you have any suggestion related to the tool usage? (open question)
Q10	Overall	What do you think is the main advantage using MSCDrawer? Would you add more information to the MSCDrawer? (open question)

References

1. PSD2.   https://eur-lex.europa.eu/legal-content/EN/TXT/?uri=CELEX %3A32015L2366 Accessed 23 Jun 2020
2. Security Considerations OAuth. https://tools.ietf.org/id/draft-bradley-oauth-jwt-encoded-state-08.html#rfc.section.6 Accessed 23 Jun 2020
3. Armando, A., Carbone, R., Compagna, L., Cuellar, J., Tobarra, L.: Formal analysis of SAML 2.0 web browser single sign-on: breaking the SAML-based single sign-on for google apps. In: Proceedings of the 6th ACM Workshop on Formal Methods in Security Engineering, pp. 1–10 (2008)
4. Bisegna, A., Carbone, R., Martini, I., Odorizzi, V., Pellizzari, G., Ranise, S.: Micro-Id-Gym: identity management workouts with container-based microservices. Int. J. Inf. Secur. Cybercrime 8(1), 45–50 (2019)
5. C. Wohlin, P. Runeson, M.H.M.O.B.R.A.W.: Experimentation in software engineering. Softw. Test., Verif. Reliab. (2001). https://doi.org/10.1002/stvr.230
6. Hardt, D.: The OAuth 2.0 Authorization Framework (RFC6749). Internet Engineering Task Force (IETF) (2012)
7. Höst, M., Regnell, B., Wohlin, C.: Using students as subjects—a comparative study of students and professionals in lead-time impact assessment. Empirical Softw. Eng. 5(3), 201–214 (2000)
8. Hughes, J., Maler, E.: Security assertion markup language (saml) v2.0 technical overview. OASIS SSTC Working Draft sstc-saml-tech-overview-2.0-draft-08 pp. 29–38 (2005)
9. Li, Wanpeng, Mitchell, Chris J.: Security issues in OAuth 2.0 SSO implementations. In: Chow, Sherman S.M., Camenisch, Jan, Hui, Lucas C.K., Yiu, Siu Ming (eds.) ISC 2014. LNCS, vol. 8783, pp. 529–541. Springer, Cham (2014). https://doi.org/10.1007/978-3-319-13257-0_34
10. Sakimura, N., Bradley, J., Jones, M., De Medeiros, B., Mortimore, C.: OpenID Connect Core 1.0 incorporating errata set 1. The OpenID Foundation, specification 335 (2014), https://openid.net/specs/openid-connect-core-1_0.html
11. Salman, I., Misirli, A.T., Juristo, N.: Are students representatives of professionals in software engineering experiments? In: 2015 IEEE/ACM 37th IEEE International Conference on Software Engineering. vol. 1, pp. 666–676. IEEE (2015)
12. Svahnberg, M., Aurum, A., Wohlin, C.: Redirect uri attack. In: Proceedings of the Second ACM-IEEE International Symposium on Empirical Software Engineering and Measurement, pp. 288–290 (2008)
13. Svahnberg, M., Aurum, A., Wohlin, C.: Using students as subjects-an empirical evaluation. In: Proceedings of the Second ACM-IEEE International Symposium on Empirical Software Engineering and Measurement, pp. 288–290 (2008)

IFTTT Privacy Checker

Federica Paci[1] , Davide Bianchin[2], Elisa Quintarelli[1] ,
and Nicola Zannone[3]( )

[1] Department of Computer Science, University of Verona, Verona, Italy
{federica.paci,elisa.quintarelli}@univr.it
[2] IFInet SRL, Verona, Italy
d.bianchin@ifinet.it
[3] Eindhoven University of Technology, Eindhoven, The Netherlands
n.zannone@tue.nl

Abstract. IFTTT is a platform that allows users to create applets for
connecting smart devices to online services, or to compose online services,
in order to provide customized functionalities in Internet of Things scenarios. Despite their flexibility and ease-of-use, IFTTT applets may create privacy risks for users, who might unknowingly share sensitive information with a wider audience than intended. In this paper, we focus on
privacy issues related to the sharing of pictures through IFTTT applets.
We propose a framework to detect when IFTTT applets violate user's
privacy, both at design-time and run-time, based on the visibility and
sensitivity of shared data. We have realized two prototypes implementing
the framework, a browser plugin to detect design-time privacy violations
and an online service to detect run-time privacy violations. We evaluate
the online service using an IFTTT applet for posting to Twitter new
pictures uploaded in Google Drive.

1 Introduction

The rapid growth of the Internet of Things (IoT) has changed the way users
daily share information, personal or not, by interacting with smart devices and
services. Trigger-Action Programming (TAP) is an emerging paradigm to allow
lay user to program and connect their services and smart devices [12] in different
IoT scenarios like smart homes, smart buildings and robots. One of the most
widely used TAP platform is IFTTT (If This Then That), which allows users
to create applets of the form IF *trigger* THEN *action*, where *trigger* is an event
that should occur for the applet to be executed and *action* is the action that
is performed when the trigger is fired. An example of IFTTT applet is IF *A
New Photo is Taken with IOS Photo* THEN *Upload It to Google Drive*, which
automatically uploads on the Google Drive folder of the user any new photo the
user takes with his IPhone.

While IFTTT applets allow users to easily automate tasks that connect their
smart devices and online services, the use of such applets expose them to security
and privacy risks [1,2,4,8,17]. For example, the execution of applet IF *A New
Photo is Taken with IOS Photo* THEN *Upload It to Google Drive* can potentially

A. Saracino and P. Mori (Eds.): ETAA 2020, LNCS 12515, pp. 90–107, 2020.
https://doi.org/10.1007/978-3-030-64455-0_6

expose a user's sensitive photos to a wider audience than intended. For instance, when a user takes a photo of his blood test results to share it with his wife via Telegram, the photo is also automatically uploaded on his Google Drive folder. If the folder is public, the execution of the applet would lead to a privacy violation. On the other hand, if the visibility of the folder is private or the photo is not sensitive, the applet's execution would not violate the privacy of the user.

Privacy violations can also be caused by a *chained execution* of two or more applets, that is a sequence of applets where the action of one applet is the trigger of the next applet [1]. For example, the applets IF *Any new Instagram Photo* THEN *Upload It to Google Drive* and IF *Any new file on Google Drive* THEN *Create a new post to Twitter* form a chained execution. The first applet does not violate user's privacy if the Google Drive folder is private, but the chained execution of the two applets leads to a privacy violation if the user's Twitter profile is public and the photo being posted is sensitive.

These examples show that, to correctly capture privacy violations related to IFTTT applet execution, it is necessary to consider *contextual information* like the *sensitivity* of the data being shared, along with the *visibility* of the data once posted on user's online services. Despite this, previous work on mitigating privacy risks related to IFTTT applets' execution (e.g., [1,2,7,9]) often only accounts for the visibility of information and proposes to block the execution of an applet when the applet results in a flow of information from a private source to a public one. This approach, however, can result in blocking legitimate information flows.

Contribution: This paper proposes a framework to alert users about privacy risks they are facing *both* when they create or install IFTTT applets and they execute such applets. In particular, our framework relies on the notion of *design-time violation* and *run-time privacy violation*. Similarly to previous work [1,2,7,9], our first notion of privacy violation flags a privacy violation when information flows from a private trigger to a public or restricted action. The notion of *run-time privacy violation*, instead, is grounded on the notion of privacy as *contextual integrity* [15], which ties privacy to the specific contexts in which the information is shared and disseminated. As contextual information we consider the *sensitivity* of the information being disseminated. Considering the sensitivity allows us to detect run-time privacy violations only when a highly sensitive data item flows from a private trigger to a restricted or public action. We have implemented a browser plugin to detect design-time privacy violations when users add an applet to their profile. We have also developed a service to detect run-time violations and tested it using an IFTTT applet for sharing new pictures posted on Google Drive to Twitter.

Outline: The structure of the paper is as follows. Section 2 provides background notions and related work on IFTTT and related privacy issues. Section 3 describes typical privacy threat scenarios in IFTTT. Section 4 introduces the notions of privacy violations at design-time and run-time and provides an overview of our framework to detect them. Section 5 describes a browser plugin to detect design-time privacy violations, and Sect. 6 an online service developed to detect run-time privacy violations. A performance evaluation of the online service is presented in Sect. 7. Finally, Sect. 8 concludes the paper and provides directions for future work.

2   Background and Related Work

2.1   IFTTT Platform

IFTTT applets enable users to connect smart devices (e.g., Fitbit, smart thermostat) to online services or online services to other online services, e.g., social network websites, cloud storage, etc. IFTTT applets are based on an emerging end-user programming paradigm [3] and follow a simple structure of the form IF *trigger* THEN *action*, where *trigger* indicates the event that should occur for the applet to be executed and *action* represents the action that is performed when the trigger is fired. The building blocks of IFTTT applets are services, each service providing its triggers, actions and APIs to interact with the service. An example of IFTTT applet is: IF *a new photo is taken in IOS Photo* THEN *upload the photo to Dropbox*. In this example, IOS Photo is the service associated with the trigger, whereas Dropbox is the service associated with the action. Triggers and actions can be customized using *ingredients* and *filter code*. Ingredients are parameters that can be passed to triggers and actions. Filter code is a Javascript snippet of code that has access to the APIs pertaining to the services used in the trigger and action of the applet. The filter code is executed after the trigger has been fired and before the action is dispatched. The filter code can use a special command, called *skip*, to stop the execution of the action in the applet.

A user needs to authorize IFTTT applets to poll the trigger's service for new data or to push data to a service in response to the execution of the action. In particular, IFTTT requires users to authenticate themselves and authorize the use of the services in the trigger and action through the OAuth 2.0 protocol when the services are selected. To pass the data from the trigger's service to the action's service, IFTTT uploads the data provided by the trigger on its own servers, generates a random public URL and passes it to the action's service.

2.2   Privacy in IFTTT

While IFTTT applets provide a simple but powerful approach to automatize a controlled response mechanism, this approach poses questions on the privacy and security guarantees offered by IFTTT. Various threat models for IFTTT applets and IoT applications, in general, have been studied [1,2,4,8,17,19], ranging from sensitive data leakages to permission misuse.

Some studies have focused on the privacy and security risks of malicious apps, where malicious applet makers engineer their applets to exfiltrate private information. For example, Bastys et al. [2] show that IFTTT applets are susceptible to two types of URL-based attacks that can lead to privacy, integrity and availability violations. Other researchers have studied the potential unintended effects of IFTTT applets by modeling the information-flow properties of IFTTT applets with respect to the *visibility* of information [1,17]. This threat model is typically described in terms of a labeling system defining the security level of events. In particular, security labels are assigned to triggers and actions based on the intended audience for an event (secrecy) or on who could have caused the event (integrity). Security policies are defined in terms of security lattices, which determine which information flows are allowed. Subtle privacy risks can arise from the interconnection between the applets employed by the user. In particular, the employed applets can form *chains* where the action of an applet fires the trigger of some other applets, leading to confidentiality and integrity violations. These privacy risks are underpinned by empirical evidence showing that a large portion of the applets currently available on the IFTTT platform might leak private information or can allow untrusted services to execute potentially risky actions [2,14,17].

Table 1. Overview of enforcement mechanisms for IFTTT applets where ● means "support", ◐ "partially support", ○ "no support".

	Approach	Enforcement	Context	Chain
Bastys et al. [2] (blocking)	Information flow	Static	○	○
Bastys et al. [2] (tracking)	Information flow	Static	○	○
Balliu et al. [1]	Information flow	Static	○	●
Enck et al. [7]	Information flow	Dynamic	◐	○
Fernandes et al. [9]	Information flow	Dynamic	◐	○
Celik et al. [6]	Permission-based	Dynamic	●	○
Jia et al. [11]	Permission-based	Static	●	○
Fernandes et al. [10]	Permission-based	Static	○	○
Celik et al. [5]	Code analysis	Static	○	●
Wang et al. [18]	Code analysis	Static	●	●

Our work mainly focuses on the second threat model, with the aim to identify which (combinations of) applets can potentially lead to privacy violations. However, we refine and extend the notion of privacy violation adopted in prior studies and ground such a notion in the realm of contextual privacy [15]. This will provide a more accurate privacy risk assessment as, without accounting for the context in which applets are executed, applets might be flagged as risky even if they do not violate the privacy of the user.

2.3 Policy Enforcement in IFTTT

Security and privacy issues in IFTTT mainly arise from the use of OAuth as this protocol has been shown to be not well-suited to deal with privacy in IoT applications [10,16]. To overcome these limitations, several researchers have proposed enforcement mechanisms to mitigate the identified security and privacy risks. An overview of existing solutions is provided in Table 1: we highlight, for each solution, the underlying *approach*, whether *enforcement* is static or dynamic, whether the *context* is accounted for to allow an action, and whether the solution is able to address violations due to applet *chains*.

A line of research aims at the design of enforcement mechanisms that prevent illegitimate information flows [1,2,7,9]. For instance, Bastys et al. [2] propose two solutions, one to block any applet that allows information to flow from private sources (e.g., user's mobile phone) to public sinks (e.g., social network profile) and one to monitor risky information flows. Balliu et al. [1] propose a semantic framework able to capture cross-app interactions and rely on a flow-sensitive type system and a security classification of services and devices to determine whether any inference between apps complies the given security classification. These proposals typically employ some form of mandatory access control for the protection of information confidentiality and integrity. Consequently, they are very rigid and do not consider the actual context in which the applets are actually used. Some work (e.g., [7,9]) addresses these shortcomings by accounting for the sensitivity of the transmitted information. However, the sensitivity is determined based on the information source rather than on the information itself, thus capturing the context of the information flow only partially.

Another stream of research focuses on the definition of dynamic permission-based systems for IoT to protect users from insecure device states [6,10,11]. For instance, Celik et al. [6] propose IoTGuard, a policy-based authorization mechanism that augments apps' source code to collect app information at run time and checks the behavior of IoT apps (i.e., triggers and actions) against safety and security policies to detect if the execution of an action leads to policy violations. Similarly, Jia et al. [11] propose ContextIoT, a permission-based system that provides contextual integrity for IoT applications. A common aspect of this research line is the central role played by context information in the verification of apps' behavior. This allows fine-grained access control capabilities, contributing to the correct operation of IoT devices. Although these frameworks allows for fine-grained access control and, in general, are able to account for context information in decision making, they typically do not consider the combined effect of multiple applications connected to the user profile.

A few works propose to identify safety and security property violations through a static analysis of the IoT applications' source code. An example of these approaches is SOTERIA [5]. This system extracts state models from IoT app code and apply static analysis techniques to find security, safety and functional errors in (a collection of) IoT applications. Wang et al. [18] propose ProvThings, a framework to capture, manage and analyze data provenance in IoT platforms. A main limitation of these approaches is their intrinsic inability to support run-time enforcement.

3   Privacy Threat Scenarios

Despite providing users a means to easily implement customized functionalities, IFTTT applets are susceptible to threats to users' privacy. As discussed in Sect. 2.2, there are two main types of threats: *intentional* and *unintentional*. Intentional threats are mainly conducted by a *malicious IFTTT applet maker*. These threats have the main goal to exfiltrate sensitive or personal information of IFTTT applet's users. The attacker exploits the fact that the services associated with the action of IFTTT applets provides URL-based APIs to connect the trigger to the applet action for uploading the content. Therefore, when new content is created by the trigger of the applet, IFTTT first uploads this new content to its servers and then creates a publicly-accessible URL to pass information to the service associated to the action of the IFTTT applet. A malicious applet maker can manipulate the public URL to send the content to his own servers. We do not discuss in details here how these attacks are conducted because they are outside of the scope of this paper. For a detail discussion we refer the reader to [2].

In this paper, we focus on unintentional privacy threat scenarios initiated by IFTTT applets' users when they install or create an applet that shares information to a different audience than what the users intended. As a running scenario we have analyzed the services that can be used by IFTTT applets to create and share photos. To this end, we implemented a web scraper to extract these services and the applets using them from the IFTTT platform. Our dataset contains applets and services available on IFTTT as of the end of February 2020. We examined 41 applets that allow users to take and share photos online. We analyzed the services that can be associated with the trigger and action of an IFTTT applet. We found that four main services can be used to take a photo: Android Photos, IoS Photos, Instagram and Camera Widget. To share a photo, instead, we found that the most picked services by users are Google Drive, Dropbox, OneDrive, Flickr, Twitter, Pinterest, WordPress, Tumblr, Telegram, Facebook Pages and Slack.

These services implement different settings to restrict the visibility of the photos published by users on their service's profile. This may expose users' photo to a wider audience than the users intended. For example, consider the applet IF *Any new foto* THEN *Back it up to Google Drive*[1], which has been connected by 114.100 users to their profile. The *Any new photo* trigger event fires not only when a new photo is made with the phone, but also when a new photo is received on the phone using other applications. For instance, any new photo received in a Whatsapp chat will be automatically downloaded on the phone and trigger the execution of the event *Any new photo*. Therefore, a photo that the user considered to be appropriate to share in a Whatsapp chat can end up in a Google Drive folder shared with another group of users, thus potentially violating the privacy of the user. Another example is the applet IF *Any new*

---

[1] https://ifttt.com/applets/113607937d-automatically-back-up-your-new-ios-photos-to-google-drive.

photo THEN *Upload it privately to Flickr*[2], which have been connected to their profile of 228 users. This applet violates user privacy because any photo taken by the user with IoS Photos is automatically uploaded to the Flickr photostream of the user, which is public. To keep the photo private, the user has to login into his Flickr account and manually change the privacy settings of the photo from public to private. However, this can be done only after the photo was uploaded and, thus, the photo could have already reached an unintended audience.

A user can also accidentally disclose sensitive data due to a chained execution of IFTTT applets associated with its IFTTT profile. We discovered 166 possible chains among the 41 applets that we analyzed. For example, consider the applets IF *Any new Instagram Photo* THEN *Post to WordPress*[3] and IF *Any new Word-Press post* THEN *Create a new post to Reddit*[4]. The execution of the first applet does not violate privacy as WordPress profiles are private. However, its execution triggers the execution of the second applet, resulting in any photo taken with Instagram to be posted on the Reddit's profile of the user. As posts, photos, comments, and messages posted on Reddit are public, the chained execution of the two applets makes public a photo that the user might want to keep private.

4 Privacy-Preserving Framework for IFTTT Applets

This section presents our framework to detect privacy violations during the installation and execution of IFTTT applets. We first introduce the notions underlying our framework and then provide an overview of its architecture.

4.1 Basic Notions

Previous approaches to privacy for IFTTT applets [1, 2, 17] define a privacy violation as a flow of information from a private source (the trigger event) to a public sink (the action event). To determine if a violation occurs, the trigger and the action of an IFTTT applet are assigned to *security labels*. The labels of the trigger and the action depends on the visibility settings of user profiles on the services associated with the trigger and the action. Intuitively, the visibility denotes the audience of the information posted on the user profile. In this paper, we apply this notion to detect a privacy violation when an IFTTT applet is created or installed by the user. If the creation/installation of an IFTTT applet violates privacy, the user is notified and can decide not to add the applet to his IFTTT profile. Next, we first introduce the notion of *IFTTT applet model* and then we formalize the notions of *design-time* and *run-time privacy violation*.

Definition 1 (IFTTT Applet Model). *The model of an IFTTT applet* app_i *is defined as a tuple:*

$$\langle T, d, A \rangle$$

---

[2] https://ifttt.com/applets/113447276d-upload-all-ios-photos-privately-to-flickr.
[3] https://ifttt.com/applets/XtwWPrki-post-your-instagram-photos-to-wordpress? term=WordPress.
[4] https://ifttt.com/applets/393774p-wordpress-to-reddit?term=WordPress.

where T is the trigger event, d is the data item disseminated by the execution of app_i, and A is the action event.

Hereafter, we represent the flow of a data item d from the trigger event T to the action event A as $T \xrightarrow{d} A$. The *visibility* of T and A is denoted v_T and v_A, respectively. We assume that the visibility can assume the values *private*, *restricted* or *public*: *public* means that the information is accessible by anyone, *restricted* indicates that the information of the user is shared only with a limited number of users, *private* means that the information is not visible to any other user. Since we focus our analysis on IFTTT applets that allow to take and share photos, and the photos once taken are accessible only by the user, we assume that the visibility of the user profile on the service associated with the trigger of the applet is always *private*. The execution of an applet violates privacy when the data item d flows from a trigger which is *private* to an action event that is either *restricted* or *public*.

Definition 2 (Design-Time Privacy Violation). *Let $app_i = \langle T, d, A \rangle$ be the model of an IFTTT applet. The flow of information $T \xrightarrow{d} A$ violates privacy when $v_T = private$ and $v_A \neq private$.*

Example 1. Let suppose that the user installs the applet IF *Any new photo with rear camera* THEN *Upload it to Google Drive*. If the Google Drive folder where the photo is posted is public, the applet violates design-time privacy.

When an applet is installed or created by the user, we can only reason about privacy in terms of the visibility of the information. This is because the information is actually created and disseminated when the IFTTT applet is executed. However, this may lead to notify the user that a flow of information violates his privacy when it does not. Suppose the user installs in his IFTTT profile the applet IF *Any New Photo on Instagram* THEN *Save it to Dropbox*: the photo taken represents a countryside landscape and the Dropbox folder where the photo is saved is public. This applet violates design-time privacy because the visibility of the action event is public. However, the photo being shared does not reveal any personal or sensitive information of the user, and thus the flow of information should not be flagged as a privacy violation.

To capture privacy violations during the execution of an IFTTT applet, we need to consider not only the audience of a data item but also the type of data being shared and whether it is appropriate to disseminate the data item from the trigger to the action. Therefore, we extend the notion of design-time privacy violation to include contextual information like the *sensitivity* of the photo. As advocated by privacy as contextual integrity [15], contextual information is important to determine whether a flow of information is appropriate and respect constraints on the dissemination of information. We first introduce the notion of *context of execution* of an IFTTT applet and then we define the notion of *run-time privacy violation*.

Definition 3 (Context of Execution of an IFTTT Applet). *Given the model of an IFTTT applet $app_i = \langle T, d, A \rangle$, the context C_{app_i} of execution of app_i is defined as a tuple:*

$$\langle u_i, \delta_d, v_T, v_A \rangle$$

where u_i is the user who runs the applet app_i, δ_d is the sensitivity of the data item d, v_T and v_A is the visibility of T and A.

To determine the sensibility of information, we adopt the taxonomy proposed in [13]. This taxonomy classifies data items in four main categories based on the type of information that reveals about a user: *simple data*, which contains simple information like the name of the user or its contact information, *behavioral data*, which comprises information like data on location or personal preferences, *financial data*, which includes information like income, financial transactions, bank statements, investments, credit cards, invoices, etc., and *sensitive data*, which comprises information like health data, political affiliations or sexual life. The *sensitivity* δ_d of a data item d represents how critical the category of a data item d is for the user. We consider three sensitivity values that can be assigned to a data item based on its category: *low* sensitivity is assigned to simple data, *medium* sensitivity is given to behavioral data, while financial and sensitive data have *high* sensitivity. The execution of an applet violates run-time privacy when the data item d is highly sensitive and it flows from a trigger which is *private* to an action which is *restricted* or *public*.

Definition 4 (Run-time Privacy Violation). *Let $app_i = \langle T, d, A \rangle$ be the model of an IFTTT applet app_i and $C_{app_i} = \langle u_i, \delta_d, v_T, v_A \rangle$ be the context of the IFTTT applet execution. The flow of information $T \xrightarrow{d} A$ violates run-time privacy in C_{app_i} when $\delta_d = high$, $v_T = private$ and $v_A \neq private$.*

Example 2. Let consider a babysitter that installed the applet IF *Any New IoS Photo* THEN *Upload it to Flickr* to automatically upload any photo taken with her iPhone to Flickr photostream in order to share them with the baby's mother. Suppose that the babysitter took a photo of the rash on the baby's leg. In this case, we have a run-time privacy violation because a highly sensitive information about the health of the baby becomes public once posted on Flickr.

The notions of *design-time privacy* and *run-time privacy* also apply to a *chain of IFTTT applets*. A chain of IFTTT applets is a sequence of IFTTT applets $T_1 \xrightarrow{d_1} A_1, T_2 \xrightarrow{d_2} A_2, \ldots, T_n \xrightarrow{d_n} A_n$ (with $n \geq 2$) where, for each pair of applets app_i and app_{i+1}, $d_i = d_{i+1}$ and $A_i = T_{i+1}$. We say that a chain of IFTTT applets $T_1 \xrightarrow{d_1} A_1, T_2 \xrightarrow{d_2} A_2, \ldots, T_n$ violates design-time privacy if $v_{T_1} = private$ and $v_{A_n} \neq private$. Similarly, a chain of IFTTT applets $T_1 \xrightarrow{d_1} A_1$, $T_2 \xrightarrow{d_2} A_2, \ldots, T_n$ violates run-time privacy when $\delta_d = high$, $v_{T_1} = private$ and $v_{A_n} \neq private$.

Example 3. Let consider two applets: IF *Any new Instagram photo* THEN *Post it on Tumblr* and IF *Any new Tumblr post* THEN *Create Twitter post*. In case, the user has set his Tumblr profile to private, the first applet does not violate design-time privacy. However, if the user has configured the privacy settings of his Twitter profile to public, the chained execution of the two applets violates design-time privacy.

Similar reasoning applies to run-time violation, but in this case we should also account for the sensitivity of the photo. If the user takes a photo of him and his boyfriend at their wedding, which reveals the sexual habit of the user, the chained execution of the applets will violate run-time privacy because the photo discloses very sensitive information of the user and the second applet posts the photo on the public Twitter profile of the user. On the other hand, if the photo shows a swan in a lake, the chain execution of the applets does not violate run-time privacy because the sensitivity of the photo is low.

It is worth noting that the notion of run-time privacy violation refines the one of design-time privacy violation. Specifically, it is easy to observe that if an applet does not violate design-time privacy, it will never violate run-time privacy. On the other hand, if an applet violates run-time privacy, it also violates design-time privacy, but the opposite is not true. In fact, we have also to account for the sensitivity of the data item shared to determine whether a run-time privacy infringement occurs.

4.2   Architecture

To detect privacy violations during the installation and execution of an IFTTT applet, we have developed two main components: a *browser plugin* and a *privacy service*. The overall architecture is presented in Fig. 1.

The browser plugin aims to detect design-time privacy violations. When the user creates a new applet, he needs to select the services he wants to associate with the trigger and action of the applet along with the corresponding events. The user is then requested to select the visibility of his profile on the service associated with the action. The user can choose among three visibility options: public, private and restricted. After the user has specified the visibility of his profile, the plugin shows whether the applet violates design-time privacy. If the applet created by the user forms a chain with other applets connected to the user profile, the plugin displays the chain and reports whether the chain violates design-time privacy.

Once the user has connected an applet to his IFTTT profile, the privacy service verifies that the execution of the applet does not breach run-time privacy. The execution of an applet is initiated by the occurrence of the event associated with the trigger of the applet, e.g., by the user taking a photo with his iPhone. The trigger event is notified to the IFTTT server that stores the photo and generates a public-accessible URL of the photo. The IFTTT server passes the URL to the privacy service along with the visibility of the user profile associated with the action of the applet. The service relies upon a classifier to assign a category to the photo that reflects the content of the photo. Based on the category

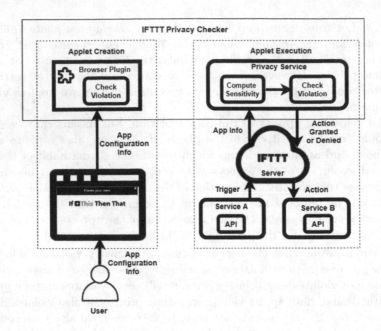

Fig. 1. IFTTT privacy checker logical architecture

the privacy service assigns a sensitivity value to the photo. Using the sensitivity of the photo and the visibility of the user profile, the privacy service checks whether the applet violates run-time privacy and communicates to the IFTTT server whether the action should be executed or not. If the privacy service has detected a run-time privacy violation, the IFTTT server blocks the execution of the action.

5   Design-Time Enforcement

In this section, we describe the implementation of the browser plugin to detect design-time privacy violations. We decided to implement the browser plugin as a Google Chrome extension for the following reasons. First, a browser extension can interact with the IFTTT web pages to create an applet and it can listen for events associated with the DOM (Document Object Model) of the web pages. Second, a browser extension allows to easily extend the functionalities of IFTTT website with the detection of privacy violations during the creation of an IFTTT. In addition, Google Chrome is the most widely adopted browser and the extensions for this browser can be easily ported to other browsers. The extension has been created with different web development technologies: HTML, CSS, and JavaScript. It consists of different components: a file manifest, a background script, a content script, and user interface elements (HTML and CSS files, and user interface Javascript). The main components of the extension are shown in Fig. 2.

manifest.json is a file that gives the browser information about the main files, the capabilities the extension might use, and the toolbar icon used by the user to access the user interface. The main files are: *content.js*, *background.js*, *popup.js* and *popup.html*.

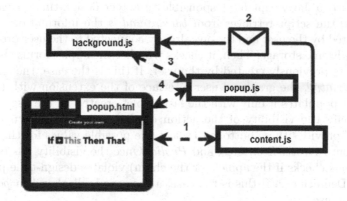

Fig. 2. Chrome extension architecture

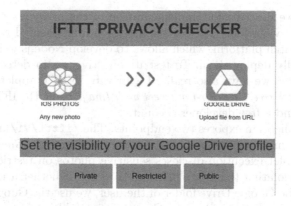

Fig. 3. Plugin interface

content.js is a Javascript file that keeps track of the different steps involved in the creation of an IFTTT applet on the IFTTT web page (https://ifft.com/ create) and registers the choices made by the user during each step of the creation, e.g., trigger and trigger event. In order to do so, the script implements listeners for the events that correspond to the different steps of the creation of an IFTTT applets. When an event is fired, the script creates a message containing the choices made by the user at that step and sends it to *background.js*.

background.js is a Javascript file used to save the information about the applets created by the user in the Google Chrome storage. The information is stored as a JSON object called *info*, which contains two main elements *trigger* and *action*. These elements specify the events associated with the trigger and the action along with their description. To save the info object into Chrome storage, the script uses the Chrome API storage.sync. This API implements two main methods: *set()* to insert data in the Chrome storage, and *get()* to retrieve data from the storage.

popup.js is a Javascript file responsible to detect design-time privacy violations. First, the script retrieves from *background.js* the information about the applet created by the user and the one already connected to the user profile saved in Google Chrome storage. Then, it checks whether the applet forms chains with other applets previously created by the user. If this is the case, the script populates *popup.html*, the graphical user interface of the extension with the chain; otherwise it populates it only with the last applet created by the user. The user has to specify the visibility of the action of the applet. As shown in Fig. 3, *popup.html* provides three buttons to select the possible values for the visibility of the action: *Private*, *Restricted*, and *Public*. Once the visibility has been specified, *popup.js* checks if the applet (or the chain) violates design-time privacy as defined in Definition 2. If this is the case, a message is displayed in *popup.html* to notify the user.

6 Run-Time Enforcement

In this section we describe the implementation of the privacy service to detect run-time privacy violations. The service has been implemented as a web application on the Glitch platform, which allows to develop Node.js web applications and automatically deploy them. To test its effectiveness in detecting run-time privacy violations, we have also realized a private IFTTT applet IF *Any New Photo on Google Drive* THEN *Post a Tweet with Image* using the IFTTT platform for developers and a free developer account.[5]

The web application exposes two endpoints. The /ifttt/v1/triggers/get_photo endpoint implements the trigger *Any New Photo on Google Drive* and checks if the applet execution discloses sensitive photos on restricted or public channels, thus violating the user's privacy. To detect whether a new photo has been added to the Google Drive folder of the user, we use the Google Drive API, which allows one to list the files in a Google Drive folder and to retrieve those files. To decide whether the disclosure of a photo on the action endpoint (i.e., Twitter in our sample applet) violates the user's privacy, the endpoint needs to determine both the visibility of the action and the sensibility of the photo. To compute the sensibility of the photo, we use the Google Vision API, which allows developers to integrate image recognition capabilities within their applications. This API uses machine learning models to classify images and assigns labels to images that reflect their content. The labels returned by the Vision API are used to assign a sensitivity value to the photo (cf. Sect. 4.1). The visibility of the

---

[5] The service is not publicly available on the IFTTT website. Publishing an IFTTT service requires a premium IFTTT developer account and applets submitted for publication have to go through a long code vetting process.

action is specified by the user when the IFTTT applet is created. The endpoint flags a run-time privacy violation if the sensitivity of the photo is high and the visibility of the action is restricted or public (cf. Definition 4).

The /ifttt/v1/actions/social_upload implements the *Post a Tweet with Image* action, which posts a tweet with the photo on Twitter. To create the tweet, it makes a POST request to the Twitter endpoint media/upload through the Twitter API twitter.post() where the body of the request contains the image encoded in base64.

It is worth mentioning that, to invoke the Google Drive, Google Vision and Twitter APIs from our application, it is necessary to generate the necessary keys and stored them in the respective configuration file, which can be done in the IFTTT developer console. To make the implemented endpoints accessible within the IFTTT platform, we created a new IFTTT service where endpoint /ifttt/v1/triggers/get_photo is specified as a trigger event and endpoint /ifttt/v1/actions/social_upload as an action event. We used this IFTTT service as a building block to create the IFTTT applet IF *Any New Photo on Google Drive* THEN *Post a Tweet with Image*. By using the trigger event and action event supported by our IFTTT service, the disclosure of photos uploaded on Google Drive to Twitter is mediated by the privacy checker.

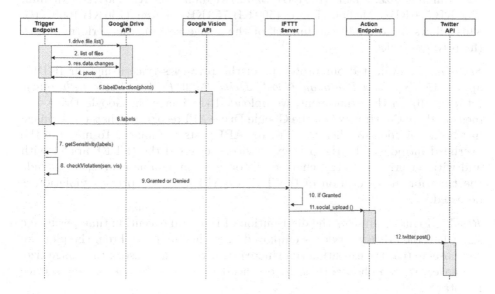

Fig. 4. Run-time privacy violation detection workflow

The interactions among the different components involved in the detection of run-time privacy violations are represented in Fig. 4. First, the trigger endpoint calls the Google Drive API drive.files.list() to retrieve the list of files contained in the user's Google Drive folder. Once the endpoint received the list, it contacts the Google Changes API to determine if new files have been added to the folder and to retrieve those files. For each new photo added to Google Drive folder, the trigger endpoint invokes the Google Vision API `labelDetection()` passing the new photo as an argument. Based on the labels returned by the Vision API, the endpoint computes the sensitivity of the photo and checks if a run-time privacy violation has occurred. The endpoints communicates to the IFTTT server if the action should be executed. If there is no violation, the IFTTT server calls the action endpoint, which invokes the Twitter API `twitter.post()` to upload a twit with the image.

7   Performance Evaluation

We have performed an experimental evaluation of the prototype implementation of the privacy service presented in Sect. 6 to understand the overhead introduced for the detection of privacy violations at run-time. In this section, we present the dataset and setting of our experiments and discuss the results.

Dataset: We created a dataset consisting of 45 images of varying size. Specifically, we selected 9 images belonging to different categories (e.g., landscape, credit cards, people, identity documents) and, for each of them, we created five copies with different size: Small (¡100 KB), Small/Medium (100 KB,250 KB), Medium (250 KB,500 KB), Medium/Large (500 KB,750 KB), Large (750 KB,1000 KB). This allows us to study the impact of the image size on the performance of the privacy service.

Settings: We evaluated our prototype of the privacy service using our IFTTT applet IF *Any New Photo on Google Drive* THEN *Post a Tweet with Image* (cf. Sect. 6). In the experiment, we uploaded the images in Google Drive and measured the time from when the Google Drive API recognizes that a new image has been uploaded to when the Twitter API posts the image. To measure the overhead introduced by the privacy service, we tested the IFTTT applet with and without privacy control enabled. To obtain comparable results, we include the time for the invocation of the Twitter API even if a privacy violation is detected.

Results: Figure 5 presents the distribution of the total execution time per image size when the privacy service is employed and when it is not. From the plot, we can observe that the execution time increases with the increase of the image size. Moreover, we can observe that the overhead introduced by the privacy service is notable.

To further investigate this, we broken down the computation time with respect to API calls (Google Drive, Twitter and Vision) at the varying of the image size. Figure 6 shows the average time for API calls along with the average total computation time per image size. We can observe that the Twitter API takes a large portion of the total computation time. In particular, the time required by the Twitter API is approximately the execution time required by the tested IFTTT applet when the privacy service is not employed. The overhead

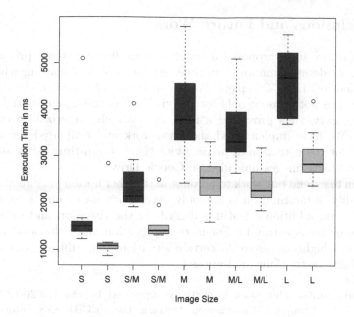

Fig. 5. Total execution time per image size with (blue boxplots) and without the privacy service (gray boxplots) (Color figure online)

introduced by the privacy service is mainly due to the Vision API for the classification of the image uploaded in Google Drive. It is worth noting that, while the performance of Twitter and Vision APIs depend on the size of the image, the Google Drive API exhibits a more stable behavior across images of different size.

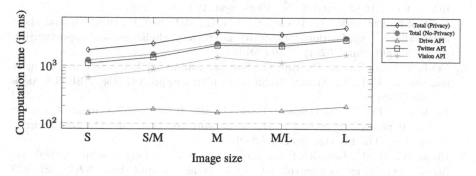

Fig. 6. Breakdown of average computation time for API calls in log scale at the varying of the image size

8   Conclusions and Future Work

In this paper, we have proposed a framework to discover users' privacy violations, both at design-time and run-time, related to image sharing when using (combinations of) IFTTT applets. For the detection of run-time violations, our framework does not account only for the visibility of the image shared but also for its sensitivity, thus providing a more accurate characterization of privacy violations. We have implemented the framework and evaluated the overhead introduced for the detection of privacy violations at run-time using an IFTTT applet that tweets images uploaded on Google Drive.

We plan to extend our work to account for a richer notion of context in which the sensibility of information is not only determined based on its content, but considering also additional features describing the situation and environment the picture owner is acting in. For instance, location and behavioral data may be considered highly sensitive in certain situations, e.g., during an emergency where mobility restrictions are imposed.

Acknowledgments. This work is partially supported by the H2020-ECSEL programme of the European Commission through the SECREDAS project (grant no. 783119).

References

1. Balliu, M., Merro, M., Pasqua, M.: Securing cross-app interactions in IoT platforms. In: Computer Security Foundations Symposium, pp. 319–334. IEEE (2019)
2. Bastys, I., Balliu, M., Sabelfeld, A.: If this then what?: controlling flows in IoT apps. In: Conference on Computer and Communications Security, pp. 1102–1119. ACM (2018)
3. Bu, L., et al.: Systematically ensuring the confidence of real-time home automation IoT systems. ACM Trans. Cyber-Phys. Syst. **2**(3), 1–23 (2018)
4. Celik, Z.B., Fernandes, E., Pauley, E., Tan, G., McDaniel, P.: Program analysis of commodity IoT applications for security and privacy: challenges and opportunities. ACM Comput. Surv. **52**(4), 1–30 (2019)
5. Celik, Z.B., McDaniel, P., Tan, G.: Soteria: automated IoT safety and security analysis. In: USENIX Annual Technical Conference, pp. 147–158. USENIX Association (2018)
6. Celik, Z.B., Tan, G., McDaniel, P.D.: IoTGuard: dynamic enforcement of security and safety policy in commodity IoT. In: Network and Distributed System Security Symposium. The Internet Society (2019)
7. Enck, W., et al.: Taintdroid: an information-flow tracking system for realtime privacy monitoring on smartphones. ACM Trans. Comput. Syst. **32**(2), 5:1–5:29 (2014)
8. Fernandes, E., Jung, J., Prakash, A.: Security analysis of emerging smart home applications. In: Symposium on Security and Privacy, pp. 636–654. IEEE (2016)
9. Fernandes, E., Paupore, J., Rahmati, A., Simionato, D., Conti, M., Prakash, A.: FlowFence: practical data protection for emerging IoT application frameworks. In: USENIX Security Symposium, pp. 531–548. USENIX Association (2016)

10. Fernandes, E., Rahmati, A., Jung, J., Prakash, A.: Decentralized action integrity for trigger-action IoT platforms. In: Network and Distributed Security Symposium. The Internet Society (2018)
11. Jia, Y.J., et al.: ContexIoT: towards providing contextual integrity to appified iot platforms. In: Network and Distributed Security Symposium. The Internet Society (2017)
12. Leonardi, N., Manca, M., Paternò, F., Santoro, C.: Trigger-action programming for personalising humanoid robot behaviour. In: Conference on Human Factors in Computing Systems. ACM (2019)
13. Manso, C.G., Górniak, S.: Recommendations for a methodology of the assessment of severity of personal data breaches. https://www.enisa.europa.eu/publications/dbn-severity
14. Mi, X., Qian, F., Zhang, Y., Wang, X.: An empirical characterization of IFTTT: ecosystem, usage, and performance. In: Internet Measurement Conference, pp. 398–404. ACM (2017)
15. Nissenbaum, H.: Privacy as contextual integrity. Washington Law Rev. **79**(1), 119–157 (2004)
16. Ravidas, S., Lekidis, A., Paci, F., Zannone, N.: Access control in internet-of-things: a survey. J. Netw. Comput. Appl. **144**, 79–101 (2019)
17. Surbatovich, M., Aljuraidan, J., Bauer, L., Das, A., Jia, L.: Some recipes can do more than spoil your appetite: analyzing the security and privacy risks of IFTTT recipes. In: International Conference on World Wide Web. pp. 1501–1510. International World Wide Web Conferences Steering Committee (2017)
18. Wang, Q., Hassan, W.U., Bates, A., Gunter, C.A.: Fear and logging in the internet of things. In: Network and Distributed System Security Symposium. The Internet Society (2018)
19. Xu, R., Zeng, Q., Zhu, L., Chi, H., Du, X., Guizani, M.: Privacy leakage in smart homes and its mitigation: IFTTT as a case study. IEEE Access **7**, 63457–63471 (2019)

A Comparison Among Policy Editors for Attributed Based Access Control Model

Fabio Martinelli[1], Christina Michailidou[1,2], Oleksii Osliak[1,3(✉)], Alessandro Rosetti[4], Antonio La Marra[4], and Theo Dimitrakos[5]

[1] Istituto di Informatica e Telematica, Consiglio Nazionale delle Ricerche, Pisa, Italy
{fabio.martinelli,christina.michailidou,oleksii.osliak}@iit.cnr.it
[2] Department of Information Engineering, University of Pisa, Pisa, Italy
[3] Department of Computer Science, University of Pisa, Pisa, Italy
[4] Security Forge srl, Pisa, Italy
{alessandro.rosetti,antonio.marra}@security-forge.com
[5] Huawei Technologies, Munich, Germany
theo.dimitrakos@huawei.com

Abstract. Attribute Based Access Control is a widely used access control model, which regulates the access to the resources by evaluating security policies which contain a number of attributes related to the subject, the object and the environment distinguishing thus from a simple access control list or a role-based model. Although, the dynamicity of today's environments requires security policies that consider a large set of attributes and conditions, making thus the policy writing an error-prone procedure. Existing policy editors are usually targeted to one particular framework and satisfy the needs of this application environment without providing the possibility of a more general use. In this paper we provide a comparison among the most known ABAC policy editors and their characteristics. Moreover, we propose an extension of one of those editors aiming at providing a more general and simple environment which supports the definition not only of attribute based access control policies, but also for Usage Control policies.

Keywords: Policy editors · ABAC · Apache hadoop · Amazon Web Services · XACML

1 Introduction

Undeniably, over the last years the amount of data being generated grows exponentially. In fact, a recent study of the International Data Corporation (IDC), predicts that the world's data will grow from 33 zettabytes this year to a 175ZB by 2025, for a compounded annual growth rate of 61% [10]. Smart devices, sensors, actuators, social media produces data with different characteristics and of various types in a per second base. The so called Big Data [11], because of their heterogeneity and the velocity with which the grow and transform, demand

© Springer Nature Switzerland AG 2020
A. Saracino and P. Mori (Eds.): ETAA 2020, LNCS 12515, pp. 108–123, 2020.
https://doi.org/10.1007/978-3-030-64455-0_7

scalable and robust systems both for their processing and also for regulating the access over them according to pre-defined security policies.

One of the existing access control models which can satisfy the needs of the aforementioned environments is the Attribute Based Access Control (ABAC) [9] which managed to differentiate from the traditional access control models, since it gives the possibility of defining security policies which consider a large set of attributes related to the subject, the object and the environment in order to grant or deny access over a resource. Hence, it provides the means of writing complex policies, which do not lack of expressiveness, in contrast to other commonly used models such as Role Based Access Control (RBAC) [7], where the only attribute under evaluation is the role of the subject.

Despite the fact that ABAC has proven to be a very powerful access control model, a big challenge which has yet to be met is the construction of appropriate, practical and user-friendly policy editors. The increased number of attributes which must be considered in an ABAC security policy, turns the process of writing the policy into an error-prone procedure and leads many times to misconfigurations, conflicts and unpredictable mistakes. The existing policy editors are mainly created by big companies who seek to provide to their security administrators a way to simply define the necessary rules for accessing their resources. Hence, these editors tend to be targeted to the specific application environment and lack of generalization. In this paper we provide a comparison among the most known ABAC policy editors and we mention some of their characteristics and the core of their functionality. In addition, we present our initial work on extending and modifying one of the existing editors, having as main goal to create a more general and simple environment which supports the definition not only of ABAC policies, but also for Usage Control policies.

The rest of the paper is structured as follows Sect. 2 presents Apache Hadoop framework and more specifically Apache Ranger policy editor. Section 3 describes the Amazon Web Services mainly focusing on Identity and Access Management. Finally Sect. 4 presents a number of XACML editors, alongside with our initial work and Sect. 5 concludes the paper.

2   Apache Hadoop

Big Data is an evolving term, which represents a field where a large volume of information, coming from various sources in a structure or unstructured form, can be processed and analyzed by machine learning algorithms or advanced analytics applications. The collection and the analysis of those data, is a common strategy followed by big companies and banks who seek to provide better customer service or to create targeted marketing campaigns, by governments who try to predict any suspicious activities and by the research community [11]. However, the volume, the variety and the velocity, which are commonly refer to as the 3Vs [12], of Big Data overcome the capabilities of the traditional data processing software [5]. Thus, new frameworks came to provide services and solutions for handling Big Data, with one of the most widely and commonly used being Apache Hadoop[1].

Hadoop provides the necessary infrastructure for storing, mining, processing and analyzing large data sets through a collection of open-source, Java-based software. The applications which form the framework of Hadoop are designed to run in clustered systems and highly distributed environments and are capable of managing various forms of data, from structured such as those coming from transactions to totally unstructured piece of information such as social media posts.

The core component of Hadoop ecosystem is its distributed file system, called Hadoop Distributed File System (HDFS), which is responsible to provide high-performance and fault-tolerant access to data across Hadoop's clusters. One of the main characteristics of HDFS is the support of a parallel processing of the data, since its functionality relies on the fact that the incoming information are broken down into separate blocks and distributed in different nodes of the cluster, making sure always that replicates and copies have been created on different servers. Other applications which form Hadoop framework and a brief description of their role are listed in Table 1.

Table 1. Applications of hadoop ecosystem

Application	Description
HIVE	Acts like an SQL database and provides an interface to the stored data. SQL-like queries can be exploited in order to interact with the data
KNOX	Constitutes the gateway of the whole ecosystem. It provides a single point of authentication and access to all the other services of the framework
KAFKA	A streaming platform which gives the possibility of a publish/subscribe process to real-time streams of records
SPARK	A powerfull analytics engine for processing stored data and applying machine learning algorithms
YARN	Is the resource management service of Hadoop, responsible for allocating resources of the system to the various applications

The access to these services and the protection of the available data is regulated through security policies, which ensure that users are assigned with the appropriate access privileges based on their authorization level. A way to write and manage the security policies across the Hadoop ecosystem is provided by Apache Ranger[2] framework which is described in the following section.

---

[1] https://hadoop.apache.org/.
[2] https://ranger.apache.org/.

2.1 Apache Ranger Policy Editor

Apache Ranger came to provide a centralized security solution for the majority of Hadoop services. This framework gives the possibility to the security administrator to define and manage policies related to Hadoop components and regulate the access over the amount of data stored in HDFS. In order to achieve this goal, Ranger comes along with a User Interface (UI), also known as Ranger Plugin, which offers the possibility to the user to create services for specific Hadoop components (i.e Hive, Kafka etc.) and define access policies. An example of the available Ranger Plugins is given in Fig. 1.

Fig. 1. Available ranger plugins.

Through the Ranger Plugins, the policy writer is able to create and manage resource-specific policies. Having as an example Hive and considering that, as mentioned above, HIVE acts as a SQL database, the Ranger Plugin for this component allows the definition of policies in a database, table and column level. Moreover, the permissions or privileges which can be assigned to a user or a group of users are related to the actions that someone can make upon a database as for example select, drop or create a table, read specific entries, execute SQL-queries etc. An overview of the interface of the policy editor and the possible privileges that can be assigned to a user who wants access to HIVE is shown in Fig. 2. For the rest of Hadoop services, a similar UI is provided, with the main difference lying in the type of access rights which can be granted to a user.

Another possible way to define security policies with Ranger is through Tag-based policies. In this case, it is not necessary for the policy writer to create policies for each component separately, but instead he/she can designate access policies to tags which can be attached to the resources (i.e. files, directories, databases etc.). Thus, whenever a resource is first introduced in Hadoop ecosystem or at any other given time, a tag can be assigned to it and automatically all the existing policies for this tag will be applied to the resource. The main advantage of the tag-based system is that it minimizes the effort of writing policies,

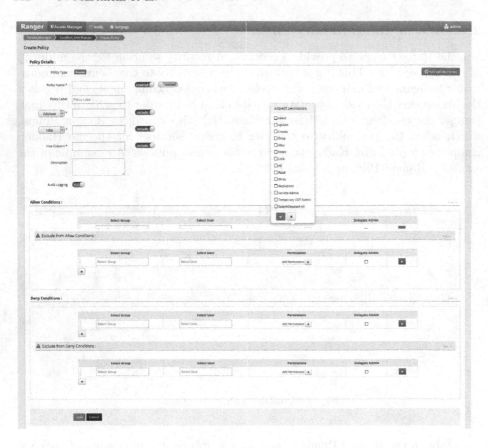

Fig. 2. Ranger policy editor for Hive.

since the process can be accomplished in a higher level and not in a per resource base. Moreover, due to the fact that tags are universal within Hadoop framework, meaning that they apply to all of the components, tagging the resources ensures the existence of an access control over them across multiple components.

A workflow of how a policy is evaluated and the access is granted or denied when Tag Policies are present, is shown in Fig. 3.

3   Amazon Web Services

In 2006 Amazon.com launched a cloud computing platform, known as *Amazon Web Services* (AWS), aiming at providing a combination of a an infrastructure as a service (IaaS) and a platform as a service (PaaS). The services which are included in AWS exceed the 100 and cover various areas such as data processing, databases, application development and security. For example, Amazon Simple Storage Service (Amazon S3[3]) allows to store data securely, while Amazon Sage-

---

[3] https://aws.amazon.com/s3/.

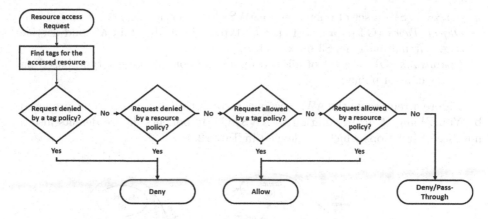

Fig. 3. Apache ranger policy evaluation flow with tags [8].

Maker[4] is a service for building, training, and deploying machine learning models. However, apart from advantages (e.g., cost-efficient, unlimited storage, backup & recovery, and easy access to information), cloud computing also has security and technical issues.

AWS cloud infrastructure was designed to be the most flexible and secure cloud network. It provides a highly reliable platform that enables customers to use applications and data quickly and in a secure way. AWS provides a variety of tools and features that customers can use to keep AWS Accounts and resources safe from unauthorized access and usage. Some of them are credentials for Access Control, HTTPS endpoints for encrypted data transmission, and user activity logging for security monitoring.

AWS utilizes several types of credentials for authorization in order to ensure that only authorized users can access and use an organization's account and resources [1]. Following, a more comprehensive description of the Access Control model used in AWS is provided.

3.1 AWS Access Control Model (AWSAC)

In 2015 Yun Zhang, Farhan Patwa and Ravi Sandhu [19] developed Access Control model for AWS cloud services (AWSAC). The AWSAC model consists of several components:

- *Accounts* (A) - a set of basic resource containers in AWS. These services allows customers to own specific cloud services;
- *Users* (U) - a set of users/individuals that can be authenticated by AWS and authorized to access cloud resources through their account;
- *Groups* (G) - a set of user groups to which user is assigned;
- *Roles* (R) - used to establish trust relationships between users and resources;

---

[4] https://aws.amazon.com/sagemaker/.

– *Services* (S) - a set of references to AWS cloud services;
– *Object Types* (OT) - a set of specific types of an object in a cloud service (e.g., virtual machine, S3 bucket, etc.);
– *Operations* (OP) - a set of allowed operations on the object type based on access control policy;

Figure 4 represents the AWS access control within a single account proposed by Yun Zhang et al. In addition to AWSAC components, figure depicts also a number of functions which are defined in Table 2.

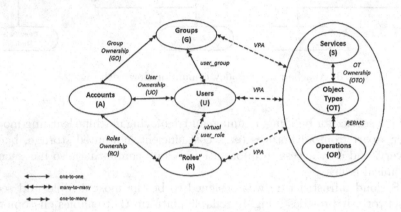

Fig. 4. AWS access control model [19].

More specifically, AWS offers *Identity and Access Management* (IAM[5]) service that allows customers to secure other Amazon cloud services by managing access control through policies and roles assigned to users.

3.2   Identity and Access Management

The main purpose of IAM is securing information and access to other Amazon services through access control policies. By using AWS IAM, customers can create/remove users, assign them individual credentials, or request temporary security credentials to provide users access to AWS services and resources. Moreover, IAM allows to create roles and manage permissions to control which operation can be performed by an entity that assumes the role. In AWS IAM, roles can be assigned either to groups or individually to the entity.

AWS IAM uses a policy-based access control mechanism where policies can be attached to users, groups, roles or a specific cloud resource. However, if the policy is attached to a resource, in this case, an account, user or role needs to be specified. Policy evaluation depends on the types of policies applied to the request context. In AWS, request context consists of *Actions*, *Resources*,

---

[5] https://aws.amazon.com/iam/.

Table 2. Functions and relationships

Function/ Relationship name	Description
User Ownership (UO)	a function mapping a user to its owning account, equivalently a many-to-one relation $UO \supseteq U \times A$
Group Ownership (GO)	a function mapping a group to its owning account, equivalently a many-to-one relation $GO \supseteq G \times A$
Role Ownership (RO)	a function mapping a role to its owning account, equivalently a many-to-one relation $RO \supseteq R \times A$
Object Type Ownership (OTO)	a function mapping an object type to its owning service, equivalently a many-to-one relation $OTO \supseteq OT \times S$
PERMS	a set of permissions $PERMS = OT \times OP$
Virtual Permission Assignment (VPA)	a many-to-many virtual relation resulting from policies attached to user, groups, roles and resources $VPA \supseteq (U \cup G \cup R) \times PERMS$
user_group	a many to many mapping between users and groups where users and groups are owned by the same account $user\_group \supseteq U \times G$
virtual user_role (VUR)	a virtual relation resulting from policies attached to various entities, where users are AssumeRole action to acquire/activate a role authorized in VUR: $VUR \supseteq U \times R$

Principal, Environment Data, and *Resource Data.* Based on this information, AWS search for specific policies that apply to the request context and evaluates request according to the defined policy. There are five policy types in AWS:

- *Identity-based policies* are attached to IAM users, groups, or roles and grand permissions to IAM users and roles;
- *Resource-based policies* grand permissions to the account, user, role or federated user specified as *principal*;
- *IAM permissions boundaries* are features for setting up maximum permissions that an identity-based policy can grant to an IAM user or role;
- *AWS Organizations service control policies (SCPs)* specify the maximum permissions for an organization or organizational unit. In AWS maximum applies to AWS root user;
- *Session policies* are advanced policies used for creating a temporary session for a role or federated user.

However, one important aspect is that all requests are implicitly denied. Meanwhile, if any related policy does not have an explicit deny statement and allows to perform an action, the user will be allowed to perform requested action.

Figure 5 depicts the policy evaluation process in AWS. In this particular case, the AWS enforcement code decides whether the request should be allowed or denied based on the user's attributes together with gathered policies that apply to the particular request context.

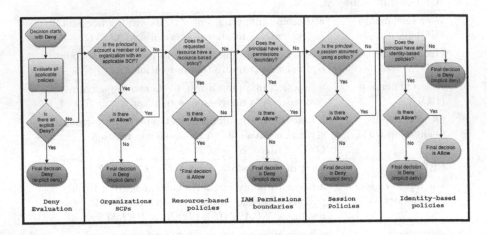

Fig. 5. Policy evaluation workflow [2].

Deny Evaluation. As it was mentioned before, all requests are denied by default. The AWS enforcement code gathers and evaluates all policies related to the particular request. Particularly, it looks for a specific statement i.e., **Deny**. Thus, if even one **Deny** statement exists in a policy, the enforcement code returns **Deny**.

Organizations SCPs. As the second step, the enforcement code evaluates AWS SCPs that is applied to the request. The request is denied if the enforcement code did not find any **Allow** statement in the SCPs. In case if SCP does not exist, or if it allows the requested action, the enforcement code continues.

Resource-Based Policies. In case where the requested source (e.g., S3, EC2, etc.) has an assigned resource-based policy that includes **Allow** statement, the enforcement code returns **Allow** as the final decision. However, if the resource-based policy does not exist or it does not include **Allow** statement, the enforcement code continues to evaluate next policies.

IAM Permissions Boundaries. As the fourth step, the enforcement code checks whether the IAM entity has a permissions boundary. The code returns **Deny** if the permissions boundary policy does not allow the requested action. Otherwise, the code continues if the permissions boundary does not exist, or if it allows the requested action.

Session Policies. The code returns **Deny** if the session policy does not allow the requested action. While if the session policy does not exist, or if the policy allows the requested action, the code continues.

Identity-Based Policies. As the final step, the enforcement code evaluates user policy and policy of the group to which user belongs to. Thus, if any policy includes **Allow** statement, the code returns **Allow** as the final decision. If any policy does not include the statement that allows to perform the requested action, the code returns **Deny**.

Finally, if an error at any point during the evaluation appears, then the enforcement code generates an exception and closes.

3.3   Managing AWS Policies

There are several options for customers to access AWS IAM in order to manage policies and users' accounts. Some of them are:

AWS Management Console[6] provides a web-based way to administrate AWS services that can be used by customers to create, list and perform other tasks with AWS services of the customers account. The AWS Management Console is a user friendly tool that allows to access the AWS account, assign existing and create custom policies based on tags.

AWS Command Line Tools is a set of command line tools including *AWS Command Line Interface* (AWS CLI[7]) and *AWS Tools for Windows PowerShell*[8]. By using AWS tools for PowerShell, customers can manage AWS resources with the same PowerShell tools for managing Windows, Linux, and MacOS environments. However, it requires to install additional components like *Microsoft .NET Framework Features, AWS SDK for .NET*, etc.

AWS CLI is a tool for managing AWS services. Before using it, customers have to download and install AWS CLI in order to control multiple AWS services from the command line and automate them through scripts.

AWS Software Development Kits[9] is a set of libraries and code samples for various programming languages including JAVA, Python, JavaScript, etc. Moreover, it also supports different platforms like iOS, Android, etc. By using this libraries, customers can mange policies, create/remove users, assign tags and perform other actions automatically/periodically.

IAM HTTPS API[10]. Finally, customers can access AWS and IAM by using IAM HTTPS API which allows to send HTTPS requests directly to Amazon cloud services.

Customers can attach existing policies to AWS entities or define custom by using one of the mechanism mentioned above. AWS policies are represented as a JSON file, which includes permissions defined on services and resources in the cloud. The policy file consist of three main components *Effect, Action*, and *Resources*, and optional *Conditions*. While each policy can have multiple permissions, each permission can include several conditions and actions.

---

[6] https://docs.aws.amazon.com/IAM/latest/UserGuide/console.html.
[7] https://aws.amazon.com/cli/.
[8] https://aws.amazon.com/powershell/.
[9] https://aws.amazon.com/tools/.
[10] https://docs.aws.amazon.com/IAM/latest/UserGuide/programming.html.

Meanwhile, one of the disadvantages of Amazon IAM is that this service was designed for managing access across Amazon services. Thus, it cannot be applied to other services that do not belong to AWS. Moreover, since Amazon services support traditional Access Control model, there is a lack of attributes values mutability control. Thus, it is impossible to revoke access to AWS service if the user's attributes values have changed during the session. In fact, AWS allows customers to monitor and log users' activity as well as analyse user behaviour (e.g., using Amazon Macie). However, session logging does not affect decision making directly and requires access control administrators to perform additional actions.

4   XACML Policy

Among the variety of XML-based access control languages [4], the *eXtensible Access Control Markup Language* (XACML) [3] is one of the most known and widely used. The first version of XACML was ratified in 2003, while the latest XACML 3.0 was standardized in 2013 by OASIS [18]. The XACML standard defines a declarative fine-grained, ABAC policy language. Moreover, as a specific case of ABAC, RBAC can be also implemented.

The policy language model includes three main components i.e., *Policy set*, *Policy*, and *Rule*. *Policy set* is a top-level element in the XACML schema that comprises a set of policies, target, policy-combining algorithm, obligation expressions, and advice expressions. *Policy* is an element in the XACML schema that comprises a target, rule-combining algorithm-identifier, a set of rules, obligation expressions, and advice expressions. Finally, *Rule* is the policy component that includes a target, effect, condition, obligation expressions, and advice expressions. More detailed information about XACML standard can be found in official specification [16].

In order to make the task of writing, managing and altering policies in XACML a number of editors has been created, which are described below.

4.1   UMU XACML Editor

The UMU XACML Editor[11] has been developed by the University of Murcia. Using this tool administrators can create or modify policies that are written in XACML 2.0/3.0. It is also possible to perform a validation of the resulting policy against the XML schema. Figure 6 depicts a *Graphical User Interface* (GUI) for the UMU XACML Editor.

The UMU XACML Editor uses a Java Swing interface that makes this editor compatible with all the main desktop operating systems. This application uses a classic tree view of the policy according to the XML structure. Each node and node property can be interacted and edited in the side panel on the right part of the application.

---

[11] http://umu-xacmleditor.sourceforge.net/.

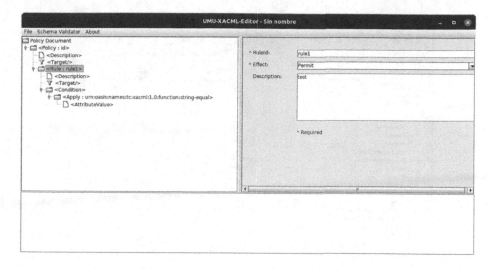

Fig. 6. UMU XACML Editor v1.3.2.

4.2 Security Policy Tool

Another tool for editing XACML policy is *Security Policy Tool* [15]. This tool helps to create, verify and test XACML policies. Similarly to the UMU XACML Editor, Security Policy Tool uses a GUI that simplifies the management of access control policies. It allows converting, importing, and exporting policies defined through XACML 2.0/3.0. Additionally, it allows policy engineers to validate and fix the faulty, unintended, misconfigured policies. Security Policy Tool has the following key functionalities:

- *Security Model and Policy Editing.* Security Policy Tool allows composing and editing Access Control Attributes of Subject, Resource, Action, and Environment as well as Conditions, Rules, Policies, and algorithms. Policy authors can effectively compose and edit policies for large organizations by using GUI represented in Fig. 7.
- *Policy Testing.* Security Policy Tool provides functions for comprehensive policy tests to verify the policies against predefined security requirements.
- *Policy Analyzing and Verification.* Security Policy Tool enables policy authors to perform analysis of rules and policies, their AC authentication consequences in responses to the various requests. Policies' potential security vulnerabilities could be detected in order to prevent AC flaws before applying these policies.
- *XACML Converter and Editor.* Security Policy Tool has an XACML 3.0 editor that helps in reducing mistakes caused by policy editing. Furthermore, it is possible to automatically convert the SPT data into XACML 3.0 policy format and output it for portability.

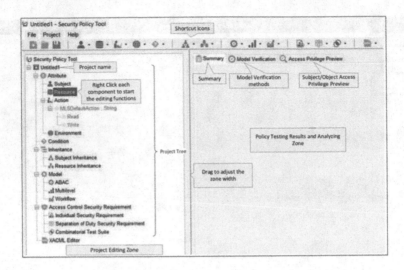

Fig. 7. The SPT policy editor.

Additionally to the editors described above, there are also *WSO2 Identity Server*[12] and *Axiomatics Policy Server*[13] tools. Unlike previous techniques, these two tools use a web user interface. By using *WSO2 Identity Server Management Console* it is possible to write XACML policies using a web interface. It allows creating an XACML policy from scratch, starting from a template, editing or importing the XML directly.

Axiomatics Policy Server is a leader in ABAC solutions. This XACML policy editor implements a rich and fast web based policy editing interface. It has the support for REST and JSON that simplifies the interaction with other applications.

4.3 Enhancing UMU XACML Policy Editor for U-XACML

In our initial work, we propose an extension of the UMU XACML editor, aiming at creating an editor which will also support *U-XACML* [6,14] which is an extension of the XACML standard. U-XACML was developed in order to support *Usage Control* systems features [13,17].

Particularly, by using the extended version of UMU XACML Editor which is depicted in Fig. 8, it is possible to add up to three XACML condition elements into a single rule. Each condition has a particular decision time to be applied depending on the status of the evaluation i.e., before, during, and after the session. Decision time can be one of the following:

– *Pre:* which represents the conditions to be applied before the access;

---

[12] https://docs.wso2.com/display/IS510/WSO2+Identity+Server+Documentation.
[13] https://www.axiomatics.com/resources/axiomatics-policy-server-product-sheet/.

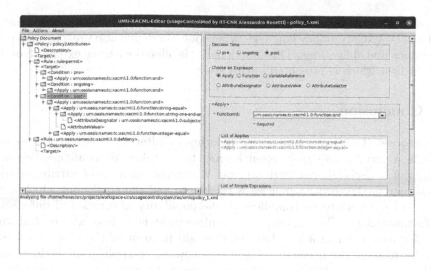

Fig. 8. Modified version of the UMU XACML Editor.

– *Ongoing:* which represents the conditions to be monitored while the access is in progress since attributes are mutable;

– *Post:* which represents conditions to be applied after the access has ended;

This editor simplifies creating and updating XACML policies and supports also U-XACML as an extension. However, the Java Swing is an old GUI library that was not considered anymore between the best practice to develop a user modern interface. As future work we are aiming at further simplifying and generalizing the editor. Moreover, we intent to publish these policies to a Policy Administration Point through REST operations and evaluate them through a Policy Decision Point, so as to assess the correct functionality.

4.4 Comparison Results

Apache Ranger and the AWS editors presented in the above sections are characterized by a user friendly environment which offers many possibilities on how to compose security policies. Although, they are two policy editors which are platform oriented and designed in order to serve the needs of those two application environments. Hence, it is not feasible to exploit those editors in order to write ABAC policies for other systems. On the other hand, the two XACML editors presented, the UMU and the Security Policy Tool, are more generalized editors and can be used in order to write policies based on the environment of the access control enforcement and the resources under protection. Among the two of them, Security Policy Tool offers more functionalities, which include policy testing and verification as long as an XACML converter which can be used to transform data into XACML 3.0 policies. Notwithstanding the fact that both of the editors offer a great solution for writing and editing policies, they do not support the U-XACML policy language, where one can define also pre/ongoing/post conditions and obligations. This functionality is offered with the extension of the UMU editor which is presented in this study.

5   Conclusion

The process of writing, managing, updating or altering security policies can become a very tedious task, often leading to mistakes, misconfigurations and conflictions. Especially in environments where the number of attributes that participate to the security policies is very large and the conditions which must be considered tend to be complicated, the possibility of errors and unforeseen conflictions grows. The existing policy editors provide an easy way to deal with the aforementioned problem, but yet they are in most of the cases developed in order to serve the needs of a specific framework or application environment. In this study, we presented a comparison among the most known policy editors for ABAC and moreover we introduced our initial work on developing a more simplified and general editor.

Acknowledgments. This paper was partially supported by the EU H2020 funded project SPARTA, ga n. 830892.

References

1. Amazon Web Services, I.: Amazon web services: Overview of security processes. https://d1.awsstatic.com/whitepapers/Security/AWS_Security_Whitepaper.pdf. Accessed 01 Jul 2019
2. Amazon Web Services, I.: Aws identity and access management: user guide. http://docs.oasis-open.org/xacml/3.0/xacml-3.0-core-spec-os-en.html. Accessed 09 Jul 2019
3. Anderson, A., et al.: Extensible access control markup language (XACML) version 1.0. OASIS (2003)
4. Ardagna, C., De, S., Vimercati, C.: Comparison of modeling strategies in defining xml-based access control languages. In: Computer Systems Science and Engineering, vol. 19, no. 3. Citeseer (2004)
5. Batty, M.: Data about cities: redefining big, recasting small. In: Data and the City, pp. 31–43. Routledge (2017)
6. Colombo, M., Lazouski, A., Martinelli, F., Mori, P.: A proposal on enhancing XACML with continuous usage control features. In: Desprez, F., Getov, V., Priol, T., Yahyapour, R. (eds.) Grids, P2P and Services Computing, pp. 133–146. Springer, Boston (2010). https://doi.org/10.1007/978-1-4419-6794-7_11
7. Ferraiolo, D.F., Sandhu, R., Gavrila, S., Kuhn, D.R., Chandramouli, R.: Proposed NIST standard for role-based access control. ACM Trans. Inf. Syst. Secur. (TISSEC) **4**(3), 224–274 (2001)
8. Hortonworks: Providing authorization with apache ranger. https://docs.hortonworks.com/HDPDocuments/HDP3/HDP-3.1.0/authorization-ranger/sec_authorization_ranger.pdf. Accessed 09 Jul 2019

9. Hu, V.C., et al.: Guide to attribute based access control (ABAC) definition and considerations (draft). NIST Special Publication **800**(162) (2013)

10. IDC: The digitization of the world: From edge to core. https://www.seagate.com/files/www-content/our-story/trends/files/idc-seagate-dataage-whitepaper.pdf. Accessed 10 Jul 2019

11. Khan, N., et al.: Big data: survey, technologies, opportunities, and challenges. Sci. World J. **2014** (2014)

12. Kitchin, R., McArdle, G.: What makes big data, big data? exploring the ontological characteristics of 26 datasets. Big Data Soc. **3**(1), 2053951716631130 (2016)

13. Lazouski, A., Martinelli, F., Mori, P.: Usage control in computer security: a survey. Comput. Sci. Rev. **4**(2), 81–99 (2010)

14. Lazouski, A., Martinelli, F., Mori, P.: A prototype for enforcing usage control policies based on XACML. In: Fischer-Hübner, S., Katsikas, S., Quirchmayr, G. (eds.) TrustBus 2012. LNCS, vol. 7449, pp. 79–92. Springer, Heidelberg (2012). https://doi.org/10.1007/978-3-642-32287-7_7

15. LLC, I.T.: Security policy tool: user manual. https://securitypolicytool.com/Content/files/Security-policy-tool-user-manual.pdf. Accessed 09 Jul 2019

16. OASIS: Extensible access control markup language (XACML) version 3.0. 22 January 2013. http://docs.oasis-open.org/xacml/3.0/xacml-3.0-core-spec-os-en.html. Accessed 09 Jul 2019

17. Park, J., Sandhu, R.: The UCON ABC usage control model. ACM Trans. Inf. Syst. Secur. (TISSEC) **7**(1), 128–174 (2004)

18. OASIS Standard: eXtensible access control markup language (XACML) version 2.0 (2005)

19. Zhang, Y., Patwa, F., Sandhu, R.: Community-based secure information and resource sharing in AWS public cloud. In: 2015 IEEE Conference on Collaboration and Internet computing (CIC), pp. 46–53. IEEE (2015)

Automatic Firewalls' Configuration Using Argumentation Reasoning

Erisa Karafili[1]([✉])(iD) and Fulvio Valenza[2]

[1] Electronics and Computer Science, University of Southampton, Southampton, UK
e.karafili@soton.ac.uk
[2] Department of Control and Computer Engineering, Politecnico di Torino,
Turin, Italy
fulvio.valenza@polito.it

Abstract. Firewalls are widely used as the first frontier to protect the network from intrusions, vulnerability exploitations, and cyber-attacks. Usually, the configuration of this critical component of network security is done manually by network administrators that introduce human errors. In this paper, we present an automatic tool that is based on a formal framework, called *ArgoFiCo*. Our tool automatically configures the distributed firewalls of the network by generating conflict-free firewalls' configuration. *ArgoFiCo* is based on abduction and argumentation reasoning and it permits the identification and resolution of anomalies in firewalls. Our tool provides an answer to the human error problem as it automatically populates the firewalls of a network, given the network topology and the high-level requirements of the network behaviour.

1 Introduction

Firewalls are widely used as the first frontier to protect the network from intrusions, vulnerability exploitations, and cyber-attacks. The firewalls are mainly configured by network administrators and these configurations suffer from human errors. The impact of the human error in network security is significant, as nearly 60% of the security breaches that occurred in 2019 were due to humans errors made by systems and network administrators [24].

The network administrators have the difficult task to ensure the networks from security breaches, and this task requires very specific skills and competencies. Their typical approach is *trial and error* by creating ad-hoc rules to correct the reported misconfigurations. This solution is not sustainable in the long run, especially when there are different network administrators. Thus, there is a need for an automatic tool that evaluates the enforced policies [2] and guarantees the networks from misconfigurations.

We introduce a tool that automatically configures conflict-free firewalls. In particular, this tool is based on a formal framework, called *ArgoFiCo*, that uses abductive and argumentation reasoning. Our tool, given as input the network topology and high-level network behaviour requirements, provides as result the firewalls' configurations.

© Springer Nature Switzerland AG 2020
A. Saracino and P. Mori (Eds.): ETAA 2020, LNCS 12515, pp. 124–140, 2020.
https://doi.org/10.1007/978-3-030-64455-0_8

The used formal framework, *ArgoFiCo*, uses *preference-based argumentation* reasoning [10,12], which permits us to deal with conflicting policies and order them by introducing preferences. In particular, our tool uses Gorgias [10] that is a preference-based argumentation reasoning tool with abduction. The anomalies identified are automatically solved by removing the unnecessary rules or proposing a novel anomaly free re-ordering based on the introduced preferences. The re-ordering is provided by following various resolution strategies. Our framework simplifies the network administrators' work, by automatically configuring the firewalls of the network. Furthermore, as the process is automatic, it reduces the chances of human errors. We use a similar methodology as the one provided in [23] for analyzing the network behaviour rules and for automatically identifying the anomalies between them.

Our tool provides to the user together with the results also an *explanation*. This explanation gives new insights to the administrator that can now check if the information provided is correct, or if further adjustments are needed. Our tool provides flexibility to the administrator that can decide between two ordering strategies (that we call configurations). The tool permits the administrator to configure the firewalls of the network to allow or deny the flow of information in all possible paths between source and destination, called *max configuration*. The second type of configuration is more restrictive, as it configures the firewalls of the network to allow or deny the traffic only for the path derived from the routing between the source and destination, called *min configuration*.

We introduce the related work for the firewall configuration in Sect. 2. In Sect. 3, we present the used formal framework. We show the main components of our tool in Sect. 4 and provide the main results in Sect. 5. We conclude and describe some future research directions in Sect. 6.

2 Related Work

In this section, we briefly report the most important related work on *policy analysis* and *policy refinement*.

2.1 Policy Analysis

The main goal of policy analysis is to detect *anomalies* in the policies of network security controls like firewalls, VPN, IDS. Specifically, this anomaly analysis[1] looks for incorrect policy specifications that administrators may introduce in the network. In our view, an anomaly can be potential errors, conflicts, and sub-optimizations affecting either a single policy or a set of security policies [22].

One of the most important works on policy analysis with filtering configurations was proposed by *Al-Shaer et al.* in [1]. In this work, the authors classify and analyze the local anomalies, arising in a single firewall (*intra-firewall*

---

[1] Sometimes anomaly analysis is also referred to as either conflict analysis or policy validation.

anomaly) and the global anomalies that arise in distributed firewalls (*inter-firewall* anomaly). Another interesting work that performs a policy analysis is introduced in [3], where the authors use an argumentation framework for specifying security requirements. In this work, the authors focus on analyzing the requirements and identifying their orderings. The work does not deal with the configuration of different firewalls inside the same network and with inter-firewall anomalies.

Another work [20] deals only with redundant policies. It focuses on detecting and removing redundant filtering rules with a data-structure named FDD (Firewall Decision Diagram). A formal model for detecting anomalies among different security functions (inter-function anomalies) is introduced in [6,23]. The proposed model detects several kinds of errors and anomalies that originate from correlations between configuration rules of different network functions. This approach is able to cope with different network functions, such as firewalls, NAT/NAPT devices, traffic monitors, and encryption devices.

In this paper, we introduce a solution that uses a similar technique as [3] (i.e., argumentation reasoning) but our solution is able to work with different firewalls and to capture and resolve also inter-firewall anomalies. Furthermore, we use the same definitions of anomalies as in [1] but we apply different resolution techniques, as we use argumentation reasoning, while [1] uses FOL formulas. Our solution is also able to deal with redundant rules and the conflicts/anomalies identification is similar to the one introduced in [23].

2.2   Policy Refinement

The *policy refinement* is the process that automatically "determines the resources needed to satisfy policy requirements and translates high-level policies into operational policies that may be enforced by the system" [21]. Policy refinement is a critical task that may lead to either incorrect or sub-optimal implementations that affect network performance and can jeopardise the overall system security.

The most significant frameworks for automatic configuration of packets filtering firewalls based on policy refinement are FIRMATO [4], FACE [25], MIRAGE [9], and VEREFOO [7]. Moreover, a refinement model that allows the translation of high-level security requirements into low-level configuration settings for the virtual network security functions was introduced in [5].

All the above introduced frameworks perform refinement using FOL (i.e, First-Order Logic), while the solution we propose in this paper uses argumentation reasoning for the policy refinement.

3   Automatic Firewalls' Configuration

Our tool automatically configures the firewalls of the network, given the network topology and the behaviour requirements of the network. The input is provided

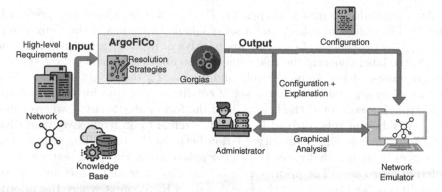

Fig. 1. An overview of our framework for Automatic Firewalls' Configuration via Argumentation Reasoning (ArgoFiCo)

by the users that are the network administrators. The outputs are the constructed firewalls' configurations that are anomaly free, i.e., no inter- or intra-firewall anomalies. An overview of the main workflow of our tool is provided in Fig. 1. The introduced tool is based on a formal framework, called *ArgoFiCo* that uses abduction and argumentation reasoning. The theoretical formalism used by *ArgoFiCo* is introduced in Sect. 3.1 and a brief introduction of *ArgoFiCo*'s preliminary results on the firewalls' configuration problem are given in [17].

Let us briefly describe how our tool operates. It starts by analyzing the high-level requirements of the network (provided in the form of behavioural rules). This analysis identifies possible existing conflicts and anomalies. The analysis, identification, and resolution of the anomalies is performed automatically using *ArgoFiCo*, as the use of argumentation permits us to identify the conflicting rules and resolve the conflicts. The next step is the resolution of anomalies, which is done by removing or reordering the rules and by taking into account also the network topology and the resolution strategies. Once the rules are ordered, then the next step is the population of all the firewalls. The population is done by avoiding the anomalies and conflicts between rules of different firewalls. The final steps of our tool are the translation of the rules into low-level firewall rules and the generation of the firewalls' configurations.

3.1 Preference-Based Argumentation Reasoning

The used formalism by *ArgoFiCo* is preference-based argumentation [10,12], which permits us to work with conflicting rules, given its *non-monotonic* nature. *ArgoFiCo* uses the Gorgias [10] tool that is a preference-based argumentation reasoning tool, which uses abduction [11]. We decided to base *ArgoFiCo* on argumentation reasoning, given the extended applicability of this reasoning, e.g., policy analysis [3], secure data sharing [13,14,16], swarm of drones [8,15], and cyber investigations [18,19].

An *argumentation theory* is a pair $(\mathcal{T}, \mathcal{P})$ of argument rules $\mathcal{T}$ and preference rules $\mathcal{P}$. The argument rules $\mathcal{T}$ are a set of labelled formulas of the form: $rule_i :$ $L \leftarrow L_1, \ldots, L_n$ where $L, L_1, \ldots, L_n$ are positive or negative ground literals, and $rule_i$ is the label denoting the rule name. In the above argument rule, L denotes the *conclusion* of the argument rule and $L_1, \ldots, L_n$ denote its *premises*. The premise of an argument rule is the set of conditions required for the conclusion to be true. Instead, for $\mathcal{P}$ the head L is of the form $rule_1 > rule_2$, where $rule_1$, $rule_2$ are labels of rules defined in $\mathcal{T}$, and $>$ refers to an irreflexive, transitive, and antisymmetric higher priority relation between the rules. The priority rule $rule_1 > rule_2$ means that $rule_1$ has *higher priority* over $rule_2$, or better $rule_1$ is preferred over $rule_2$. The priority rule is true always or under certain contexts or conditions. The premise of the rule describes the context where the priority rule is true and when the premise is empty it means that the priority rule is always true.

Our approach uses abduction [11]. The ability to work with incomplete information makes *abduction* suitable to capture anomalies in case not all the rules are provided. By introducing a set of *abducible* predicates Ab, abduction allows us to make assumptions $\triangle$ ($\triangle \subseteq Ab$), for reaching a conclusion L, as long as the assumptions $\triangle$ satisfy the *integrity constraints*. Integrity constraints are conditions that every admissible set of arguments must satisfy.

In our framework the preference-based reasoning rules are the high-level requirements of the network and are denoted as follows:

$$req(\text{allow/deny, source, destination, type of traffic}).$$

The premises of the above rule are the *source*, *destination*, *type* of traffic, and information related to the location of the source and destination, and the conclusion is the decision of *allowing* or *denying* the traffic. The preferences between rules are represented with the order between the rules. In particular, the priority rules permit us to order the rules and to have a total order for the set of rules. The preferences are introduced automatically by *ArgoFiCo*, by applying the conflicts resolution strategies.

3.2   Inputs and Outputs

In this section, we describe more in detail the inputs and outputs of our tool. Currently, the inputs are provided by the network administrator/s and in the future, we plan on fully automating this process. The provided inputs are the network behaviour policies, which are given in the form of high-level requirements of the network, the network topology, which includes the components of the network together with their containing relations, and also the resolution strategies. The user can decide the strategies or in case no strategy is provided by the user, a "default" mode is selected where the resolution strategies are decided by *ArgoFiCo* depending on the *configuration* (*max* or *min*). The outputs are the firewalls' low-level configurations. These configurations are generated automatically and are composed of all the ordered rules that should apply in each firewall.

High-Level Requirements The high-level network requirements describe the behaviour rules of the network. These requirements specify which communications are allowed and which are denied. Given the high complexity of the network, we permit the user to specify these requirements using statements that are close to natural language and are user-friendly. In particular, the user can provide requirements like: *"All internal hosts of the subnet can reach Server Mail"*, *"The ciphered outgoing communications are denied"*. The use of high-level requirements permits the user to provide the network requirements by avoiding human errors.

Network Topology and Knowledge Base. Another important input for our tool is the network topology, where the users provide information about the network. In particular, they provide information about the topology of the network, with its components (hosts and firewalls), their positions, containing relations, and the routing tables. The *knowledge base* contains the map from high-level terms to low-level network layer information, where the information is given in the form of IP-tables and the names used to describe the network components are translated into IPs. The network topology and knowledge base are needed by *ArgoFiCo* to correctly derive from the high-level requirements the low-level configuration for every firewall.

Low-level Configurations The low-level configurations are the outputs of our tool. These configurations are generated automatically and are composed of all the ordered rules that need to apply in each firewall.

3.3   Resolution Strategies

The resolution strategies describe how the anomalies should be solved in the policy specifications. Some of the implemented strategies are presented below[2]:

- *Allow Takes Precedence* (ATP) in case of contradicting actions that are simultaneously activated, we enforce the Allow rule over the Deny one;
- *Deny Takes Precedence* (DTP) in case of contradicting actions that are simultaneously activated, we enforce the Deny rule over the Allow one (this is a restrictive strategy);
- *Most Specific Takes Precedence* (MSTP) in case two conflicting rules are applied, we give priority to the most specific rule;
- *Least Specific Takes Precedence* (LSTP) in case two conflicting rules are applied, we give priority to the less specific rule.

ArgoFiCo applies different strategies for different types of anomalies.

---

[2] The presented strategies are some of the standard strategies. Further resolution strategies can be integrated into *ArgoFiCo*.

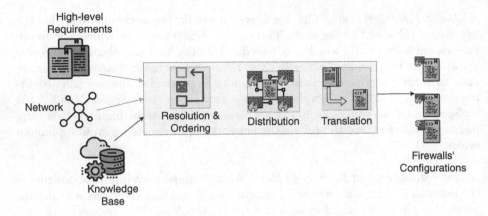

Fig. 2. The main components of *ArgoFiCo*

4   *ArgoFiCo*'s Components

Let us now describe in detail the main components of *ArgoFiCo*. We present in Fig. 2 a general overview of the various components of our tool and how they interact with each other. The inputs are provided by the user and are shown on the left side. Our tool, shown in the center, is composed of three main components: the resolution and ordering module, the distribution module, and the translation module. The inputs are passed to the resolution and ordering module, which automatically checks the rules for anomalies, and orders them. The ordered high-level firewall rules are then passed to the distribution module, which distributes the rules to the various firewalls of the network. Finally, the rules for each firewall are translated into low-level firewall rules using the translation module, which generates for each firewall its configuration file, shown on the right side of Fig. 2. Let us now describe in detail these three modules.

4.1   Resolution and Ordering Module

The high-level requirements, provided by the user, are passed to the resolution and ordering module. The high-level requirements have the following form:

$$req(allow/deny, source, destination, type\ of\ traffic).$$

These requirements are analyzed in order to identify possible anomalies. This module is able to resolve all the anomalies between rules of the same firewall. In particular, *ArgoFiCo* avoids all the anomalies introduced in [1] e.g., the *shadowing* anomaly, i.e., a rule is shadowed when a previous rule matches all its packets, and the shadowed rule is never activated, the *correlation* anomaly, i.e., two rules with conflicting actions match some packets of each other, the *generalization* anomaly, i.e., two rules with conflicting actions, where all the packets matched from one of the rules are a subset of the packets of the second rule, the *redundancy* anomaly, i.e., two rules with the same actions have matching or partially matching packets, the *irrelevance* anomaly, i.e., a rule that does not match any traffic that might flow in that network. Algorithm 1 shows the pseudo-code of the process that identifies the potential anomalies.

The potential anomalies are avoided using the resolution strategies, which in some cases remove rules and in other cases order them by introducing priorities. The use of argumentation reasoning permits us to work with conflicting rules by introducing priorities. These priorities are used to order the rules, where the ordering of the rules is performed by clustering the rules that have sources and destinations that are in relation[3] between each other. The rules between different clusters are not related, therefore, the order between them is irrelevant. Algorithm 1 shows the resolution strategies applied to avoid the anomalies, i.e., removal of rules or introduction of priorities.

```
1  // p₁ and p₂ are policy rules part of the high-level requirements given as input
2  if !topology(p₁.src) ∨ !topology(p₁.dst) then
3  |    remove p₁
4  end
5  if !topology(p₂.src) ∨ !topology(p₂.dst) then
6  |    remove p₂
7  end
8  if exactmatch(p₁, p₂) then
9  |    if p₁.action == p₂.action then remove p₂ else if p₁.action = "allow" then remove
        p₁ else remove p₂
10 end
11 else if inclusion(p₁, p₂) then
12 |    if
        p₁.action == p₂.action∧ ∄ p₃ s.t., inclusion(p₃, p₂) ∧ inclusion(p₁, p₃) ∧ p₂.order >
        p₃.order ∧ p₃.order > p₁.order then   remove p₂ else
13 |    |   p₂.order > p₁.order
14 |    end
15 end
16 else if intersection(p₁, p₂) ∧ p₁.action! = p₂.action then
17 |    if (p₁.action = "allow") then  p₂.order > p₁.order else p₁.order > p₂.order
18 end
```

Algorithm 1: Anomalies identification and resolution algorithm

Example 1. We now show with the use of an example how the resolution and ordering module works. Our example is a cyclic network topology, shown in Fig. 3 that is composed of three different subnetworks. Each subnetwork contains different hosts and is connected to the others through the use of three firewalls. The high-level requirements provided by the administrator are presented below:

1. $req_1(deny, subnet1, subnet2, all)$
2. $req_2(allow, bob, david, tcp)$
3. $req_3(allow, bob, subnet2, tcp)$
4. $req_4(deny, subnet1, subnet3, all)$

---

[3] We use the same definitions of *relations* between firewall rules as in [1].

5. $req_5(deny, eve, subnet4, all)$
6. $req_6(allow, subnet1, subnet3, all)$

The source and destination names are already provided in the topology and the protocols are tcp, udp, and all.

The above requirements are analyzed by the ordering and resolution module, which provides the following potential anomalies together with their resolution:

- Conflict 1 - redundancy: rule req_2 is included[4] in rule req_3 and their actions are the same. Since req_2 is more specific and it does not exist any rule req_x with a different action, included in req_3 and that includes req_2, then req_2 is removed [see line 13–14 of Algorithm 1];
- Conflict 2 - shadowing: rule req_3 is included in rule req_1 but they have different actions. Since rule req_3 is more specific, it has a higher priority with respect to rule req_1, $(req_3 > req_1)$ [see line 13–18 of Algorithm 1];
- Conflict 3 - irrelevance: rule req_5 has as source and destination hosts that are not in the topology. Thus, this rule is irrelevant and is removed [see line 2–7 of Algorithm 1];
- Conflict 4 - shadowing: req_6 is exactly matching req_4 but they have different actions. Thus, req_6 is removed [see line 8–12 of Algorithm 1].

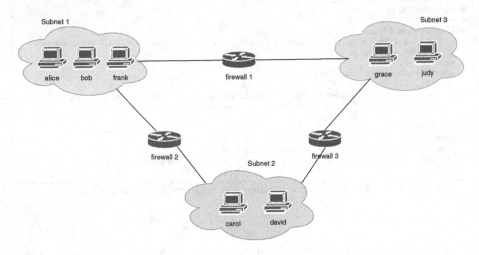

Fig. 3. Network topology for Example 1 and 2

The result of the resolution and ordering module is as below:

1. $req_3(allow, bob, subnet2, tcp)$
2. $req_1(deny, subnet1, subnet2, all)$
3. $req_4(deny, subnet1, subnet3, all)$

where req_2, req_5, and req_6 are removed.   □

---

[4] In Algorithm 1, $inclusion(p_1, p_2)$ means that all the packets matched by rule p_2 are included in the packets matched by rule p_1.

4.2   Distribution Module

The distribution module is the second process of our tool. It gets as input the ordered rules, from where the intra-firewall anomalies are removed. The distribution module, given the input, analyzes the rules and gives as result the high-level configuration for each firewall. We call it a high-level configuration as the provided rules are in high-level form and not low-level network format. This module is able to identify and avoid all the potential anomalies between rules of different firewalls (inter-firewall anomalies). In particular, our tool avoids all the inter-firewall anomalies introduced in [1] e.g., the *shadowing* anomaly, i.e., an upstream firewall blocks the traffic accepted by a downstream firewall, the *spuriousness* anomaly, i.e., an upstream firewall permits the traffic denied by a downstream firewall, the *redundancy* anomaly, i.e., a downstream firewall blocks the traffic already blocked by an upstream firewall, the *correlation* anomaly, i.e., two rules with conflicting actions, where all the packets matched by one of the rules are a subset of the packets of the second one, where one rule is in an upstream firewall and the other is in a downstream firewall. Algorithm 2 shows the pseudo-code of the process that distributes the rules in the various firewalls by avoiding all the above anomalies.

The distribution module provides two types of high-level firewalls' configurations to the user that can decide which one to apply. Algorithm 2 shows the pseudo-code for the distribution module, where both ordering configurations are included. The first configuration is the *max configuration* and provides the firewalls' configurations that allow or deny the sources to send messages to the destinations, by using *all possible paths*. This configuration is the ideal one when we want to configure a robust network. In case a particular part of the network is unavailable, then the packets can use alternative routes. The firewalls of these alternative routes are prepared to route/filter the traffic appropriately. In the max configuration, we expect redundancies between firewalls as this configuration generates repetitions of rules. The second configuration is the *min configuration* and provides the firewalls' configurations that allow or deny the sources to send messages to the destinations, by using *a specific path*. This configuration populates the firewalls only with the needed rules and avoids all types of inter-firewalls anomalies. In this case, we expect the traffic flow to be faster and efficient but the traffic cannot be routed/filtered by alternative firewalls in case of unavailable paths.

Example 2. Let us now continue with the example introduced in Example 1 and show the application of the distribution module that creates the firewalls' high-level configurations. The results are passed to the distribution module, and the max configuration is selected. The first step is to understand which are the paths for a certain package to go from the source to the destination. For req_3 we have two paths: the first uses Fw_1[5] and Fw_3 and the second uses Fw_2; for req_1 we have two paths: the first uses Fw_1 and Fw_3 and the second uses Fw_2; and for req_4 we have two paths: the first uses Fw_1 and the second uses Fw_2 and Fw_3.

---

[5] For the sake of simplicity we denote the firewalls with Fw.

```
1  // p is a policy rule
2  if configuration== "max" then
3      foreach path in paths(p.source, p.dest) do
4          if p.action== "allow" then
5              foreach f in firewall(path)// firewall(path) is the set of all the
                     firewalls in path
6              do
7                  |  f.rule.add(p)
8              end
9          end
10         else most_upstream(firewall(path)).rule.add(p)
11     end
12 end
13 if configuration== "min" then
14     path = routing(p.source, p.dest)
15     if p.action== "allow" then
16         foreach f in firewall(path) do
17             |  f.rule.add(p)
18         end
19     end
20     else most_upstream(firewall(path)).rule.add(p)
21 end
```

Algorithm 2: Firewalls' population algorithm

req_3 should be applied in all paths, as it is an "*allow*" action, thus, it should be placed in all firewalls. For req_1 and req_4 because their action is "*deny*", the rules are put in the most upstream firewall along each path. The output of the distribution module, with max configuration, is as follows:

Fw_1
    1. $req_3(allow, bob, subnet2, tcp)$
    2. $req_1(deny, subnet1, subnet2, all)$
    3. $req_4(deny, subnet1, subnet3, all)$
Fw_2
    1. $req_3(allow, bob, subnet2, tcp)$
    2. $req_1(deny, subnet1, subnet2, all)$
    3. $req_4(deny, subnet1, subnet3, all)$
Fw_3
    1. $req_3(allow, bob, subnet2, tcp)$

In case the min configuration is selected, the result is:

1. $req_3(allow, bob, subnet2, tcp)$

where req_1 and req_4 are removed, as there is no rule with a lower priority than them that "allows" a related requirement, and we expect to have the "deny all" rule at the end of the firewalls. The distribution module puts req_3 in Fw_2. □

4.3   Translation Module

The results of the distribution module are passed to the translation module. The inputs of the translation module are the high-level configurations for each firewall. This module translates the high-level configurations into low-level network layer information. The terms used in the high-level requirements refer to the names of sources, destinations, and specific services, while the low-level network layer terms are the traditional IP addresses, port numbers, and protocols used by the firewall rules. The translation is performed using information from the network topology and the knowledge base. For example, "Employees" is mapped to a set of IP addresses, "College Subnet" is mapped to a subnetwork, and "illegal sites" is a set of IP addresses and ports. The results of this module are the configuration files for each firewall, that can be loaded to the various firewalls.

5   Implementation and Validation

The main component of *ArgoFiCo* is the resolution and ordering module, which finds the various anomalies and orders the rules. The ordering of the rules is made through the use of argumentation reasoning. Our tool permits the user to provide the various high-level requirements and the network topology. The user gets as result from our tool the firewalls' configurations. *ArgoFiCo* implements the argumentation reasoning through the use of the Gorgias tool. In order for the administrator to simulate the *ArgoFiCo* results, we provide a direct call to an open-source network emulator, called *Core*[6]. The use of the network emulator provides the administrator with a graphical representation of the flow of information and how the network requirements are applied.

The use of argumentation reasoning permits *ArgoFiCo* to provide *explanations* together with the given results. The explanations are provided in the form of text, explaining why certain requirements were removed, changed, or ordered in a particular way, by giving the solved anomalies and the used resolution strategies. The explanations make the administrator part of the process and provide insights for possible errors or correctness of the given high-level requirements.

We tested our framework using various realistic scenarios. *ArgoFiCo* always configured correctly the rules of the firewalls, for both max and min configurations. The given firewalls' configurations were tested using the network emulator that confirmed the correctness of the rules.

Example 3. Let us now show with the use of a more complex example how our tool is able to automatically generate the distributed firewalls' configurations. We provide the network topology of our case study in Fig. 4, where there are six subnetworks and six different firewalls. In particular, the scenario described previously in Example 1 and 2 is a small part of this example.

We present below all the provided high-level requirements:

1. $req_1(allow, grace, peggy, all)$
2. $req_2(deny, grace, peggy, all)$
3. $req_3(allow, olivia, david, all)$
4. $req_4(allow, subnet4, subnet1, all)$
5. $req_5(deny, subnet4, alice, udp)$

---

[6] https://github.com/coreemu/core.

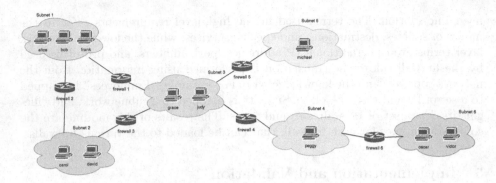

Fig. 4. Network topology for Example 3

6. $req_6(allow, subnet4, bob, tcp)$
7. $req_7(allow, subnet6, judy, udp)$
8. $req_8(deny, oscar, subnet3, all)$
9. $req_9(allow, alice, subnet5, all)$
10. $req_{10}(allow, alice, michael, tcp)$
11. $req_{11}(deny, peggy, david, all)$
12. $req_{12}(allow, victor, bob, udp)$
13. $req_{13}(allow, victor, bob, udp)$

We present below the identified anomalies and their resolution strategies:

- Conflict 1 - shadowing: req_1 is exactly matching with req_2 and their actions are different. Due to the strategy resolution employed, req_1 is removed;
- Conflict 2 - irrelevance: req_3 contains a host that is not in the current topology, thus this requirement is irrelevant and is removed;
- Conflict 3 - shadowing: req_5 is included in req_4 and their actions are different. Since req_5 is more specific, then it has higher priority than req_4, ($req_5 > req_4$);
- Conflict 4 - redundancy: req_6 is included in req_4 and their actions are the same. Since req_6 is more specific and allows the traffic, then it is removed;
- Conflict 5 - correlation: there is an intersection between the packets of req_7 and req_8 and their actions are different. Due to the resolution strategy employed, req_8 has higher priority than req_7, ($req_8 > req_7$);
- Conflict 6 - redundancy: req_{10} is included in req_9 and their actions are the same. Since req_{10} is more specific and allows the traffic, then it is removed;
- Conflict 7 - redundancy: req_{12} is exactly matching with req_{13} and their actions are the same. Thus, req_{12} is removed.

We present below the results of the resolution and ordering module that provide the ordered high-level requirements.

1. $req_2(deny, grace, peggy, all)$
2. $req_5(deny, subnet4, alice, udp)$
3. $req_4(allow, subnet4, subnet1, all)$

4. $req_8(deny, oscar, subnet3, all)$
5. $req_7(allow, subnet6, judy, udp)$
6. $req_9(allow, alice, subnet5, all)$
7. $req_{11}(deny, peggy, david, all)$
8. $req_{13}(allow, victor, bob, udp)$

where req_1, req_3, req_6, req_{10}, req_{12} are removed.

This ordered list of requirements is passed to the distribution module, which for the max configuration gives the following high-level firewalls' configurations.

Fw_1
1. $req_4(allow, subnet4, subnet1, all)$
2. $req_9(allow, alice, subnet5, all)$
3. $req_{13}(allow, victor, bob, udp)$

Fw_2
1. $req_4(allow, subnet4, subnet1, all)$
2. $req_9(allow, alice, subnet5, all)$
3. $req_{13}(allow, victor, bob, udp)$

Fw_3
1. $req_4(allow, subnet4, subnet1, all)$
2. $req_9(allow, alice, subnet5, all)$
3. $req_{13}(allow, victor, bob, udp)$

Fw_4
1. $req_2(deny, grace, peggy, all)$
2. $req_5(deny, subnet4, alice, udp)$
3. $req_4(allow, subnet4, subnet1, all)$
4. $req_7(allow, subnet6, judy, udp)$
5. $req_{11}(deny, peggy, david, all)$
6. $req_{13}(allow, victor, bob, udp)$

Fw_5
1. $req_9(allow, alice, subnet5, all)$

Fw_6
1. $req_8(deny, oscar, subnet3, all)$
2. $req_7(allow, subnet6, judy, udp)$
3. $req_{13}(allow, victor, bob, udp)$

When the min configuration is called, the results are as below:

Fw_2
1. $req_4(allow, subnet4, subnet1, all)$
2. $req_9(allow, alice, subnet5, all)$
3. $req_{13}(allow, victor, bob, udp)$

Fw_4
1. $req_5(deny, subnet4, alice, udp)$
2. $req_4(allow, subnet4, subnet1, all)$
3. $req_7(allow, subnet6, judy, udp)$
4. $req_{13}(allow, victor, bob, udp)$

Fw_5

    1. $req_9(allow, alice, subnet5, all)$

Fw_6

    1. $req_8(deny, oscar, subnet3, all)$
    2. $req_7(allow, subnet6, judy, udp)$
    3. $req_{13}(allow, victor, bob, udp)$

The min configuration removes the requirements: req_2, req_{11}, as they cannot be triggered, given that there is no relevant "allow" requirement after them, and the default "*deny all*" rule will be added in all the firewalls. Fw_1 and Fw_3 are not populated and have the default configuration that is the "*deny all*" rule. $\square$

6   Conclusion and Future Work

In this paper, we introduced a tool that automatically configures distributed firewalls in a network. This tool will alleviate the work of network administrators, as it permits to configure anomaly free firewalls given the network topology and its high-level requirements. Our approach provides the administrators the needed level of flexibility when configuring the firewalls, as they can decide how the ordering of the rules is done, by specifying the distribution option. The administrators can choose i.f they want to focus on the reachability aspects of the network and make it more robust by using the max configuration, or if they want to have a more slim and fast routing/filtering by using the min configuration. The main goal of the tool is to help the administrators during the firewalls' configuration by avoiding human errors.

    The introduced automatic tool is based on a formal framework, called *ArgoFiCo* that uses abduction and argumentation reasoning. We presented the three modules that compose *ArgoFiCo*: the resolution and ordering module, the distribution module, and the translation module. The use of argumentation permits *ArgoFiCo* to provide an explanation together with the given result in order to explain to the administrators the configurations and to provide further help to them. The explanations provide the administrators with new insights and can be used to capture any human error in the high-level requirements. We also provide a direct execution to an open-source network emulator that shows graphically how the network will behave.

    Currently, the inputs for *ArgoFiCo* are provided by the network administrators. We plan to fully automate this process and to integrate it with a reinforcement learning algorithm, in order to learn from the administrators' experience the best resolution strategy to use. The current version of our tool is able to generate firewalls' configurations by scratch (for empty or not yet configured firewalls) or by replacing the old configurations with the new ones. In the future, we plan to extend the tool to update existing firewalls' configurations, without the need for re-configuring all the firewalls. It would be interesting to apply this tool in high complexity commercial networks and to perform usability testing.

Acknowledgments. Erisa Karafili was partially supported by the European Union's H2020 research and innovation programme under the Marie Skłodowska-Curie grant agreement No. 746667.

References

1. Al-Shaer, E., Hamed, H., Boutaba, R., Hasan, M.: Conflict classification and analysis of distributed firewall policies. IEEE J. Sel. Areas Commun. **23**(10), 2069–2084 (2005)
2. Arunkumar, S., et al.: Next generation firewalls for dynamic coalitions. In: IEEE SmartWorld/SCALCOM/UIC/ATC/CBDCom/IOP/SCI, pp. 1–6 (2017)
3. Bandara, A.K., Kakas, A., Lupu, E.C., Russo, A.: Using argumentation logic for firewall policy specification and analysis. In: Large Scale Management of Distributed Systems, pp. 185–196 (2006)
4. Bartal, Y., Mayer, A., Nissim, K., Wool, A.: Firmato: a novel firewall management toolkit. ACM Trans. Comput. Syst. **22**(4), 381–420 (2004)
5. Basile, C., Valenza, F., Lioy, A., Lopez, D.R., Pastor Perales, A.: Adding support for automatic enforcement of security policies in NFV networks. EEE/ACM Trans. Netw. **27**(2), 707–720 (2019)
6. Basile, C., Canavese, D., Lioy, A., Valenza, F.: Inter-technology conflict analysis for communication protection policies. In: Lopez, J., Ray, I., Crispo, B. (eds.) CRiSIS 2014. LNCS, vol. 8924, pp. 148–163. Springer, Cham (2015). https://doi.org/10.1007/978-3-319-17127-2_10
7. Bringhenti, D., Marchetto, G., Sisto, R., Valenza, F., Yusupov, J.: Automated optimal firewall orchestration and configuration in virtualized networks. In: NOMS 2020 - IEEE/IFIP Network Operations and Management Symposium, Budapest, Hungary, April 20–24, 2020, pp. 1–7. IEEE (2020)
8. Cullen, A., Karafili, E., Pilgrim, A., Williams, C., Lupu, E.: Policy support for autonomous swarms of drones. In: ETAA@ESORICS 2018, pp. 56–70 (2018)
9. Garcia-Alfaro, J., Cuppens, F., Cuppens-Boulahia, N., Preda, S.: Mirage: a management tool for the analysis and deployment of network security policies. Data Privacy Manag. Auton. Spontaneous Secur. **6514**, 203–215 (2011)
10. Kakas, A., Moraitis, P.: Argumentation based decision making for autonomous agents. In: AAMAS 2003, pp. 883–890 (2003)
11. Kakas, A.C., Kowalski, R.A., Toni, F.: Abductive logic programming. J. Log. Comput. **2**(6), 719–770 (1992)
12. Kakas, A.C., Mancarella, P., Dung, P.M.: The acceptability semantics for logic programs. In: ICLP, pp. 504–519 (1994)
13. Karafili, E., Kakas, A., Spanoudakis, N., Lupu, E.: Argumentation-based Security for Social Good. In: AAAI Fall Symposium Series (2017)
14. Karafili, E., Lupu, E.: Enabling data sharing in contextual environments: policy representation and analysis. In: SACMAT 2017, pp. 231–238 (2017)
15. Karafili, E., Lupu, E., Arunkumar, S., Bertino, E.: Argumentation-based policy analysis for drone systems. In: IEEE SmartWorld/SCALCOM/UIC/ATC/CBDCom/IOP/SCI, pp. 1–6 (2017)
16. Karafili, E., Spanaki, K., Lupu, E.: An argumentation reasoning approach for data processing. Comput. Ind. **94**, 52–61 (2018)
17. Karafili, E., Valenza, F., Chen, Y., Lupu, E.: Towards a framework for automatic firewalls configuration via argumentation reasoning. In: NOMS 2020 - IEEE/IFIP Network Operations and Management Symposium, Budapest, Hungary, 20–24 April 20020, pp. 1–4. IEEE (2020)
18. Karafili, E., Wang, L., Kakas, A., Lupu, E.: Helping forensic analysts to attribute cyber-attacks: an argumentation-based reasoner. In: PRIMA 2018, pp. 510–518 (2018)

19. Karafili, E., Wang, L., Lupu, E.: An argumentation-based reasoner to assist digital investigation and attribution of cyber-attacks. Forensic Sci. Int. Dig. Invest. **32**, 300925 (2020)
20. Liu, A.X., Gouda, M.G.: Complete redundancy detection in firewalls. In: DBSeC, pp. 193–206 (2005)
21. Moffett, J., Sloman, M.: Policy hierarchies for distributed systems management. IEEE J. Sel. Areas Commun. **11**(9), 1404–1414 (1993)
22. Valenza, F., Basile, C., Canavese, D., Lioy, A.: Classification and analysis of communication protection policy anomalies. IEEE/ACM Trans. Netw. **25**(5), 2601–2614 (2017)
23. Valenza, F., Spinoso, S., Basile, C., Sisto, R., Lioy, A.: A formal model of network policy analysis. In: RTSI, pp. 516–522 (2015)
24. Verizon: Data Breach Investigations Report (2019)
25. Verma, P., Prakash, A.: FACE: a firewall analysis and configuration engine. In: SAINT05, pp. 74–81 (2005)

On Results of Data Aggregation Operations

Francesco Di Cerbo$^{(\boxtimes)}$ ⑩, Marco Rosa ⑩, and Rocío Cabrera Lozoya ⑩

SAP Security Research, Mougins 06250, France
{francesco.di.cerbo,marco.rosa,rocio.cabrera.lozoya}@sap.com

Abstract. Be it in services or as part of software features, the adoption of machine learning techniques brings new challenges to access control systems. Considering an operation that uses as operands multiple datasets of fragmented ownership or terms, its result may reveal protected information, although each of the datasets was legitimately accessed. To counter this threat, we propose an obligation model based on Attribute-Based Access Control (ABAC), to allow data owners to express access control constraints on the operation and its operands, but also the formalization of requirements on operation results. Such requirements must be automatically verified by the underlying AC mechanism. We illustrate our approach with a case study.

Keywords: Access control · Machine Learning · Data aggregation

1 Introduction

Machine Learning (ML) and Artificial Intelligence (AI) are popular nowadays in many software projects. One of the key factors for successful ML/AI approaches consists of an effective training of their generally huge amount of parameters, that in turn depends on the availability of high-quality datasets. In order to train new ML/AI models to improve their competitiveness, companies may use their customers' data, confidential business information, acquire or harvest information on the Internet to curate the most effective datasets. However, this process can lead to significant risks. For example, numerous attacks aim at inferring and/or reconstructing parts of the original training set (e.g., [8,22]), others aim at understanding whether one or more records were part of the training set for a model (i.e., the so-called membership inference attacks [11,24]). Other significant risks consist in violation of usage terms of datasets, and in hiding the way and purpose a dataset is used from its data owner.

To address these risks that we identified as significant, in [21] we proposed a solution to allow data owners to express machine-enforceable security policies (based on an ABAC model[12]) to regulate the access and usage to their datasets when aggregated and/or analyzed together with other datasets. Examples may be any operation considering multiple datasets as input, such as *map-reduce*, *k-means* for data clustering, etc. We did so by enabling data owners to express

© Springer Nature Switzerland AG 2020
A. Saracino and P. Mori (Eds.): ETAA 2020, LNCS 12515, pp. 141–153, 2020.
https://doi.org/10.1007/978-3-030-64455-0_9

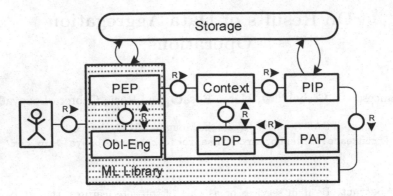

Fig. 1. The proposed system architecture (including "ML Library", "Obl-Eng" (Obligation Engine) and "Storage" components integrated with those of OASIS XACMLv3 standard)

conditions on the characteristics of the not-owned pieces of information used together with the owned data. For instance, if *CompanyA* owns *dataset1*, they can express a policy that prevents its use from anyone but *CompanyC*. In this case, if a subject requests *dataset1* to be used with *dataset2* and *dataset3*, belonging respectively to *CompanyB* and *CompanyC*, a trusted entity will ensure that *CompanyA*'s policy is respected, and the subject's request can only be fulfilled for the resource clusters {*dataset1, dataset3*} and/or {*dataset2, dataset3*}.

In this work, we elaborate on the use of obligations for data aggregation operations. In particular, we observed that some of abovementioned attacks can still result viable if no control on the result of data aggregation operations can be effectively applied. Analyzing datasets from fragmented ownership can reveal sensitive characteristics of the data and allow, for example, company benchmarking or to re-identify anonymized datasets with side knowldege [10]. We claim that access control obligations can fill this gap; this article details our contribution towards an obligation model to express obligations for data aggregation operations, discussing their characteristics and presenting a case study to counter re-identification attacks.

2   Basic Concepts

In [21], we presented a formalism derived from [9]. We extend it to include a definition of aggregation function. Given a set of subjects S, a set of actions A, a set of resources R, and an environment e, we define the request of a subject s to perform an action a on a resource r in a certain environmental setting e as an *access control request*, in two variants for single and multiple resources.

Definition 1 (Access Control Request Types). *An access control request request or request-Multi is a tuple*

$$request = \{s, a, r, e\}$$
$$request-Multi = \{s, a, [r_1, \dots, r_n], e, responseType\}$$

where $s \in S, a \in A, r \in R$, $r_1, \dots, r_n$ *are a set of resources of multiple data owners and responseType is a parameter to specify the desired response flavor.*

Each of the entities in S, A, R, e have *attributes (attr)* that characterize them (e.g., a name and a role for a subject, an owner specification for a resource, etc.). The logic and conditions that determine how to evaluate an access control request is formalized in an *access control policy* that we adapt from [9], adding the notion of obligation O part of a policy P.

Definition 2 (Access Control Policy). *An access control policy P is an expression of the form:*

$$P = Permit \mid Deny \mid Permit, O \mid Deny, O \mid (T, P) \mid (ca, [P, \dots, P])$$
$$T = attr \; \varphi \; v \mid T \wedge T \mid T \vee T \mid \neg T$$
$$O = op(attr) \mid O \wedge O$$

where *Permit* and *Deny* represent the effects of a policy, (T, P) is a *targeted policy* where T describes the entity(-es) controlled by the policy (the "target"); $(ca, [P, \dots, P])$ represents a *composite policy* where ca is the policy processing algorithm (also called *policy combining algorithm*). An exhaustive explanation can be found in the original paper [9]. An extension of the original model is represented by O: it represents one or a set of operations op that must be mandatory performed by the requestor or by the controlled system as part of the authorization decision.

Let us consider the following policy and its formalization: "Cyber Threat Information of *Company1* can only be processed by users with role *analyst* with the obligation of logging such processing" (Listing 1.2).

Listing 1.1. An example of AC policy

```
(permit-overrides,
    [(r.type="Cyber Threat Information" ∧
        r.owner="Company1" ∧ s.role="analyst",
        Permit, log(s,a,r,e)),
    Deny])
```

2.1 XACML

XACML [20] is a standard based on XML, published by OASIS that defines a language for access control policies as well as an enforcement architecture. XACML is a flexible, well-known and widespread language. XACML can be used to express policies based on ABAC models, it is the conceptual basis of the work [21] of which the current obligation model is an extension. For the sake of this exposition, we will focus on the XACML architecture and on the execution flow among the different components.

An XACML architecture is composed by the following elements: **PAP (Policy Administration Point)**: the component that manages the policies and makes them available when needed for evaluation. **PDP (Policy Decision Point)**: the component that evaluates requests against the applicable policies and makes the access control decisions. **PEP (Policy Enforcement Point)**: the component that receives the request from the user and returns a response, even if it delegates the access control decision to the PDP. Moreover, the PEP is the component in charge of executing Obligations and Advices. **PIP (Policy Information Point)**: the component that retrieves further attributes related to the subject, action, resource and environment of the request from their respective repositories. **Context Handler**: the component that is responsible for maintaining a set of attributes, coming from PEP request and PIP, necessary for PDP evaluation.

An example of our reference architecture is shown in Fig. 1, using the FMC notation [20].

XACML also provides a definition for *obligations*, that are actions that a policy dictates to be executed under certain conditions. Park and Sandhu [16] defines 3 types of obligations: *pre-obligations* (in the following, abbreviated as *pre-obl*) are actions that must be implemented before the actual execution of the requested operation, while conversely *post-obligations* (abbr. *post-obl*) must be executed just after the requested operation. *Ongoing* obligations must be executed during the execution of the requested operation, and they can only be supported in a special family of AC models called Usage Control models.

We foresee the use of the PAP, PDP, PEP, PIP and Context Handler as described above, but our reference architecture also relies on: an *Obigation Engine*, a component that is devoted to the implementation of a set of obligations as deemed necessary by the system owner. A *Storage* module, i.e., a component in charge of storing datasets, and a *ML Library* module, i.e., a library able to perform aggregation operations (for example, an ML library like Tensorflow [1]).

Whenever a PDP is asked to make a decision, it relies on the information made available by the Context Handler, i.e., the *Context*: it consists of a container for all the attributes extracted from the PEP-prepared request and complemented with additional necessary attributes by the PIP. Then, the PDP matches the context with the attributes derived from the policy provided by the PAP and evaluates the request against the policy, returning a response to PEP and thus to the requestor.

3   Controlling Results of Aggregation Operation

Let us define an aggregation operation and consider its generic operation workflow when regulated by an AC system as in [21] based on XACML architecture , where multiple policies are applicable for the operation's input resources.

Definition 3 (Aggregation Operation). *An aggregation operation y can be defined as*

$$y \mapsto f(r_1 , \ldots , r_n , params) = result$$

where $f \in A$ is a mathematical function, $r_1, \ldots, r_n \in R$ is a set of resources, result is the result of the operation, and params represents the functional parameters of the operation.

Definition 4 (Aggregation Operation Workflow).

opRequest. A requestor *s* issues a request to a mathematical component to compute an operation $y = f(r_1 , \ldots , r_n)$.

acRequest. The PEP intercepts the request and submits an AC request *request − Multi* to the PDP.

acDecision. The PDP computes and sends to the PEP an AC response to the *request − Multi* as in [21], deriving possible aggregation-specific obligations.

acObligations. If the response is Permit, the PEP allows the computation of *f* and executes the obligations, if they were notified.

resultReturn. Operation's result is returned to the requestor by the PEP.

Traditional AC systems normally terminate their role after allowing the controlled system to perform an operation, while in our case we require that the AC system controls all interactions with *s*.

Requirements for Controlling Aggregation Results. As we have discussed, data aggregation operations produce results derived from a set of different input resources. An access control system can be expected to regulate multiple aspects of such operations:

R1 determine whether an operation *f* can be allowed and, in this case, force the execution of obligations before or after the processing of *f*;

R2 determine whether a piece of information r_i can be used as part of the input set of an operation *f*, also considering the qualities of the other operands $(r_1 , \ldots , r_n) \setminus (r_i)$;

R3 determine whether *result* of *f* has/does not have certain sensitive qualities;

R4 associate a new (possibly derived) policy to *result* and (possibly) use such policy for a new AC assessment.

Implementation Strategies. Let us focus on *R3* and let us consider the different implementation strategies.

Let us start considering approaches based on XACML access control policies as in [21], where a data owner policy can declare constraints on attributes of the other data part of the same operation.

Given the flexible definition of obligations, data owners may potentially specify:

Table 1. Classification of obligations considered in this work

name	target		AC	UC
Obl-standard	Data owner's resource		pre-obl	pre-obl, ongoing
Obl-other	Other resources part of the same request-Multi		pre-obl	pre-obl, ongoing
Obl-action	Aggregation function		pre-obl	pre-obl, ongoing
Obl-result	Result		post-obl	ongoing

Timestamp	Host	src	IP	Longitude	Latitude	ISP
t_1	H_1	s_1	IP_1	x_1	y_1	A
t_2	H_2	s_2	IP_2	x_2	y_2	B
t_3	H_3	s_3	IP_3	x_3	y_3	C
...	...	...	...	...	...	...

Fig. 2. Subsample of dataset of attacks to several providers' honeypots

- Obligations on their own data, as in the standard profile [20] (*obl-standard*). Examples: "my data must be anonymized before operation takes place" (pre-obligation) or "log request if access is denied" (post-obligation).
- Obligations on other operands (*obl-other*). Example: "other pictures aggregated with mine must be resized to the same resolution as mine". The system owners are demanded to decide whether such option can be viable or not for their system.
- Obligations on the operation (e.g., setting boundaries for its parameters) (*obl-action*). Example: "number of target clusters k must not be higher than N".
- Obligations on the *result* of f. Example: "result y must be anonymized".

Therefore, **R3** can be successfully implemented as *obl-action*, as a post-obligation. According to the capabilities of the access control system, one could specify to evaluate the attributes of the result and deny access in case they are not meeting expectations. In case of more sophisticated access control systems with usage control functionalities, one could specify to evaluate conditions on *result* and, if needed, to execute an obligation, or to enable a dynamic control on the resource to ensure that subsequent operations still preserve the desired result attributes or qualities (ongoing or continuous conditions and/or obligations [7, 15]).

Figure 1 shows a classification of the different obligations that we consider in this work, together with the indication whether they could be applied before or after the access control response (i.e., pre-, ongoing or post-obligations for access control (AC) systems, ongoing obligations for usage control (UC) systems).

4   Case Study

In this section we present our paradigmatic example to introduce our discussion on obligations for aggregation operations.

We will perform a clustering operation on a combined dataset D created from a number of datasets d_i of multiple owners. We will consider two personas in order to analyse the role and impact of obligations in this example: **Alice**, the *data analyst* requesting an aggregation operation and **Lucy**, one of the *data owners*.

The data we used for our experimental evaluation is derived from a publicly available dataset [13] of about 450,000 samples of attacks to multiple honeypots. Figure 2 depicts the structure of D: it represents malicious connections to the honeypots, with the recorded attack IP address and its approximate geographic location. We supplemented the original dataset by adding the column "ISP", obtained by querying the Internet service WHOIS and assigning a random identifier for each discovered ISP. We did not work with actual ISP names as deemed unnecessary to exemplify our approach. From this dataset, we extracted 10 evaluation datasets d_i of about 50k entries representing attacks to honeypots, as if they were provided by different entities. We also associated to each dataset d_i a set of attributes like owner (e.g., Company1, Company2, ...), an identifier. Lucy works for one of these ISP and determines the access control policy for her d_i, assuming that other data owners define a different access control policy, to allow the evaluation of access requests using our approach. Their objective is to release attack data but to prevent the re-identification of the ISP. In our case study, Alice issues a request to compute an aggregation (a k-means clustering [1]) on D.

In particular, Alice filters D in order to keep only entries corresponding to attacks performed to honeypots in a specific geographical location, i.e., eastern Asia. Successively, Alice computes the k-means of the targets of the attacks (each target appears with its latitude and longitude). Finally, we show how Alice, with her analysis, could identify some of the providers (i.e., individual disclosure from aggregated data such as in [5,6,26]). Lucy will be able to state a policy to counter this situation.

K-means [2] is a clustering algorithm whose goal is to partition a dataset of N samples into k clusters given a feature space. Since k is an input parameter of the algorithm, its optimal value can be chosen using the elbow method. This method relies on the minimization of inertia, also known as the within-cluster sum of squared criterion. The inertia can be interpreted as a measure of internal cluster coherence.

For a dataset with N samples defined by their feature vector x which is separated into k clusters C with mean μ, the inertia is defined as:

$$I = \sum_{i=0}^{N-1} \min_{\mu_j \in C}(\|x_i - \mu_j\|^2) \tag{1}$$

where $\|x_i - \mu_i\|$ represents the Euclidean distance of sample i to its closest cluster centroid μ_j.

The inertia is computed and plotted for a set of plausible values of k. The location of a bend (elbow) in the plot indicates an appropriate number of clusters for the given problem.

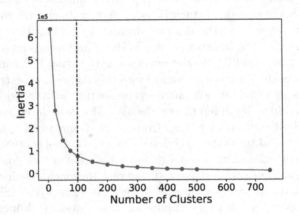

Fig. 3. Elbow method for the selection of k, suggesting $k = 100$ for the current application

For the current application, only geographical location features were used. Therefore, each sample in the database was represented by the feature vector $x = (longitude, latitude)$. Figure 3 shows the inertia for a range of tested values of k in our application, with 100 being the suggested number of clusters to be used. Figure 4 shows the k resulting cluster centroids in our dataset color-coded by their cluster identifier. The marker size is proportional to the number of samples contained within each cluster.

Alice then analyses the composition of each of the clusters. We define the Maximum Contribution MC in a cluster c as the largest percentage of samples in a cluster belonging to an individual ISP p.

$$MC_c = \max_{p_j \in ISP} \left(\frac{|c \cap p_j|}{|c|} \right) \tag{2}$$

If a cluster has a prominent single contributor, it means that the ISP is easily re-identified. To counter this situation, Lucy can either force a maximal value for k or express an obligation to drop a cluster if MC_c is greater than a threshold, as follows.

The policy in Listing 1.2 allows resources with attribute type "cyber threat information" belonging to Company1 to be analyzed by requestors of role "analyst" with operation "k-means", however with an obligation (to be enforced by the Obligation Engine) that forces the value of k to k_{max} as upper bound. The Obligation Engine must be able to alter k before its execution.

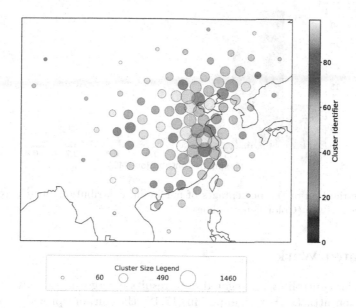

Fig. 4. Cluster centroids color-coded by their cluster identifier

Listing 1.2. Access control policy example with *obl-action* to override k-means parameter.

```
( permit−overrides ,
    [( r . type=''Cyber  Threat  Information"  ∧
        r . owner=''Company1"  ∧  s . role =''analyst"  ∧  a . name=''k−means" ,
        Permit ,  OverrideKIfGreaterThan ( k_max )) ,
    Deny])
```

Similarly, policy in Listing 1.3 again permits that resources with attribute type "cyber threat information" belonging to Company1 are analyzed by requestors of role "analyst" with operation "k-means"; this time, the obligation states that the Obligtion Engine must check the clusters being returned and drop from the result set those with MC value over the threshold *threshold*. The Obligation Engine must be able to compute such value on demand.

Listing 1.3. Access control policy example with *obl-result* to control aggregation result

```
( permit−overrides ,
    [( r . type=''Cyber  Threat  Information"  ∧
        r . owner=''Company1"  ∧  s . role =''analyst"  ∧  a . name=''k−means" ,
        Permit ,  DropClusterIfMCOver ( threshold )) ,
    Deny])
```

with k_{max} and *threshold* selected according to Lucy's directives. While the mentioned Fig. 3 gives indications for selecting k_{max}, Fig. 5 and Fig. 6 represent the clusters' results according to their MC value, yellow and red colors show growing individual contributions per cluster.

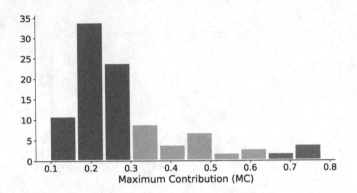

Fig. 5. Distribution of the percentages of maximum contributions for clusters, color-coded by sensitivity (Color figure online)

5 Related Work

The need for controlling aggregated data results emerges in many works on re-identification attacks. For example, in [17,18] the authors provide a study on membership inference attacks on aggregated data (users' location). They prove the effectiveness of their attacks on small groups of users with regular habits, and they prove it is hard to reach the same results on differentially private data. These works differ from ours because they focus on statistical methods that can be leveraged to leak information, and not on the regulation of the access of the input datasets using policies. Yet, these works can be considered as practical use cases proving the need of our solution.

Other works considered regulating aggregation operations, with different approaches. In [25], the authors focus on map-reduce in Apache Hadoop and enhanced it to support dynamic filtering of processed resources using a Role-Based Access Control model, also providing an implementation. Their work essentially focuses on filtering input data for a requestor and not on the operation results. The work described in [19] adopts obligations to perform actions when certain time-based conditions happen, then obligations determine the operation to be performed, potentially altering the operation result. However, while this work adopts an approach that can be represented with our obligation model, their approach is used to implement a functional behavior in a system and not to provide any access control functionality.

Looking closely at the different requirements, **R1** is a standard functionality of any AC system that directly materialises in the steps *acRequest, acDecision, acObligations*. **R2** is fulfilled with approaches focusing on regulating

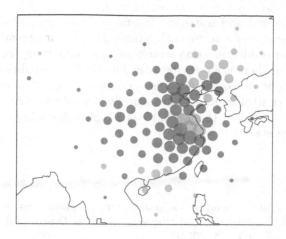

Fig. 6. Cluster centroids color-coded by their MC value (Color figure online)

data mash-ups, data fusion or data aggregation operations during *acDecision*, as in [9,21]. The latter **R3** is more challenging, both from a model and implementation perspective. It actually implies that the result of a previously approved operation is evaluated before being released to the operation requestor. Conceptually speaking, this new evaluation stems from the original AC evaluation in that it shares with the first certain characteristics, like the same requestor and environment, and the AC directives assessed in the second evaluation are dictated by the outcomes of the first.

The described situation for **R3** differs from approaches based on policy combination/integration/derivation (e.g., [3,4,23]) that are in scope of **R4**. **R3** foresees a form of "temporary-extended" assessment of the original access control request, that comprises the execution of the controlled operation. **R3** can be seen as a form of "post-obligations", i.e., an obligation that is executed after the evaluation of $request - Multi$. However, in this case the temporal trigger for the obligation execution is f, and the action to be executed is actually a re-evaluation of the qualities of the result. **R3** shares some similarities with the usage control obligations $UCON_{onB}$ [16] in that, the authorization given to s to compute f is valid until certain attributes of $result$ holds, otherwise the authorization is revoked[1].

6   Conclusion

Expressing constraints on the results of aggregation operations can effectively help to counter threats coming from data analysis/profiling. We proposed a model for AC obligations to serve this purpose, provided that they cater for

---

[1] For this reason, approaches like [7,14] can be applied, both with obligations or *continuous* or *ongoing* conditions. However this latter aspect is deemed out of scope of the current work.

a set of mathematical and statistical functions. From our initial observations, we distilled a use case where two obligations part of our obligation model can effectively counter re-identification attacks using a popular aggregation function, k-means. However, there is a need for extending the functionalities of access control systems, in order to cover a broader spectrum of the data analysis operation workflow. Usage control solutions can naturally control processes stemming from access control requests and they seem to offer higher flexibility in policy expression and enforcement.

References

1. Abadi, M., et al.: Tensorflow: a system for large-scale machine learning. In: 12th {USENIX} Symposium on Operating Systems Design and Implementation ({OSDI} 16), pp. 265–283 (2016)
2. Arthur, D., Vassilvitskii, S.: k-means++: the advantages of careful seeding. In: Proceedings of the 18th Annual ACM-SIAM Symposium on Discrete Algorithms (SODA), pp. 1027–1035. New Orleans, LA, USA, January 2007
3. Bertolissi, C., den Hartog, J., Zannone, N.: Using provenance for secure data fusion in cooperative systems. In: Proceedings of the Symposium on Access Control Models and Technologies (SACMAT), pp. 185–194. Toronto, Canada, June 2019
4. Bonatti, P., De Capitani di Vimercati, S., Samarati, P.: An algebra for composing access control policies. ACM Trans. Inf. Syst. Security (TISSEC) 5(1), 1–35 (2002)
5. Brownstein, J., Cassa, C., Kohane, I., Mandl, K.: An unsupervised classification method for inferring original case locations from low-resolution disease maps. Int. J. Health Geographics 5, 56 (2006)
6. Curtis, A., Curtis, J., Leitner, M.: Spatial confidentiality and GIS: re-engineering mortality locations from published maps about hurricane katrina. Int. J. Health Geographics 5, 44 (2006)
7. Di Cerbo, F., Lunardelli, A., Matteucci, I., Martinelli, F., Mori, P.: A declarative data protection approach: from human-readable policies to automatic enforcement. In: International Conference on Web Information Systems and Technologies (WEBIST), pp. 78–98. Seville, Spain, September 2018
8. Gambs, S., Gmati, A., Hurfin, M.: Reconstruction attack through classifier analysis. In: Proceedings of the 26th Annual IFIP WG 11.3 Working Conference on Data and Applications Security (DBSec), pp. 274–281. Paris, France, July 2012
9. den Hartog, J., Zannone, N.: A policy framework for data fusion and derived data control. In: Proceedings of the 2016 ACM International Workshop on Attribute Based Access Control (ABAC), pp. 47–57. New Orleans, LA, USA, March 2016
10. Hay, M., Miklau, G., Jensen, D., Towsley, D., Weis, P.: Resisting structural re-identification in anonymized social networks. Proc. VLDB Endowment 1(1), 102–114 (2008)
11. Hayes, J., Melis, L., Danezis, G., De Cristofaro, E.: Logan: membership inference attacks against generative models. Proc. Privacy Enhancing Technol. (PoPETs) 2019(1), 133–152 (2019)
12. Hu, C.T., et al.: Guide to attribute based access control (ABAC) definition and considerations [includes updates as of 02–25–2019]. Tech. rep, NIST (2019)
13. Jacobs, J.: The Marx-Geo Dataset. https://datadrivensecurity.info/blog/pages/dds-dataset-collection.html (2014)

14. Lazouski, A., Mancini, G., Martinelli, F., Mori, P.: Usage control in cloud systems. In: Proceedings of the 2012 International Conference for Internet Technology and Secured Transactions (ICITST), pp. 202–207. London, UK (2012)
15. Martinelli, F., Mori, P., Saracino, A., Di Cerbo, F.: Obligation management in usage control systems. In: Proceedings of the 27th Euromicro International Conference on Parallel, Distributed and Network-Based Processing (PDP). pp. 356–364. Pavia, Italy (February 2019)
16. Park, J., Sandhu, R.: The uconabc usage control model. ACM Trans. Inf. Syst. Security (TISSEC) **7**(1), 128–174 (2004)
17. Pyrgelis, A., Troncoso, C., Cristofaro, E.D.: What does the crowd say about you? evaluating aggregation-based location privacy. In: Proceedings of the Privacy Enhancing Technologies Symposium (PETS), pp. 156–176. Minneapolis, MN, USA July 2017
18. Pyrgelis, A., Troncoso, C., Cristofaro, E.D.: Knock knock, who's there? membership inference on aggregate location data. In: Proceedings of the Network and Distributed System Security Symposium (NDSS). San Diego, CA, USA, February 2018
19. Reiff-Marganiec, S., Tilly, M., Janicke, H.: Low-latency service data aggregation using policy obligations. In: 2014 IEEE International Conference on Web Services, pp. 526–533. IEEE (2014)
20. Rissanen, E., et al.: Extensible access control markup language (xacml) version 3.0. OASIS standard 22 (2013)
21. Rosa, M., Di Cerbo, F., Lozoya, R.C.: Declarative access control for aggregations of multiple ownership data. In: Proceedings of the 25th ACM Symposium on Access Control Models and Technologies (SACMAT), pp. 59–70. Barcelona, Spain, June 2020
22. Salem, A., Bhattacharya, A., Backes, M., Fritz, M., Zhang, Y.: Updates-leak: data set inference and reconstruction attacks in online learning. arXiv preprint arXiv:1904.01067 (2019)
23. Scalavino, E., Gowadia, V., Lupu, E.C.: A labelling system for derived data control. In: Proceedings of the 24th Annual IFIP WG 11.3 Working Conference on Data and Applications Security (DBSec). pp. 65–80. Rome, Italy, April 2010
24. Shokri, R., Stronati, M., Song, C., Shmatikov, V.: Membership inference attacks against machine learning models. In: Proceedings of the 2017 IEEE Symposium on Security and Privacy (S&P), pp. 3–18. San Jose, CA, USA, May 2017
25. Ulusoy, H., Colombo, P., Ferrari, E., Kantarcioglu, M., Pattuk, E.: Guardmr: fine-grained security policy enforcement for mapreduce systems. In: Proceedings of the 10th ACM Symposium on Information, Computer and Communications Security, pp. 285–296 (2015)
26. Yan, Y., Ni, B., Song, Z., Ma, C., Yan, Y., Yang, X.: Person re-identification via recurrent feature aggregation. In: European Conference on Computer Vision (ECCV). pp. 701–716. Amsterdam, Netherlands, October 2016

The Cost of Having Been Pwned: A Security Service Provider's Perspective

Gergely Biczók[1]([✉]), Máté Horváth[1], Szilveszter Szebeni[2], István Lám[2], and Levente Buttyán[1]

[1] CrySyS Lab, Department of Networked Systems and Services,
Budapest University of Technology and Economics,
Budapest, Hungary
{biczok,mhorvath,buttyan}@crysys.hu
[2] Tresorit, Budapest, Hungary
{szebeni,lam}@tresorit.com

Abstract. Account information from major online providers are getting exposed regularly; this gives rise to PWND services, providing a smart means to check whether a password or username/password tuple has already been leaked, rendering them "pwned" and therefore risky to use. However, state-of-the-art PWND mechanisms leak some information themselves. In this paper, we investigate how this minimal leaked information can speed up password cracking attacks of a powerful adversary, when the PWND mechanism is implemented on-premise by a service provider as an additional security measure during registration or password change. We analyze the costs and practicality of these attacks, and investigate simple mitigation techniques. We show that implementing a PWND mechanism can be beneficial, especially for security-focused service providers, but proper care needs to be taken. We also discuss behavioral factors to consider when deploying PWND services.

Keywords: Pwned accounts · Credential leakage · Leaked password · Dictionary attack · Data breach · Security service provider

1 Introduction

Data breaches at major online service providers exposing account information are increasingly prevalent. As a result of these breaches, many millions of user accounts, including usernames and passwords, have been *"pwned"*. In fact, as of June 2020, the number of pwned accounts is reported to be around 9.7 billion [6]; this number is based on already discovered incidents, therefore it should be treated as a a conservative lower bound. Such data leaks and the challenges they have been posing have not gone unanswered by the security community. Privately and publicly curated databases containing records of pwned accounts have emerged, providing a means to check if a given account(email address or

© Springer Nature Switzerland AG 2020
A. Saracino and P. Mori (Eds.): ETAA 2020, LNCS 12515, pp. 154–167, 2020.
https://doi.org/10.1007/978-3-030-64455-0_10

email address/password tuple) is affected. Prominent examples include http://www.haveibeenpwned.com [6], SpyCloud [18] and Google's own database [20]. Services based on these repositories implement privacy-preserving mechanisms, which we term as *PWND mechanisms*, enabling their users (both end-users and service providers) to check whether certain passwords or full login credentials are already known to be leaked without revealing them to the service.

A security Service Provider's Perspective. Online service providers are able to check whether a user registering to their service is re-using a pwned password; this could improve account security and avoid potential reputation loss stemming from account compromise such as with iCloud[1]. Similarly, providers could use the same PWND mechanism for password change and logins of existing users to protect against the usage of a leaked password. We emphasize that here the goal of such checkup is not to alert users when their credentials become known to be leaked, but rather to avoid the potential reuse of a leaked password, regardless who used the password when it was leaked. Consequently, *we focus on checking passwords only*, to make pwned password lists useless in dictionary attacks. (Of course, incorporating the PWND mechanism is not enough; providers should take extra care with how they present the results of such checks to the user [5]). Providers of security services, such as end-to-end encrypted file storage or secure collaboration, are under even more scrutiny regarding incidents involving user accounts; hence, they have a strong incentive to implement PWND measures. However, not all PWND integration options [10,20] are equal in their potential appeal to such a provider. We argue that an on-premise PWND solution, built on downloadable public databases and run by the provider itself, might be preferable. Such a solution i) does not require trusting an explicit third party ii) works also with desktop and mobile apps, not just with browser-based service access iii) gives the control to the service provider, and requires no user action.

Information Leakage. Proper PWND services obviously never require the client to send its cleartext password, moreso, they do not require the full (e.g., SHA-1) hash either; that would provide too much information and allow an adversary to reconstruct the original password. Instead, only the leading few[2] bytes of the password hash is sent upstream that enables the server to send down a filtered (therefore much smaller) version of the list of pwned password hashes. Then, the client can check locally whether the hash of his own password is in the received pwned password hash list. Such filtering greatly accelerates the checking process, however, it also leaks some information [10]. Obviously, a few bytes of the password hash is not enough to be used directly for reversing the original password, but it can accelerate password cracking.

Strong Adversary and Expedited Attacks. When considering security services (e.g., secure storage), from the user's perspective *the service provider is*

---

[1] https://mashable.com/2014/08/31/celebrity-nude-photo-hack/.

[2] e.g., 5 half-bytes for http://www.haveibeenpwned.com and 2 bytes for Google's Password Checkup.

the strongest potential adversary who claims protection even from itself. In the corresponding security model the adversary obtains every bit of leaked information related to a specific user; such a model has not yet been analyzed in the context of PWND services in related work [10,20]. Such an adversary can launch a sped-up password cracking attack: given a targeted user he computes a simple SHA-1 hash of the password candidate; if the first few bytes do not match with the leaked bytes, the adversary can skip to the next password. This can accelerate the cracking process by a significant factor, in the order of thousands or millions depending on the actual extent of information leakage. Variants of this idea can be used both for dictionary and brute force attacks; furthermore, a non-targeted brute force attack could also be carried out with increased speed. Note that such an adversary is not slowed down by rate limiting API calls.

Our Contribution. In this paper, focusing on PWND mechanisms using only password hashes, we analyze expedited dictionary and brute force attacks by a strong adversary against users of an online service provider utilizing an on-premise PWND mechanism. We characterize attack costs for each attack and password strength category, and take a look at simple potential countermeasures. Our quantitative results indicate that i) public PWND databases can be used as dictionaries for password cracking attacks, and ii) the proposed hash stretc.hing indeed renders brute force attacks on "medium-strength" passwords impractical. Furthermore, we discuss how user behavior and the composition of a given service provider's user base affects the introduction of a PWND mechanism from a cost-benefit standpoint. Finally, we discuss why a PWND solution based on Private Set Membership (PSM) protocols is not (yet) practical.

The rest of the paper is organized as follows. Section 2 describes potential PWND implementation alternatives for online service providers and the details of the most popular PWND mechanisms. Section 3 introduces and analyzes the potential attacks in detail and discusses simple mitigation techniques. Section 4 takes a look at the expected costs of the above attacks and the trade-off associated with deploying a PWND mechanism with regard to both service providers and end-users. Section 5 discusses the limitations of a potential PWND mechanism based on PSM protocols. Finally, Sect. 6 concludes the paper.

2   Background

Here we introduce the most important concepts regarding PWND services and position our contributions with respect to related work.

2.1   PWND: Architectural Alternatives

From the service provider's aspect, a PWND service can be realized in a variety of ways. Figure 1(a) and 1(b) represent solutions where checking is initiated by the user (e.g., by using a specific browser (extension) [20] or password manager [7] that alerts in case of a password becoming leaked). While these solutions have

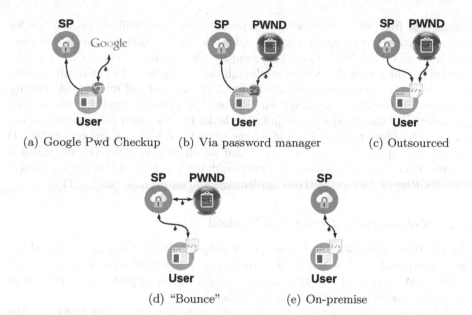

(a) Google Pwd Checkup   (b) Via password manager   (c) Outsourced

(d) "Bounce"   (e) On-premise

Fig. 1. PWND architectural alternatives: initiated either by the user or by the service provider

their own merits, they also have inherent weaknesses. In these scenarios, the service provider has no influence over whether the user has checked his candidate password against a PWND database. The provider may display a recommendation in its registration dialogue, and nudge the user towards checking, but nothing more. Therefore, the service provider relies on the voluntary actions of the user and either risks account compromise, or is forced to also implement his own PWND mechanism. Furthermore, if the service requires a desktop or mobile app for client access, browser extensions and non-system level password managers will not work. Last, but not least, a major issue is trust: a provider with mostly security-conscious users (whether end-users or enterprises) will find it hard to justify opting for a PWND mechanism administered by a third party.

Contrarily, Fig. 1(c), 1(d) and 1(e) depict checking mechanisms triggered by the service provider. In such cases, the control is with the service provider, so that it can enforce PWND, requiring no action from the user. This can be especially crucial for providers of security-related services, such as end-to-end encrypted file storage, online virus checking, secure collaboration, etc. Also, requiring no extra functionality at the client side, these solutions handle client heterogeneity inherently. The outsourced and "Bounce" [17] alternatives still suffer from the third party trust issue mentioned above. In addition, the outsourced case presents a sizable challenge in terms of API keys to the PWND service: since PWND-related data do not flow through the service provider, the API is either public and free (which is shown to be problematic[3]), or utilizes an API key for authentication (and usually charges a fee for API usage). In the latter case, the outsourced PWND architecture requires the sharing of the API key of the service provider with all its users; although this is doable, it might result in complex policies at the service provider's side and does not fall under best security practice. Furthermore, assuming an adversary who sees everything the service provider sees, the "Bounce" architecture leaks just as much information as the on-premise solution, but with adding the trust issue with a third party PWND service. Based on the above, we argue that an on-premise PWND mechanism is a sensible choice for providers of security-related services and/or with security-conscious users. In fact, GitHub implements the on-premise model [11].

2.2 K-Anonymity Preserving Method

We say that some data has K-anonymity property [15] if the information about any entry, contained in the data cannot be distinguished from at least $K - 1$ other entries. [1] used this type of privacy guarantee to protect the process of testing password leakage with the algorithm in Fig. 2.

We recall the most notable instantiations of the idea of [1]. The first one is the http://www.haveibeenpwned.com[4] website, which uses the SHA-1 hash function that has an output of 40 hexadecimal digits (thus $m = 160$) out of which a 5 digit long prefix ($n = 20$) is used for the partitioning of the database. In Google's Password Checkup Chrome extension, the same K-anonymity based method guarantees the privacy of user credentials (see Subsect. 2.3 for differences). The extension relies on the Argon2 hash function with $m = 128$ bit output length

---

Let $H : \{0,1\}^* \rightarrow \{0,1\}^m$ be a hash function and L a database of leaked passwords.
Input / Output:
   Server: A list L of leaked passwords / -
   Client: Password p^* to be checked / {0,1}
Protocol:

Offline phase For all $p^i \in L$, the server computes $H(p^i) = h^i$ and organizes
   the resulting hash values into 2^n sets based on their length n prefixes i.e.,
   $S_{\mathsf{pref}^j} = \{h^i | h^i_\ell = \mathsf{pref}^j_\ell$ for $\ell = 0, \ldots, n - 1\}$.
Online phase :
   1. Client computes $H(p^*) = h^*$ and sends pref^*, its first n bits to the Server.
   2. Based on pref^*, the Server sends S_{pref^*} to the Client.
   3. The Client checks if $h^* \in S_{\mathsf{pref}^*}$. If yes, the password is a leaked one and
      outputs 1, otherwise $p^* \notin L$ and returns 0.

Fig. 2. K-anonymity preserving protocol for checking whether a password has already been leaked (for $K = 2^{m-n}$).

---

[3] https://www.troyhunt.com/authentication-and-the-have-i-been-pwned-api/.
[4] For details: https://haveibeenpwned.com/API/v2#PwnedPasswords.

and a configuration using a single thread, 256 MB of memory, and a time cost of three [20]. This results in a computationally expensive calculation (modelled by an inefficient oracle) that is unnoticeable for honest users performing a single query but causes significant slowdown for brute force attackers (see details in Sect. 3.3). The prefix length, sent by the client, is 2 bytes ($n = 16$).

2.3 Related Work

In February 2019, Google has introduced a Chrome extension[5], called Password Checkup, with the goal of enabling users to check whether their credentials were part of a former data breach. The extension checks possible data leakage in a privacy-preserving manner, whenever the user registers or logs in to a third party service. While Password Checkup offers a service similar to the one we are considering in this paper, it is important to notice the essential differences in their objectives. Password Checkup handles usernames and passwords together aiming to alert the user only if she or he was involved in a data breach [20]. Contrarily, we are not interested in detecting whether a specific user is affected by any of the breaches. Our goal is to make users avoid the use of leaked passwords regardless of where, when and who used the specific password. Our motivation for avoiding leaked passwords, even for different usernames, roots in the considered scenario. In case of security-focused services, like the end-to-end encrypted file sharing service provided by Tresorit[6] or the private-by-design collaboration platform CryptPad[7], the service provider often wants to prove that their users are not only protected from outside attackers but also from inside attacks (i.e. from the service provider itself). While in the former case dictionary and brute force attacks can be easily prevented, e.g. by limiting the number of failed log in attempts, this is not straightforward when the attacker is the service provider itself (or, equivalently, bears the entire knowledge of the service provider). Assuming that users are exposed in such a manner, it becomes important to protect against attacks that make use of leaked data, e.g., by building a dictionary from it. In this paper, we focus on this scenario by choosing to protect users who would reuse already leaked passwords (even under different usernames) [19].

Furthermore, as we argued in Sect. 2.1, an on-premise PWND solution, built on downloadable public databases and run by the provider itself, could be the preferred implementation alternative to providers of security-focused services. Such a scenario has not been analyzed before with respect to information leakage [10] Another difference between our work and [20] is that we consider the use of publicly available databases of leaked passwords; obtaining access to a private database either costs significant money [18] or is just plain unlikely to happen [20]). Google uses its own database, consequently, their attacker model is stricter than ours as it also aims to protect the database besides the user's credentials during the checkup.

---

[5] https://chrome.google.com/webstore/detail/password-checkup-extensio/
pncabnpcffmalkkjpajodfhijclecjno.
[6] https://tresorit.com.
[7] https://cryptpad.fr.

3 PWND: Security Issues and Mitigation Techniques

3.1 Scenario Description and Assumptions

Our investigation is motivated by the applicability of a PWND mechanism by
Tresorit, an end-to-end encrypted cloud data storage, syncing and sharing service
provider. In the Tresorit system [21], user passwords are stretched and used as
input for encrypting randomly generated private keys with which all user-related
data is encrypted in an end-to-end manner. Neither unencrypted user data, nor
user passwords, nor private keys leave the devices of users at any time. Given
that Tresorit sells a value-added storage service with a distinct focus on security,
in line with our argument is Sect. 2.1, we assume that the PWND service runs
directly at Tresorit following the on-premise model (see Fig. 1(e)). Tresorit's
own PWND database can be built by obtaining the SHA-1 hashes of pwned
passwords from the http://www.haveibeenpwned.com service database and/or
compiling their own from various sources. Naturally, the PWND database is
updated continuously.

We assume an incremental roll-out of the PWND mechanism: already registered users are only checked when their session expires and they have to log in
with their password again; before doing so, Tresorit does not have extra information about their password hashes. Since Tresorit does not store password
hashes, offline checking of existing users, and selectively triggering password
change for pwned accounts is technically infeasible. Triggering session expiration for the whole existing user base upon the introduction of PWND is not a
realistic option, because Tresorit users expect their data to be continually synced
with the service. Of course, users can change their passwords voluntarily; in such
a case, the PWND mechanism could be triggered.

Note, that in case of finding a pwned password, the service provider forces
the user to choose another password. We also assume that weak passwords
are rejected during registration via a combination of rule-based and client-side
(small) dictionary based filtering; in this case the use is prompted for another
password of adequate strength. Note that we assume no mandatory 2-factor
authentication for user login [13].

3.2 Potential Attacks

Attacker Model. Motivated by the service provider's point of view, we assume
a powerful adversary. Such an adversary is assumed to break into the service
provider's system gaining access to all the information stored at and communi-
cated by the provider. In this context, the adversary has the same capabilities as
the service provider. Even though the adversary has the same access to resources
as the service provider, neither can access user data due to the end-to-end encryption (see Sect. 3.1). The adversary's aim is to crack user passwords in order to
get access to user accounts and the data stored there. It is worth noting that any
mitigation technique proposed for the attacks below should make user passwords
and data more secure against both the adversary *and* the service provider. We

also assume that the attacker does have access to public PWND databases (even if the service provider does not implement any PWND mechanism). Note that traditional API security measures, such as account locking and rate limiting, do not protect against such an adversary, as the attacker is equivalent to an insider.

There are three types of password cracking attacks which can benefit directly from the extra information revealed by the PWND mechanism. The first two attacks are sped up by filtering out potential password candidates quickly, while the third attack is accelerated by shrinking the set of users who can potentially own a given candidate password. Note that only users who registered or changed their passwords after the roll-out of the PWND service are affected.

Dictionary Attack. The objective of this attack is to crack the password of a given individual user and gain access to the data stored at her account. The dictionary attack uses an existing list of popular passwords which the adversary tries systematically; e.g., the PWND database itself or the list of the 10 million most popular passwords[8]. In our case, the adversary observes the top-n bits of the hash. Based on these the adversary filters out candidate passwords (starting with the top-n bits) from its dictionary. It then tests the candidate passwords by stretching them and trying to decrypt the encrypted private key of the user according to Tresorit's process [21]. Once done, the adversary tries to decrypt the given user's data stored at Tresorit with the derived candidate private key. If this attempt is successful, i.e., it yields meaningful data, then the password is valid[9]. The extra information from the PWND mechanism accelerates this attack. The acceleration factor depends on the composition of the dictionary; assuming uniformity across the top-n bits, the speedup is by a factor of 2^n. Note that only users, whose password appeared in the list of pwned passwords *after* they had registered (following an update of the PWND database), are affected. (Obviously, their password would have been rejected during registration otherwise.)

Brute Force Attack A. This attack is similar to the dictionary attack both in its objective and speedup factor. The only difference is that there is no pre-computed database of candidate passwords: the adversary generates the candidate password on-the-fly using a structured approach (aided by tools such as John the Ripper[10]). This attack can also be accelerated by discarding potential candidate passwords quickly by hashing the password and calculating its top-n bits and comparing it to the leaked bit of the particular user. If the top-n bits match, the attacker can test the password which is more expensive. Ignoring the small cost of the top-n bit test leads to an acceleration factor of 2^n.

Brute Force Attack B. This attack is not targeted: the objective here is to crack the password of an arbitrary user or group of users. The adversary partitions the users into 2^n groups based on the leaked top-n bits. When trying a password candidate the adversary looks up the top-n bits and tries the candidate only for users

---

[8] https://github.com/danielmiessler/SecLists/tree/master/Passwords.
[9] all three attacks follow this logic for checking if a password candidate is valid.
[10] https://www.openwall.com/john/.

in the given group. The extra information from the PWND mechanism accelerates this attack to the realm of being practical for non-pwned passwords which are neither particularly weak nor particularly strong[11]. The acceleration factor depends on the distribution of actual end-users across the top-n bits; assuming uniformity of users across top-n bit induced groups and at least 2^n affected users, this method accelerates password cracking by a factor of 2^n.

Note, that rainbow table based attacks [12] are not accelerated in this context. Rainbow tables are based on pre-computed chains of available password candidates and hashes, however, the PWND service eliminates those. If the user's registration password is pwned, i.e., the service provider's PWND database contains it, the service provider forces the user to choose another password. If the password is not pwned, there is no complete leaked hash value to build the rainbow table on. The top-n bits of the password hash, leaked by the PWND mechanism, do not help enough in the creation of the rainbow table, as the non-leaked part is still dominant.

3.3   Mitigation

Stretching. A simple way to prevent the acceleration of potential attacks is to use basic key stretching [8]. The user computes a stretched hash, iterating over a hash several thousand times, i.e., taking the output hash and feeding it back into the algorithm as an input. Such a stretched hash takes a set amount of time to complete, which will be several thousand times larger than for single iteration. Afterwards, the user sends the top-n bit of the stretched hash to the on-premise PWND service, and the rest of the PWND protocol continues according to Fig. 2. As such, the privacy-preserving manner of the password checking process is conserved.

On the one hand, this slowdown is easily tolerable for both end-users and service provider, as it is done in a one-off manner when registering for the service or changing passwords; also, calculating such a stretc.hed hash takes typically from a few hundred milliseconds to a few seconds. On the other hand, the attacker suffers as he has to compute the same stretched hash for every step of the dictionary and brute force attacks. In fact, stretching gives the service provider a flexible "pacing" tool that can be adjusted as its system (number of users, PWND mechanism, etc.) evolves. Note that since rainbow table attacks are not accelerated in our application scenario, salting is not needed.

Increasing Anonymity Set Size. Recall that the reason of leaking information during the checkup is to keep the overhead of the protocol unnoticeable for the user. Consequently, the choice of protocol parameters is a trade-off between password privacy and user experience. In order to minimize the number of false positives, the probability of hash collisions should be kept minimal (when modeling the hash function with a random oracle, it means that its output length should be long enough), so that different passwords can be represented with

---

[11] e.g., 8-character extended alphanumeric passwords.

different hash values. The prefix length determines the size of the anonymity set that belongs to a given password and also the number of hash values the server has to transmit to the user to detect password leakage (the shorter the prefix is, the bigger the anonymity set and the communication cost). One could increase the anonymity set size either by increasing false positive probability (applying shorter hash values) or by increasing the protocol overhead. As the latter one is undesirable, we investigate the other opportunity. Shortening the leaked hash prefix with n' bits reduces the attackers advantage with a factor of $2^{n'}$ by increasing the anonymity set size with the same factor. To preserve the original communication costs the server can either use a hash function with shorter output length or does not change the hash itself, but returns only a part of the hash values that match with the prefix of the user.

Note that we include stretching in our cost analysis, but leave the numerical investigation of manipulating anonymity sets to future work.

4 Cost-Benefit Analysis

4.1 Attack Cost Estimation

Here we estimate the cost of attacks defined in Sect. 3.2 in case of different versions of the on-premise PWND mechanism in terms of effort and monetary cost needed by the attacker to crack a single password. The basis of our simple calculations are the following: the size of the pwned password database, categories of password strengths and the number of potential password candidates in each category, hash computation times and the cost of CPU time.

Parameters. At the time of writing this article, the popular site http://www. haveibeenpwned.com claims to know about more than 8 billion pwned accounts. Accounting for the significant overlap among actual passwords, we estimate the number of pwned passwords at 600 million. We assume that PWND mechanisms use a 16-bit prefix, i.e., this characterizes the information leakage. We also assume that a PWND database update brings with itself 10% new password hashes, i.e., 60 million new hashes in our case. In our scenario, it is sensible to take into account four different password strength categories: pwned passwords, passwords that were not pwned at the time of registration but have become pwned since then (we refer to those as Δpwned), "medium" strength passwords (defined as 8-character-long alphanumeric passwords with basic special characters) and "good" passwords (conservatively defined as having 64 bits of entropy, corresponding to 10–11 character long extended alphanumeric passwords). Note that weak passwords are excluded in line with our assumption on the service provider's policy. As the computation time of an SHA-1 hash is in the order of a few milliseconds we take it as zero, while we parametrize our stretched hashing in a way that it takes exactly 1 s to perform (inclusive of the decryption attempt of the user's data, see Sect. 3.1). To estimate the cost of CPU time, we turn to the price list of publicly available cloud computation instances, where a 16-core processor can be rented for \$4 per hour, which equals to \$2, 190 for a single core per year. Note that here we omit attack preparation costs, such as acquiring/compiling a dictionary (anyway, the public PWND database is readily available to the attacker).

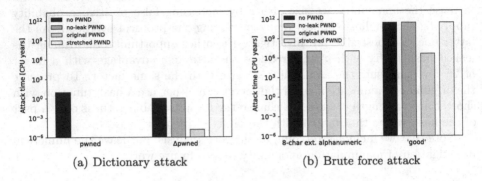

(a) Dictionary attack   (b) Brute force attack

Fig. 3. Expected attack times in CPU years

We consider 4 different PWND versions: i) a baseline with no PWND implemented, ii) an ideal, no-leak PWND (not practical owing to the large amount of data transfer that interferes with user experience), iii) the original PWND detailed in Fig. 2, and iv) a version with stretched hashing. Figure 3 shows the expected required resources for a successful attack on a single user in CPU years. Note that both plots use the same log y-axis for the sake of comparison. Also note that attack times and costs for the two different brute force attacks are the same, albeit the two attacks are different (targeted vs. non-targeted) and also accelerated differently (see Sect. 3.2).

Figure 3(a) shows that not implementing any PWND mechanism allows a dictionary attack using the public PWND database as a dictionary of hashes to be completed in less than 10 CPU years ($21,900) on average; this works only for pwned passwords, of course. Any PWND mechanism would mitigate this special case. On the other hand, for passwords that have become pwned after they were used for registration (Δpwned), quick attacks can be mounted. This follows from the fact that the adversary can construct the Δ between the two versions of the database, and use this shorter list as its attack dictionary. Specifically, if the provider implements the regular PWND mechanism detailed in Fig. 2, the attack requires roughly 8 min to succeed on a single CPU core, for this special case. Stretched hashing increases the attack cost, but does not make the attack impractical ($\approx$1 CPU year or $2,190).

Clearly, implementing a PWND mechanism is advisable, especially for encrypted cloud storage, where the sensitive content is likely to be stored. Furthermore, additional safeguards for database updates are needed; note that the adversary learns about the updates of public databases at the same time as the provider. Designing such safeguards constitute important future work.

Regarding brute force attacks, a "good" password can be considered safe against a brute force attack as it would take $\approx$4.5 $\cdot10^6$ CPU years even with the original, top-n bit leaking PWND mechanism to crack such a password. Clearly, the most interesting case concerns "medium-strength", 8-character-long extended alphanumeric passwords. In this case, when using the state-of-the-art PWND mechanism, it would take $\approx$175 CPU years on average to crack one password; this amounts to $\approx$ \$382,500. Such monetary cost can be considered borderline practical; more so with the declining cost of computation resources. We observe that stretching the hash mitigates the information leakage issue successfully in this case, increasing the cost of a successful attack to $1.15 \cdot 10^7$ CPU years and more than \$25 billion. We can conclude that utilizing an on-premise PWND mechanism with stretching allows for a milder password strength policy that users may like.

4.2   User Behavior

User behavior when facing forced password change and stricter security policies is shown to be mixed [16]. Users of a service provider can be partitioned into multiple categories with respect to their password habits and willingness to comply with an additional security mechanism such as compulsory password change. As such, some users get increased security from a deployed PWND mechanism, while some could actually suffer a decrease in security (users with "medium-strength" passwords, if the provider utilizes the regular PWND mechanism). In addition, even with benefiting from better security, users forced to change passwords may just leave the service altogether because of the bother[12].

Obviously, a service provider can suffer the costs of users leaving (either because of bother or decreased security), but may pay a larger reputation cost if an attacker can access a user account with a pwned password. In fact, providers selling a security-related service are probably better off deploying an enhanced PWND mechanism. Ultimately, the actual benefit of a proper PWND mechanism depends on the composition of the service provider's user base with regard to password habits.

5   Discussion

The cost of checking whether a password is known to be pwned can also be computational and/or communication overhead besides the investigated security loss, caused by the k-anonymity approach. However, the efficiency of cryptographic protocols, called Private Set Intersection or more specifically Private Set Membership (PSM), that could eliminate the information leakage entirely, seem to be prohibitive in case of the considered application.

The goal of PSM protocols is to enable two parties (typically a server and a user) to securely decide whether a value, determined by one of them (user), is an element of a set belonging to the other (server). The security guarantee of PSM

---

[12] This seems to be an existing threat: the online payment website of a major Hungarian mobile provider offers the alternative to the user to keep their old password even after prompting them to change it due to expiration!.

informally says that from their interaction, neither the user nor the server should learn anything about the other's input beyond the result[13] of the membership test. Authors of [3] studied PSM first, and showed its connection to Oblivious Transfer (OT), a fundamental cryptographic protocol.

When trying to apply PSM protocols for password verification, the main source of inefficiency is that both communication and computational costs depend on the set size, the order of magnitude of which is upwards of 10^8. According to the measurements of [14, Table 5–6] on desktop PCs, for passwords of 8 characters it would take 13.8 sec and a communication cost of 78.3 MB to check membership in a set of only 2^{18} elements; far less than the PWND database. We consider such a delay already impractical [4].

6   Conclusion

In this paper, we investigated the effect of information leakage when using state-of-the-art PWND mechanisms implemented at the service provider itself. We also presented simple techniques based on hash stretching and anonymity set design that could negate the acceleration of password cracking attacks owing to the usage of PWND. Our attack cost calculation showed that i) public PWND databases can be used as dictionaries for password cracking attacks ii) stretching-based mitigation is effective concerning the potentially vulnerable users using "medium strength" passwords. We also discussed how cryptographic solutions leaking no information are not yet practical in the PWND context. We have barely scratched the surface: as future work, we plan to analyze PWND mechanisms based on full account information, improve existing schemes by anonymity set engineering and handling PWND database updates, conduct a survey on PWND usage among users and service providers, and devise a formal, in-depth cost-benefit analysis.

References

1. Ali, J.: Validating leaked passwords with k-anonymity, February 2018. https://blog.cloudflare.com/validating-leaked-passwords-with-k-anonymity/. Accessed: 15 Jun 2020
2. Ciampi, M., Orlandi, C.: Combining private set-intersection with secure two-party computation. In: Catalano, D., De Prisco, R. (eds.) SCN 2018. LNCS, vol. 11035, pp. 464–482. Springer, Cham (2018). https://doi.org/10.1007/978-3-319-98113-0_25
3. Freedman, M.J., Ishai, Y., Pinkas, B., Reingold, O.: Keyword search and oblivious pseudorandom functions. In: Kilian, J. (ed.) TCC 2005. LNCS, vol. 3378, pp. 303–324. Springer, Heidelberg (2005). https://doi.org/10.1007/978-3-540-30576-7_17
4. Galletta, D.F., Henry, R., McCoy, S., Polak, P.: Web site delays: how tolerant are users? J. Assoc. Inf. Syst. 5(1), 1 (2004)

---

[13] Different variants exist based on who receives the output: only the user [14], only the server [9] or both of them in a secret shared form [2].

5. Habib, H., et al.: Password creation in the presence of blacklists. In: Proceedings of USEC 2017, p. 50 (2017)
6. Have I Been Pwned. Website. https://haveibeenpwned.com. Accessed 15 Jun 2020
7. Hunt, T.: Have i been pwned is now partnering with 1password (2018). https://www.troyhunt.com/have-i-been-pwned-is-now-partnering-with-1password/. Accessed 15 Jun 2020
8. Kelsey, J., Schneier, B., Hall, C., Wagner, D.: Secure applications of low-entropy keys. In: Okamoto, E., Davida, G., Mambo, M. (eds.) ISW 1997. LNCS, vol. 1396, pp. 121–134. Springer, Heidelberg (1998). https://doi.org/10.1007/BFb0030415
9. Kolesnikov, V., Rosulek, M., Trieu, N., Wang, X.: Scalable private set union from symmetric-key techniques. In: Galbraith, S.D., Moriai, S. (eds.) ASIACRYPT 2019. LNCS, vol. 11922, pp. 636–666. Springer, Cham (2019). https://doi.org/10.1007/978-3-030-34621-8_23
10. Li, L., Pal, B., Ali, J., Sullivan, N., Chatterjee, R., Ristenpart, T.: Protocols for checking compromised credentials. In: Proceedings of ACM CCS (2019)
11. Matatall, N.: New improvements and best practices for account security and recoverability (2018). https://bit.ly/3ftvCcA. Accessed 15 Jun 2020
12. Oechslin, P.: Making a faster cryptanalytic time-memory trade-off. In: Boneh, D. (ed.) CRYPTO 2003. LNCS, vol. 2729, pp. 617–630. Springer, Heidelberg (2003). https://doi.org/10.1007/978-3-540-45146-4_36
13. Petsas, T., Tsirantonakis, G., Athanasopoulos, E., Ioannidis, S.: Two-factor authentication: is the world ready?: quantifying 2FA adoption. In Proceedings of the 8th European Workshop on System Security, p. 4. ACM (2015)
14. Pinkas, B., Schneider, T., Zohner, M.: Faster private set intersection based on OT extension. In: USENIX Security Symposium, pp. 797–812. USENIX Association (2014)
15. Samarati, P., Sweeney, L.: Protecting privacy when disclosing information: k-anonymity and its enforcement through generalization and suppression. Technical report, SRI International (1998)
16. Shay, R., et al.: Encountering stronger password requirements: user attitudes and behaviors. In: Proceedings of the 6th Symposium on Usable Privacy and Security, p. 2. ACM (2010)
17. Sherry, J., Hasan, S., Scott, C., Krishnamurthy, A., Ratnasamy, S., Sekar, V.: Making middleboxes someone else's problem: network processing as a cloud service. ACM SIGCOMM Comput. Commun. Rev. **42**(4), 13–24 (2012)
18. SpyCloud. Website. https://spycloud.com/. Accessed 15 Jun 2020
19. Stobert, E., Biddle, R.: The password life cycle: user behaviour in managing passwords. In: 10th Symposium On Usable Privacy and Security (SOUPS-2014), pp. 243–255 (2014)
20. Thomas, K., et al.: Protecting accounts from credential stuffing with password breach alerting. In: Proceedings of the USENIX Security Symposium (2019)
21. Tresorit. White Paper. https://tresorit.com/files/tresoritwhitepaper.pdf. Accessed 15 Jun 2020

Author Index

Printed in the United States
By Bookmasters